ANSI/NISO/ISO 12083-1995
(Revision and redesignation of ANSI Z39.59-1988)

ISSN: 1041-5653

Electronic Manuscript Preparation and Markup

Abstract: To assist in the transfer of electronic text, four document type definitions (DTDs) are presented. Standard Generalized Markup Language (SGML) declarations are specified for the following DTDs: (1) Books, (2) Articles, (3) Serials, and (4) Mathematics. Annex A describes the structure and additional facilities of the DTDs. Annex B is a description of SGML elements. Annex C includes examples of marked-up text.

Developed by the
National Information Standards Organization

Approved April 17, 1995 by the
American National Standards Institute

Bethesda, Maryland, U.S.A.

Published by
NISO Press
4733 Bethesda Avenue, Suite 300
Bethesda, MD 20814

ISSN: 1041-5653
ISBN: 1-880124-20-3

Printed in the United States of America

 This paper meets the requirements of ANSI/NISO Z39.48-1992 (Permanence of Paper).

National Information Standards Organization (U.S.)
Electronic manuscript preparation and markup/developed by the National Information Standards Organization.
p. cm. — (National information standards series, ANSI/NISO/ISO 12083)
"Approved April 17, 1995 by the American National Standards Institute."
Replaces standard Z39.59-1988.
ISBN 1-880124-20-3
1. SGML (Computer program language) —Standards—United States. 2. Electronic publishing —Standards—United States. 3. Manuscript preparation (Authorship) —Data processing —Standards —United States. I. American National Standards Institute. II. Title. III. Series.
QA76.76.H94N38 1995 95-33008
005.7'2—dc20 CIP

Contents

List of Figures

Foreword

(This foreword is not part of American National Standard ANSI/NISO/ISO 12083-1995. This standard is identical to ISO 12083: 1993 and the following four paragraphs are the original foreword as it appeared in that document.)

ISO (the International Organization for Standardization) is a worldwide federation of national standards bodies (ISO member bodies). The work of preparing International Standards is normally carried out through ISO technical committees. Each member body interested in a subject for which a technical committee has been established has the right to be represented on that committee. International organizations, governmental and non-governmental, in liaison with ISO, also take part in the work. ISO collaborates closely with the International Electrotechnical Commission (IEC) on all matters of electrotechnical standardization.

Draft International Standards adopted by the technical committees are circulated to the member bodies for voting. Publication as an International Standard requires approval by at least 75% of the member bodies casting a vote.

International Standard ISO 12083 was prepared by Technical Committee ISO/TC 46, Information and documentation, Subcommittee 4, Computer applications in information and documentation.

Annexes A, B, and C of this International Standard are for information only.

Suggestions for improving this standard are welcome. They should be sent to the National Information Standards Organization, 4733 Bethesda Avenue, Bethesda, MD 20814, (301) 654-2512.

This standard was processed and approved for submittal to ANSI by the National Information Standards Organization. NISO approval of this standard does not necessarily imply that all Voting Members voted for its approval. At the time it approved this standard, NISO had the following members:

NISO Voting Members

NISO Board of Directors

At the time NISO approved this standard, the following individuals served on its Board of Directors:

Information and documentation — Electronic manuscript preparation and markup

1 Scope

This International Standard presents four document type definitions and additional facilities conforming to ISO 8879. This International Standard is intended to provide document architectures for the creation and interchange of books, articles and serial publications.

It specifies:

a) the SGML declaration defining the syntax used by the document type definitions and document instances;

b) the document type definitions for the following document classes:

   i) Books;

   ii) Articles;

   iii) Serials, which are collections of articles;

c) a document type definition for Mathematics which may be embedded in other SGML applications.

This International Standard provides a toolkit for developers of these types of publications to use as a basis for developing custom applications. The applications developed may be for authors, publishers, libraries, their users, and/or their database vendors. The document type definitions included in this International Standard have been designed to be flexible enough to expand or limit markup depending on the use of the application. For example, if the application is intended for authors, the copyright information could be removed. The markup is sufficiently general to enable its use for similarly structured documents, e.g. the Book DTD can also be used for technical reports.

2 Normative references

The following standards contain provisions which, through reference in this text, constitute provisions of this International Standard. At the time of publication, the editions indicated were valid. All standards are subject to revision, and parties to agreements based on this International Standard are encouraged to investigate the possibility of applying the most recent editions of the standards indicated below. Members of IEC and ISO maintain registers of currently valid International Standards.

ISO 8879:1986, *Information processing - Text and office systems - Standard Generalized Markup Language (SGML).*

ISO/IEC TR 9573:1988, *Techniques for applying SGML.*

ISO/IEC 10744:1992, *Information Technology - Hypermedia/Time based Structuring Language (HyTime).*

ISO 8601:1988, *Data elements and interchange formats - Information interchange - Representation of dates and times.*

ISO 5127-2:1983, *Documentation and information - Vocabulary - Part 2: Traditional documents.*

ISO/IEC 9070:1991, *Information technology - SGML support facilities - Registration procedures for public text owner identifiers.*

ISO 3166:1994, *Codes for the representation of names of countries.*

3 Definitions

For the purposes of this International Standard, the definitions given in ISO 8879, ISO/IEC TR 9573 and ISO 5127/2 apply.

4 Conformance

The intent of this International Standard is to provide a base set of elements to support the production and delivery cycle of a publication. Elements (e.g. table), or references to (e.g. mathematics) entity sets may be removed or modified as necessary for a specific application. The application should satisfy the following conditions to comply with this International Standard. It should:

a) use the reference concrete syntax;

b) declare user-defined elements in external parameter entities;

c) identify use of this International Standard as a base by using the appropriate public identifier;

d) override parameter entities defined in this International Standard to specify different order and occurrence or to specify user-defined elements or attributes;

e) not allow user-defined elements to specify an alias of an element already defined in this International Standard;

f) follow consistent naming conventions found in the document type definitions of this International Standard when creating new elements or attributes;

g) conform to ISO 8879.

If the application is developed for interchange purposes, it is recommended that the DTD be registered following ISO/IEC 9070.

5 SGML declaration

The document type definitions in this International Standard use the reference concrete syntax.

The document type definitions in this International Standard are intended for use with basic SGML documents. These documents should use the SGML declaration in ISO 8879:1986, figure 8, subclause 15.1.1. Note that OMITTAG and SHORTTAG are allowable minimization features.

Use of the SGML Document Access or HyTime facilities may necessitate a change of the APPINFO parameter in the SGML declaration, replacing the keyword NONE by SDA or HYTIME or both (see Annex A Clauses 8.5 and 9.1):

```
APPINFO "SDA HYTIME"
```

6 The Book DTD

```
<!-- This is the ISO12083:1994 document type definition for Books.       -->
<!-- Copyright: (C) International Organization for Standardization 1994.
Permission to copy in any form is granted for use with conforming SGML
systems and applications as defined in ISO 8879:1986, provided this notice
is included in all copies.                                                -->


<!-- ================================================================== -->
<!--    PUBLIC DOCUMENT TYPE DEFINITION SUBSET                          -->
<!-- ================================================================== -->

<!-- Typical invocation:
<?HyTime VERSION "ISO/IEC 10744:1992" HQCNT=32                           >
<?HyTime MODULE base                                                      >
<?HyTime MODULE locs multloc anydtd mixspace                              >
<?HyTime MODULE links                                                     >
```

```
<!DOCTYPE book PUBLIC "ISO 12083:1994//DTD Book//EN"
 [<!ENTITY % ISOnum PUBLIC "ISO 8879:1986//ENTITIES Numeric and
         Special Graphic//EN"                                      >
  <!ENTITY % ISOpub PUBLIC "ISO 8879:1986//ENTITIES
         Publishing//EN"                                           >
  <!ENTITY % ISOtech PUBLIC "ISO 8879:1986//ENTITIES
         General Technical//EN"                                    >
  <!ENTITY % ISOdia PUBLIC "ISO 8879:1986//ENTITIES
         Diacritical Marks//EN"                                    >
  <!ENTITY % ISOlat1 PUBLIC "ISO 8879:1986//ENTITIES
         Added Latin 1//EN"                                        >
  <!ENTITY % ISOlat2 PUBLIC "ISO 8879:1986//ENTITIES
         Added Latin 2//EN"                                        >
  <!ENTITY % ISOamso PUBLIC "ISO 8879:1986//ENTITIES
         Added Math Symbols: Ordinary//EN"                         >
  <!ENTITY % ISOgrk1 PUBLIC "ISO 8879:1986//ENTITIES
         Greek Letters//EN"                                        >
  <!ENTITY % ISOgrk3 PUBLIC "ISO 8879:1986//ENTITIES
         Greek Symbols//EN"                                        >
  %ISOnum;
  %ISOpub;
  %ISOtech;
  %ISOdia;
  %ISOlat1;
  %ISOlat2;
  %ISOamso;
  %ISOgrk1;
  %ISOgrk3;
  <!ENTITY % ereview PUBLIC "-//USA-DOD//DTD
         SUP MIL-M-28001 EREVIEW REV B//EN"                        >
  %ereview;
]>                                                                         -->

<!-- NOTES: 1. ISO/IEC TR 9573 Parts 12-16 are currently under review and will
              contain complete special character entity sets.
           2. MIL-M-28001 EREVIEW are the CALS facilities for electronic
              review.                                                      -->

<!-- ==================================================================== -->
<!--    Entity Naming Conventions                                          -->
<!-- ==================================================================== -->

<!-- Prefix = where used:
     p.  = in paragraphs (also in phrases if .ph suffix)
     s.  = in sections (i.e., among paragraphs)
     i.  = where allowed by inclusion exceptions
     m.  = content model or declared content
     a.  = attribute definition
     NONE= specific use defined in models
```

```
    Suffix = allowed content:
    .ph = elements whose content is %m.ph;
    .d  = elements whose content has same model as defaults
    .zz = for subelements
    NONE= individually defined elements
  -->

<!ENTITY % doctype  "book" -- default document type generic identifier    -->


<!-- +++++++++++++++++++++++++++++++++++++++++++++++++++++++++++++++++++++ -->
<!--     Specialized Elements                                               -->
<!-- +++++++++++++++++++++++++++++++++++++++++++++++++++++++++++++++++++++ -->

<!ENTITY % ade.ph     "street|city|state|country|postcode|san|email|postbox|
                      phone|fax" -- address elements                       -->
<!ENTITY % bib        "author|corpauth|msn|sertitle|location|date|pages|subject|
                      othinfo" -- bibliographic, date is the publication date-->

<!-- The following 5 declarations are specific to Books                   -->
<!ENTITY % bmsec.d  "afterwrd|notes|vita" -- back matter sections          -->
<!ENTITY % bmsec.i  "glossary|index" -- indexes and glossary               -->
<!ENTITY % fmsec.d  "foreword|intro|preface|ack|ded|abstract|supmatl"
                                      -- front matter sections             -->
<!ENTITY % pub        "sponsor|contract|reprint|cpyrt|date|pubname|location|
                      confgrp|avail" -- pubfront, date is publication date  -->
<!ENTITY % pub.ph     "coden|acqno|isbn|lccardno|reportid|edition|volid|catalog|
                      acidfree|price|extent|package|pubid"
                      -- publication related front matter material         -->


<!-- ===================================================================== -->
<!--     Basic Document Elements                                           -->
<!-- ===================================================================== -->

<!ENTITY % i.float  "figgrp|footnote|note"          -- floating elements -->
<!ENTITY % p.el       "deflist|orgaddr|indaddr|artwork|bq|lit|date|biblist|
                      author|corpauth|keyword|keyphras|poem|nameloc|indxflag"
                      -- general                                           -->
<!ENTITY % p.em.ph  "emph" -- emphasis                                     -->
<!ENTITY % p.lst.d  "list" -- list                                         -->

<!-- The following declaration is specific to Books                        -->
<!ENTITY % p.rf.ph  "noteref|fnoteref|figref|tableref|artref|appref|citeref|
                      secref|formref|glosref|indexref" -- references       -->

<!ENTITY % p.tbl      "table" -- table matter                              -->
<!ENTITY % p.form     "formula|dformula|dformgrp" -- mathematical formulas  -->
<!ENTITY % p.zz       "(%p.el;)|(%p.tbl;)|(%p.lst.d;)|(%p.form;)" -- paragraph
                      subelements                                          -->
<!ENTITY % p.zz.ph  "q|pages|(%p.em.ph;)|(%p.rf.ph;)" -- phrases           -->
<!ENTITY % s.zz       "p|(%p.zz;)" -- section subelements                  -->
```

```
<!-- ++++++++++++++++++++++++++++++++++++++++++++++++++++++++++++++++++++++ -->
<!--      Models                                                            -->
<!-- ++++++++++++++++++++++++++++++++++++++++++++++++++++++++++++++++++++++ -->

<!ENTITY % m.addr  "(%ade.ph;)*" -- address (no name)                       -->
<!ENTITY % m.bib   "(no?, title, (%bib;)*)" -- bibliographic entry          -->
<!ENTITY % m.copy  "(date|cpyrtnme|cpyrtclr)+" -- copyright notice data     -->
<!ENTITY % m.date  "(#PCDATA)" -- date                                      -->
<!ENTITY % m.fig   "EMPTY" -- default FIG content                           -->
<!ENTITY % m.sec   "(title?, (%s.zz;)*, section*)" -- section               -->
<!ENTITY % m.name  "((fname? & surname), (degree|school)*, role*,(%ade.ph;)*,
                   aff?)" -- name components                                -->
<!ENTITY % m.org   "(orgname, orgdiv*, %m.addr;)" -- organization name      -->
<!ENTITY % m.ph    "(#PCDATA|(%p.zz.ph;)|(%p.form;))*" -- phrase model      -->
<!ENTITY % m.pseq  "(p, (p|(%p.zz;))*)" -- P with sequence                  -->
<!ENTITY % m.poem  "(stanza+|poemline+)" -- poetry sub-elements             -->


<!-- ++++++++++++++++++++++++++++++++++++++++++++++++++++++++++++++++++++++ -->
<!--      Attribute Definitions                                             -->
<!-- ++++++++++++++++++++++++++++++++++++++++++++++++++++++++++++++++++++++ -->

<!ENTITY % a.id     "id ID #IMPLIED" -- ID attribute definition             -->
<!ENTITY % a.rid    "rid IDREF #REQUIRED" -- IDREF attribute definition     -->
<!ENTITY % au.rid   "rids IDREFS #IMPLIED" -- to refer to a unique id of
                                            an affiliation                  -->
<!ENTITY % a.sizes "sizex NUTOKEN #IMPLIED
                    sizey NUTOKEN #IMPLIED
                    unit CDATA #IMPLIED"
                    -- unit must be specified if sizex or sizey are.        -->
<!ENTITY % a.types "(latin|greek|cyrillic|hebrew|kanji) latin"
                    -- Indicates which alphabet is used in the element
                    (title, p, q). This may be changed to a notation
                    attribute, where the notation could describe a keyboard
                    mapping. Modify the set as necessary.                   -->
<!ENTITY % d.types "(1|2|3|4|5) #IMPLIED"
                    -- Suggestions for date types:
                    1=ISO 8601:1988, 2=mm-dd-yy, 3=mm/dd/yy, 4=dd-mm-yy,
                    5=month day year; if more needed (e.g. day month year)
                    modify or extend this list as necessary.                -->
<!ENTITY % e.types "(1|2|3|4|5|6) #IMPLIED"
                    -- Suggestions for emphasis types:
                    1=bold, 2=italic, 3=bold italic, 4=underline,
                    5=non proportional, 6=smallcaps; if more needed
                    modify or extend this list as necessary.                -->
<!ENTITY % l.types "(1|2|3|4|5|6) #IMPLIED"
                    -- Suggestions for list types:
                    1=arabic, 2=uppercase alpha, 3=roman, 4=bullet, 5=dash,
                    6=unlabelled; if more needed (e.g. lower alpha)
                    modify or extend this list as necessary.                -->

<!-- The following 2 declarations are specific to Books                     -->

<!ENTITY % m.idx    "(%m.sec;|((indxname|indxsubj)*,pages*))"
                    -- model for indexes and glossary                       -->
```

```
<!ENTITY % m.toc      "EMPTY" -- table of contents; automatic generation
                      assumed, add a specific content model if required      -->


<!-- ++++++++++++++++++++++++++++++++++++++++++++++++++++++++++++++++++++++ -->
<!--        Accessible Document Parameter Entities                          -->
<!-- ++++++++++++++++++++++++++++++++++++++++++++++++++++++++++++++++++++++ -->

<!ENTITY % SDAFORM  "SDAFORM   CDATA     #FIXED"                             >
<!ENTITY % SDARULE  "SDARULE   CDATA     #FIXED"                             >
<!ENTITY % SDAPREF  "SDAPREF   CDATA     #FIXED"                             >
<!ENTITY % SDASUFF  "SDASUFF   CDATA     #FIXED"                             >
<!ENTITY % SDASUSP  "SDASUSP   NAME      #FIXED"                             >


<!-- ====================================================================== -->
<!--     DATA CONTENT NOTATIONS                                             -->
<!-- ====================================================================== -->

<!-- These are examples. Add other public notations as required.           -->

<!NOTATION eps       PUBLIC
"+//ISBN 0-201-18127-4::Adobe//NOTATION Postscript Language Reference
 Manual//EN"                                                                 >
<!NOTATION tex       PUBLIC
"+//ISBN 0-201-13448-9::Knuth//NOTATION The TeXbook//EN"                     >
<!NOTATION cgmchar   PUBLIC      "ISO 8632/2//NOTATION Character encoding//EN" >
<!NOTATION cgmclear  PUBLIC      "ISO 8632/4//NOTATION Clear text encoding//EN">
<!NOTATION tiff      PUBLIC      "ISO 12083:1993//NOTATION TIFF-1//EN"        >


<!-- ====================================================================== -->
<!--     THE DOCUMENT STRUCTURE                                             -->
<!-- ====================================================================== -->

<!--        ELEMENT                MIN  CONTENT                 (EXCEPTIONS)   -->
<!ELEMENT (%doctype;)              - -  (front, body, appmat?, back?)
                                                            +(%i.float;)     >


<!-- ====================================================================== -->
<!--      FRONT MATTER ELEMENTS                                             -->
<!-- ====================================================================== -->

<!-- The following 2 declarations are specific to Books                     -->
<!ELEMENT front                    O O  (titlegrp, authgrp, date?, pubfront?,
                                        (%fmsec.d;)*, toc?)                  >
<!ELEMENT (%fmsec.d;)              - O  %m.sec;                              >


<!-- ++++++++++++++++++++++++++++++++++++++++++++++++++++++++++++++++++++++ -->
<!--     Title Group                                                        -->
<!-- ++++++++++++++++++++++++++++++++++++++++++++++++++++++++++++++++++++++ -->

<!ELEMENT titlegrp                 O O  (msn?, sertitle?, no?, title, subtitle?) >
```

```
<!ELEMENT (title|subtitle)      - O  %m.ph;                                   >


<!-- ++++++++++++++++++++++++++++++++++++++++++++++++++++++++++++++++++++++ -->
<!--     Author Group                                                       -->
<!-- ++++++++++++++++++++++++++++++++++++++++++++++++++++++++++++++++++++++ -->

<!ELEMENT authgrp               O O  (author|corpauth|aff)*                    >
<!ELEMENT author                - O  %m.name;                                 >
<!ELEMENT (fname|surname|role|degree|orgname|orgdiv)
                                - O  (#PCDATA)                                >
<!ELEMENT (aff|corpauth|school)
                                - O  %m.org;                                  >
<!ELEMENT (%ade.ph;)            - O  (#PCDATA)                                >


<!-- ++++++++++++++++++++++++++++++++++++++++++++++++++++++++++++++++++++++ -->
<!--     Publisher's Front Matter                                           -->
<!-- ++++++++++++++++++++++++++++++++++++++++++++++++++++++++++++++++++++++ -->

<!ELEMENT pubfront              - O  ((%pub;)|(%pub.ph;))*                    >
<!ELEMENT (%pub.ph;|contract)   - O  (#PCDATA)                                >
<!ELEMENT (pubname|avail|sponsor)
                                - O  %m.org;                                  >
<!ELEMENT reprint               - O  (%m.org;|%m.name;)                       >


<!-- ++++++++++++++++++++++++++++++++++++++++++++++++++++++++++++++++++++++ -->
<!--     Copyright                                                          -->
<!-- ++++++++++++++++++++++++++++++++++++++++++++++++++++++++++++++++++++++ -->

<!ELEMENT cpyrt                 - -  %m.copy;                                 >
<!ELEMENT cpyrtclr              - -  %m.org;                                  >
<!ELEMENT cpyrtnme              - -  (%m.org;|%m.name;)                       >


<!-- ++++++++++++++++++++++++++++++++++++++++++++++++++++++++++++++++++++++ -->
<!--    Conference Group                                                    -->
<!-- ++++++++++++++++++++++++++++++++++++++++++++++++++++++++++++++++++++++ -->

<!ELEMENT confgrp               - -  (no?, confname, date?, location?,
                                     sponsor?)                                >
<!ELEMENT confname              - O  (#PCDATA)                                >


<!-- ++++++++++++++++++++++++++++++++++++++++++++++++++++++++++++++++++++++ -->
<!--     Date                                                               -->
<!-- ++++++++++++++++++++++++++++++++++++++++++++++++++++++++++++++++++++++ -->

<!ELEMENT date                  - O  %m.date;                                 >
```

```
<!-- ++++++++++++++++++++++++++++++++++++++++++++++++++++++++++++++++++++ -->
<!--    Table of Contents                                                 -->
<!-- ++++++++++++++++++++++++++++++++++++++++++++++++++++++++++++++++++++ -->

<!ELEMENT toc                - O  %m.toc;                                  >


<!-- ==================================================================== -->
<!--    BODY ELEMENTS                                                     -->
<!-- ==================================================================== -->

<!-- ++++++++++++++++++++++++++++++++++++++++++++++++++++++++++++++++++++ -->
<!--    Body Structure                                                    -->
<!-- ++++++++++++++++++++++++++++++++++++++++++++++++++++++++++++++++++++ -->

<!ELEMENT body               O O  (part+|chapter+)                         >
<!ELEMENT part               - O  (no?, title?, (%s.zz;)*, chapter+)       >
<!ELEMENT chapter            - O  (no?, %m.sec;)                           >
<!ELEMENT section            - O  (no?, title?, (%s.zz;)*, subsect1*)      >
<!ELEMENT subsect1           - O  (no?, title?, (%s.zz;)*, subsect2*)      >
<!ELEMENT subsect2           - O  (no?, title?, (%s.zz;)*, subsect3*)      >
<!ELEMENT subsect3           - O  (no?, title?, (%s.zz;)*, subsect4*)      >
<!ELEMENT subsect4           - O  (no?, title?, (%s.zz;)*, subsect5*)      >
<!ELEMENT subsect5           - O  (no?, title?, (%s.zz;)*, subsect6*)      >
<!ELEMENT subsect6           - O  (no?, title?, (%s.zz;)*)                 >
<!ELEMENT no                 - O  (#PCDATA)                                >


<!-- ++++++++++++++++++++++++++++++++++++++++++++++++++++++++++++++++++++ -->
<!--    Section Subelements                                               -->
<!-- ++++++++++++++++++++++++++++++++++++++++++++++++++++++++++++++++++++ -->

<!ELEMENT p                  - O  (#PCDATA|(%p.zz.ph;)|(%p.zz;))*          >

<!-- ++++++++++++++++++++++++++++++++++++++++++++++++++++++++++++++++++++ -->
<!--    Paragraph Subelements                                             -->
<!-- ++++++++++++++++++++++++++++++++++++++++++++++++++++++++++++++++++++ -->

<!ELEMENT bq                 - -  %m.pseq;                                 >
<!ELEMENT indaddr            - O  %m.name; -- individual address          -->
<!ELEMENT orgaddr            - O  %m.org;  -- organization address        -->
<!ELEMENT artwork            - O  EMPTY                                    >

<!ELEMENT lit                - -  RCDATA                                   >

<!ELEMENT (%p.lst.d;)        - -  (head?, item)*                           >
<!ELEMENT item               - O  %m.pseq;                                 >

<!ELEMENT deflist            - -  ((head, ddhd)?, term, dd)*               >
<!ELEMENT (term|head|ddhd)   - O  %m.ph;                                   >
<!ELEMENT dd                 - O  %m.pseq;                                 >

<!ELEMENT biblist            - O  (head?, citation)*                       >
<!ELEMENT citation           - O  %m.bib;                                  >
```

```
<!ELEMENT (othinfo|subject|sertitle)
                                - O  %m.ph;                                   >

<!ELEMENT location               - O  %m.addr;                                 >
<!ELEMENT (msn|pages)            - O  (#PCDATA)                                >
<!ELEMENT keyword                - O  (#PCDATA)                                >
<!ELEMENT keyphras               - O  (#PCDATA)                                >
<!ELEMENT indxflag               - O  EMPTY                                    >

<!-- ++++++++++++++++++++++++++++++++++++++++++++++++++++++++++++++++++++++ -->
<!--     Poetry                                                             -->
<!-- ++++++++++++++++++++++++++++++++++++++++++++++++++++++++++++++++++++++ -->

<!ELEMENT poem                   - O  %m.poem;                                 >
<!ELEMENT stanza                 - O  (poemline)+                              >
<!ELEMENT poemline               - O  (#PCDATA|cline|%p.em.ph;)*               >
<!ELEMENT cline                  - O  (#PCDATA|%p.em.ph;)*                     >

<!-- ++++++++++++++++++++++++++++++++++++++++++++++++++++++++++++++++++++++ -->
<!--     Phrases                                                            -->
<!-- ++++++++++++++++++++++++++++++++++++++++++++++++++++++++++++++++++++++ -->

<!ELEMENT q                      - -  %m.ph;                                   >
<!ELEMENT (%p.em.ph;)            - -  %m.ph;                                   >
<!ELEMENT (%p.rf.ph;)            - -  (#PCDATA)                                >

<!-- ++++++++++++++++++++++++++++++++++++++++++++++++++++++++++++++++++++++ -->
<!--     For HyTime Links                                                   -->
<!-- ++++++++++++++++++++++++++++++++++++++++++++++++++++++++++++++++++++++ -->

<!ELEMENT nameloc                - O (nmlist*) -- assigns a local ID to
                                   named objects                            -->
<!ELEMENT nmlist                 - O (#PCDATA) -- list of local ID or entity
                                   names                                    -->

<!-- ++++++++++++++++++++++++++++++++++++++++++++++++++++++++++++++++++++++ -->
<!--     Floating Elements                                                  -->
<!-- ++++++++++++++++++++++++++++++++++++++++++++++++++++++++++++++++++++++ -->

<!ELEMENT figgrp                 - -  (title? & fig*)                          >
<!ELEMENT fig                    - O  %m.fig;                                  >
<!ELEMENT footnote               - -  (no?, %m.pseq;)        -(%i.float;)      >
<!ELEMENT note                   - -  (no?, %m.pseq;)                          >

<!-- ++++++++++++++++++++++++++++++++++++++++++++++++++++++++++++++++++++++ -->
<!--     Tables                                                             -->
<!-- ++++++++++++++++++++++++++++++++++++++++++++++++++++++++++++++++++++++ -->

<!ELEMENT table                  - -  (no?, title?, tbody)   -(%i.float;)      >
<!ELEMENT tbody                  - O  (head*, tsubhead*, row*)                 >
```

```
<!ELEMENT row                  - O  (tstub?, cell*)                      >
<!ELEMENT tsubhead             - O  %m.ph;                               >
<!ELEMENT (tstub|cell)         - O  %m.pseq;                             >


<!-- +++++++++++++++++++++++++++++++++++++++++++++++++++++++++++++++++++++ -->
<!--    Mathematics                                                        -->
<!-- +++++++++++++++++++++++++++++++++++++++++++++++++++++++++++++++++++++ -->

<!ENTITY % maths PUBLIC "ISO 12083:1994//DTD Mathematics//EN"           >
%maths;

<!-- Remove these comments if the formula's follow a NOTATION rather than
     SGML.
<!ELEMENT dformgrp             - O  (dformula)+                          >
<!ELEMENT (formula|dformula)   - -  CDATA                                >
-->


<!-- ===================================================================== -->
<!--    APPENDIX ELEMENTS                                                  -->
<!-- ===================================================================== -->

<!ELEMENT appmat               - O  (appendix+)                          >
<!ELEMENT appendix             - O  (no?, %m.sec;)                       >


<!-- ===================================================================== -->
<!--    BACK MATTER ELEMENTS                                               -->
<!-- ===================================================================== -->

<!-- The following 3 declarations are specific to Books                 -->
<!ELEMENT back                 - O  ((%bmsec.d;)|(%bmsec.i;)|biblist)*   >
<!ELEMENT (%bmsec.d;)          - O  %m.sec;                              >
<!ELEMENT (%bmsec.i;)          - O  %m.idx;                              >

<!ELEMENT (indxname|indxsubj)  - O  (#PCDATA)                            >


<!-- ===================================================================== -->
<!--    ATTRIBUTE DEFINITION LISTS                                         -->
<!-- ===================================================================== -->

<!-- HyTime attributes were added to all references,
     the citation and doclink elements                                  -->

<!-- The SGML Document Access attributes for Braille, large print
and voice synthesis markup have been added to the attributes already
declared in this DTD in the first section following, and then for
all elements which have no attributes except for the SDA set.           -->

<!--      ELEMENT   NAME        VALUE          DEFAULT                   -->
<!ATTLIST abstract  %a.id;
          %SDAPREF;                            "<h1>Abstract</h1>"       >
```

```
<!ATTLIST ack       %a.id;
          %SDAPREF;                              '<h1>Acknowledgements</h1>'   >

<!ATTLIST aff       %a.id;                                                     >

<!ATTLIST afterwrd  %a.id;
          %SDAPREF;                              '<h1>Afterword</h1>'          >

<!ATTLIST appendix  %a.id;
          %SDAPREF;                              '<h1>Appendix</h1>'           >

<!ATTLIST artwork   %a.id;
                    %a.sizes;
                    name        ENTITY           #IMPLIED
          %SDAFORM;                              'fig #attrib ID'              >

<!ATTLIST author    %au.rid;
          %SDAFORM;                              'au'                          >

<!ATTLIST biblist   file        ENTITY           #IMPLIED
          %SDAFORM;                              'list'
          %SDAPREF;                              'Bibliography'                >

<!ATTLIST chapter   %a.id;
          SDABDY    NAMES       #FIXED           'title h1'
          SDAPART   NAMES       #FIXED           'title h2'                    >

<!ATTLIST citation  id          ID               #REQUIRED
                    HyTime      NAME             #FIXED bibloc
          %SDARULE;                              'title it
                                                 author para
                                                 corpauth para
                                                 sertitle it'                  >

<!ATTLIST corpauth  %a.id;
          %SDAFORM;                              'au'                          >

<!ATTLIST country   cnycode     NAME             #IMPLIED
                                                --name should follow ISO 3166-->

<!ATTLIST date      type        %d.types;
          %SDAPREF;                              'Date:'                       >

<!ATTLIST dd        %a.id;
          %SDAFORM;                              'para'                        >

<!ATTLIST ded       %a.id;
          %SDAPREF;                              '<h1>Dedication</h1>'         >

<!ATTLIST deflist   %a.id;
          %SDAFORM;                              'list'
          %SDAPREF;                              '<?SDATRANS>Definitions '     >
```

```
<!ATTLIST %doctype; %a.id;
                    HyTime      NAME            #FIXED HyDoc
                    %SDAFORM;                   "book"                  >

<!ATTLIST fig       %a.id;
                    %a.sizes;
                    name        ENTITY          #IMPLIED
                    scale       NUMBER          100
          %SDAPREF;                             "<?SDATRANS>Figure: "   >

<!ATTLIST figgrp    %a.id;
          %SDARULE;                             "title para"            >

<!ATTLIST footnote  %a.id;
          %SDAFORM;                             "fn"                    >

<!ATTLIST foreword  %a.id;
          %SDAPREF;                             "<h1>Foreword</h1>"     >

<!ATTLIST glossary  %a.id;
          %SDAPREF;                             "<h1>Glossary</h1>"     >

<!ATTLIST index     %a.id;
          %SDAPREF;                             "<h1>Index</h1>"        >

<!ATTLIST indxflag  ref1        CDATA           #IMPLIED
                    ref2        CDATA           #IMPLIED
                    ref3        CDATA           #IMPLIED
                    ref4        CDATA           #IMPLIED                >

<!ATTLIST intro     %a.id;
          %SDAPREF;                             "<h1>Introduction</h1>" >

<!ATTLIST item      %a.id;
          %SDAFORM;                             "litem"                 >

<!ATTLIST note      %a.id;
          %SDAFORM;                             "note"                  >

<!ATTLIST nameloc   HyTime      NAME            nameloc
                    id          ID              #REQUIRED
                    -- multloc attributes --
                    ordering    (ordered|noorder)
                                                noorder
                    -- is ordering of locations significant? --
                    set         (set|notset)    notset
                    -- make multiple a set by ignoring duplicates --
                    aggloc      (aggloc|agglink|nagg)
                                                nagg
                    -- are multiple locations an aggregate? --
          %SDAPREF;                             "<?SDATRANS>Nameloc:"   >
```

```
<!ATTLIST nmlist     HyTime      NAME              nmlist
                     nametype   (entity|element) entity
                     -- entity names or IDs of elements --
                     obnames  (obnames|nobnames) nobnames
                     -- objects treated as names? --
                     docorsub    ENTITY            #IMPLIED
                     dtdorlpd    NAMES             #IMPLIED
          %SDAPREF;                                "<?SDATRANS>Namelist:"          >

<!ATTLIST p          %a.id;
                     alphabet    %a.types;
          %SDAFORM;                                "para"                          >

<!ATTLIST part
          %SDARULE;                                "chapter #use SDAPART"          >

<!ATTLIST preface    %a.id;
          %SDAPREF;                                "<h1>Preface</h1>"              >

<!ATTLIST %p.em.ph;  type        %e.types;
          %SDARULE;                                "[emph type=1] b
                                                    [emph type=2] it
                                                    [emph type=(3|4|5|6)] other"  >

<!ATTLIST %p.lst.d;  %a.id;
          type       %l.types;
          %SDAFORM;                                "list"
          %SDAPREF;           "[list type=1]#set (item,#count(item,1))
                              [list type=2]#set (item,#count(item,A))
                              [list type=3]#set (item,#count(item,I))
                              [list type=4]#set (item,#count(item,'* '))
                              [list type=5]#set (item,#count(item,'- '))"        >

<!ATTLIST (%p.rf.ph;)
                     %a.id;
                     %a.rid;
                     HyTime      NAME              #FIXED clink
                     HyNames     CDATA             #FIXED "rid linkend"
          %SDAFORM;                                "xref #attrib IDREF"           >

<!ATTLIST %p.tbl;    %a.id;
          %SDAFORM;                                "table"
          %SDARULE;                                "title h3
                                                    head hdcell"
          %SDAPREF;                                "<?SDATRANS>"                  >

<!ATTLIST q          %a.id;
                     alphabet    %a.types;
          %SDAPREF;                                "'"
          %SDASUFF;                                "'"                            >

<!ATTLIST section    %a.id;
          SDABDY     NAMES       #FIXED            "title h2"
          SDAPART    NAMES       #FIXED            "title h3"                     >
```

```
<!ATTLIST subsect1  %a.id;
         SDABDY     NAMES      #FIXED          'title h3'
         SDAPART    NAMES      #FIXED          'title h4'              >

<!ATTLIST subsect2  %a.id;
         SDABDY     NAMES      #FIXED          'title h4'
         SDAPART    NAMES      #FIXED          'title h5'              >

<!ATTLIST subsect3  %a.id;
         SDABDY     NAMES      #FIXED          'title h5'
         SDAPART    NAMES      #FIXED          'title h6'              >

<!ATTLIST subsect4  %a.id;
         SDABDY     NAMES      #FIXED          'title h6'
         SDAPART    NAMES      #FIXED          'title b'               >

<!ATTLIST (subsect5|subsect6)
                    %a.id;
         SDABDY     NAMES      #FIXED          'title b'
         SDAPART    NAMES      #FIXED          'title b'               >

<!ATTLIST term      %a.id;
         %SDAFORM;                             'term'                  >

<!ATTLIST title     alphabet   %a.types;
                    purpose    (normal|run)    normal
         %SDAFORM;                             'ti'                    >


<!-- ============================================================== -->
<!--      SDA ATTRIBUTES                                                -->
<!-- ============================================================== -->

<!-- The following declarations support elements whose only
     attributes are SDA attributes:                                 -->

<!ATTLIST acqno
         %SDAFORM;                             'para'
         %SDAPREF;                             'Acquisition/order number: ' >

<!ATTLIST avail
         %SDAFORM;                             'para'
         %SDAPREF;                             'Available from: '      >

<!ATTLIST body
         %SDARULE;                             'chapter #use SDABDY '  >

<!ATTLIST bq
         %SDAFORM;                             'bq'                    >

<!ATTLIST cpyrtclr
         %SDAFORM;                             'para'
         %SDAPREF;                             'Copyright clearance center: '>
```

```
<!ATTLIST coden
          %SDAFORM;                    'para'
          %SDAPREF;                    'CODEN: '                         >

<!ATTLIST contract
          %SDAFORM;                    'para'
          %SDAPREF;                    'Contract or grant number: '      >

<!ATTLIST sponsor
          %SDAFORM;                    'para'
          %SDAPREF;                    '(Contract or grant) sponsor:'>

<!ATTLIST catalog
          %SDAFORM;                    'para'
          %SDAPREF;                    '<?SDATRANS>Cataloguing in
                                       publication information: '        >

<!ATTLIST cell
          %SDAFORM;                    'cell'                            >

<!ATTLIST confgrp
          %SDAFORM;                    'para'
          %SDAPREF;                    'Conference group: '              >

<!ATTLIST confname
          %SDAFORM;                    'para'
          %SDAPREF;                    'Conference name: '               >

<!ATTLIST cpyrt
          %SDAFORM;                    'para'
          %SDAPREF;                    '<?SDATRANS>Copyright notice:'>

<!ATTLIST ddhd
          %SDAFORM;                    'lhead'                           >

<!ATTLIST email
          %SDAFORM;                    'para'
          %SDAPREF;                    'Electronic address: '            >

<!ATTLIST edition
          %SDAFORM;                    'para'
          %SDAPREF;                    '<?SDATRANS>Edition: '            >

<!ATTLIST extent
          %SDAFORM;                    'para'
          %SDAPREF;                    'Number of pages: '               >

<!ATTLIST fax
          %SDAFORM;                    'para'
          %SDAPREF;                    'Fax number: '                    >

<!ATTLIST head
          %SDAFORM;                    'lhead'                           >
```

```
<!ATTLIST (indaddr|orgaddr)
          %SDAFORM;                    "para"
          %SDAPREF;                    "Address: "                >

<!ATTLIST (indxname|indxsubj)
          %SDAFORM;                    "term"                     >

<!ATTLIST isbn
          %SDAFORM;                    "para"
          %SDAPREF;                    "ISBN: "                   >

<!ATTLIST (keyphras|keyword)
          %SDAFORM;                    "term"                     >

<!ATTLIST lccardno
          %SDAFORM;                    "para"
          %SDAPREF;                    "LC card number: "         >

<!ATTLIST lit
          %SDAFORM;                    "lit"                      >

<!ATTLIST location
          %SDAFORM;                    "para"
          %SDAPREF;                    "Location: "               >

<!ATTLIST notes
          %SDAPREF;                    "<h1>Notes</h1>"           >

<!ATTLIST othinfo
          %SDAFORM;                    "para"                     >

<!ATTLIST acidfree
          %SDAFORM;                    "para"
          %SDAPREF;                    "Acid free paper indicator: " >

<!ATTLIST phone
          %SDAFORM;                    "para"
          %SDAPREF;                    "Phone: "                  >

<!ATTLIST pubid
          %SDAFORM;                    "para"
          %SDAPREF;                    "Publisher's ID number: "  >

<!ATTLIST package
          %SDAFORM;                    "para"
          %SDAPREF;                    "Packaging method: "       >

<!ATTLIST pubname
          %SDAFORM;                    "para"
          %SDAPREF;                    "Publisher: "              >

<!ATTLIST pages
          %SDAFORM;                    "pp"                       >
```

```
<!ATTLIST price
          %SDAFORM;                       "para"
          %SDAPREF;                       "Price: "                     >

<!ATTLIST reportid
          %SDAFORM;                       "para"
          %SDAPREF;                       "Report identifier: "         >

<!ATTLIST reprint
          %SDAFORM;                       "para"
          %SDAPREF;                       "Reprint source: "            >

<!ATTLIST row
          %SDAFORM;                       "row"                         >

<!ATTLIST san
          %SDAFORM;                       "para"
          %SDAPREF;                       "Standard address number: "   >

<!ATTLIST subtitle
          %SDAFORM;                       "h1"                          >

<!ATTLIST subject
          %SDAFORM;                       "it"                          >

<!ATTLIST supmatl
          %SDAFORM;                       "para"
          %SDAPREF;                       "Supporting material: "       >

<!ATTLIST sertitle
          %SDAFORM;                       "ti"                          >

<!ATTLIST tbody
          %SDAFORM;                       "tbody"                       >

<!ATTLIST tstub
          %SDAFORM;                       "stubcell"                    >

<!ATTLIST tsubhead
          %SDAFORM;                       "hdcell"                      >

<!ATTLIST toc
          %SDAFORM;                       "list"
          %SDAPREF;                       "<?SDATRANS>Contents"         >

<!ATTLIST volid
          %SDAFORM;                       "para"
          %SDAPREF;                       "Volume identifier: "         >

<!-- Remove the comment declaration around the next three declarations
     if formulas follow a notation rather than SGML
```

```
<!ATTLIST formula
          %a.id;
          notation NOTATION (tex)              #IMPLIED
          alphabet %a.types;
          %SDAPREF;                            "<?SDATRANS>Inline formula: "
          %SDASUSP;                            "SUSPEND"                    >

<!ATTLIST dformula
          %a.id;
          alphabet %a.types;
          notation NOTATION (tex)              #IMPLIED
          num      CDATA                       #IMPLIED
          align    (left|center|right)         center
          %SDAPREF;                            "<?SDATRANS>Display formula: "
          %SDASUSP;                            "SUSPEND"                    >

<!ATTLIST dformgrp
          %a.id;
          num      CDATA                       #IMPLIED
          align    (left|center|right) center
          %SDAPREF;                      "<?SDATRANS>Display formula group: ">
-->
```

7 The Article DTD

```
<!-- This is the ISO12083:1994 document type definition for an Article.
     It can be embedded in a Serial.                                    -->
<!-- Copyright: (C) International Organization for Standardization 1994.
Permission to copy in any form is granted for use with conforming SGML
systems and applications as defined in ISO 8879:1986, provided this
notice is included in all copies.                                       -->

<!-- ================================================================== -->
<!--    PUBLIC DOCUMENT TYPE DEFINITION SUBSET                          -->
<!-- ================================================================== -->

<!-- Typical invocation:
<?HyTime VERSION "ISO/IEC 10744:1992" HQCNT=32                           >
<?HyTime MODULE base                                                     >
<?HyTime MODULE locs multloc anydtd mixspace                             >
<?HyTime MODULE links                                                    >
<!DOCTYPE article PUBLIC "ISO 12083:1994//DTD Article//EN"
 [<!ENTITY % ISOnum PUBLIC "ISO 8879:1986//ENTITIES Numeric and
             Special Graphic//EN"                                 >
  <!ENTITY % ISOpub PUBLIC "ISO 8879:1986//ENTITIES
             Publishing//EN"                                      >
  <!ENTITY % ISOpub PUBLIC "ISO 8879:1986//ENTITIES
             Publishing//EN"                                      >
  <!ENTITY % ISOtech PUBLIC "ISO 8879:1986//ENTITIES
             General Technical//EN"                               >
```

```
   <!ENTITY % ISOdia PUBLIC "ISO 8879:1986//ENTITIES
              Diacritical Marks//EN"                                >
   <!ENTITY % ISOlat1 PUBLIC "ISO 8879:1986//ENTITIES
              Added Latin 1//EN"                                    >
   <!ENTITY % ISOlat2 PUBLIC "ISO 8879:1986//ENTITIES
              Added Latin 2//EN"                                    >
   <!ENTITY % ISOamso PUBLIC "ISO 8879:1986//ENTITIES
              Added Math Symbols: Ordinary//EN"                     >
   <!ENTITY % ISOgrk1 PUBLIC "ISO 8879:1986//ENTITIES
              Greek Letters//EN"                                    >
   <!ENTITY % ISOgrk3 PUBLIC "ISO 8879:1986//ENTITIES
              Greek Symbols//EN"                                    >
   %ISOnum;
   %ISOpub;
   %ISOtech;
   %ISOdia;
   %ISOlat1;
   %ISOlat2;
   %ISOamso;
   %ISOgrk1;
   %ISOgrk3;
   <!ENTITY % ereview PUBLIC "-//USA-DOD//DTD
           SUP MIL-M-28001 EREVIEW REV B//EN"                       >
   %ereview;
]>                                                                      -->

<!-- NOTES: 1. ISO/IEC TR 9573 Parts 12-16 are currently under review and will
              contain complete special character entity sets.
           2. MIL-M-28001 EREVIEW are the CALS facilities for electronic
              review.                                                   -->

<!-- ================================================================== -->
<!--     Entity Naming Conventions                                      -->
<!-- ================================================================== -->

<!-- Prefix = where used:
      p.  = in paragraphs (also in phrases if .ph suffix)
      s.  = in sections (i.e., among paragraphs)
      i.  = where allowed by inclusion exceptions
      m.  = content model or declared content
      a.  = attribute definition
      NONE= specific use defined in models

     Suffix = allowed content:
      .ph = elements whose content is %m.ph;
      .d  = elements whose content has same model as defaults
      .zz = for subelements
      NONE= individually defined elements                               -->

<!ENTITY % doctype   "article" -- default document type generic identifier -->
```

```
<!-- ++++++++++++++++++++++++++++++++++++++++++++++++++++++++++++++++++++++ -->
<!--    Specialized Elements                                                -->
<!-- ++++++++++++++++++++++++++++++++++++++++++++++++++++++++++++++++++++++ -->

<!ENTITY % ade.ph   "street|city|state|country|postcode|san|email|postbox|
                    phone|fax"  -- address elements                         -->
<!ENTITY % bib      "author|corpauth|msn|sertitle|location|date|pages|subject|
                    othinfo" -- bibliographic, date is the publication date -->

<!-- The following 4 declarations are specific to Articles                 -->
<!ENTITY % bmsec.d "ack|vita"            -- back matter cps elements        -->
<!ENTITY % fmsec.d "ded|abstract|supmatl" -- front matter sections          -->
<!ENTITY % pub      "sponsor|contract|reprint|cpyrt|date|pubname|location|
                    confgrp|avail|history"
                    -- pubfront, date is the publication date               -->
<!ENTITY % pub.ph   "fpage|lpage|coden|acqno|issn|acidfree|price|extent|artid|
                    category|pubid"
                    -- publication related front matter material            -->


<!-- ====================================================================== -->
<!--    Basic Document Elements                                             -->
<!-- ====================================================================== -->

<!ENTITY % i.float "figgrp|footnote|note" -- floating elements              -->
<!ENTITY % p.el     "deflist|orgaddr|indaddr|artwork|bq|lit|date|biblist|author
                    |corpauth|keyword|keyphras|poem|nameloc|indxflag"
                    -- general                                              -->
<!ENTITY % p.em.ph "emph" -- emphasis                                       -->
<!ENTITY % p.lst.d "list" -- list                                           -->

<!-- The following declaration is specific to Articles                      -->
<!ENTITY % p.rf.ph "noteref|fnoteref|figref|tableref|artref|appref|citeref|
                    secref|formref" -- references                           -->

<!ENTITY % p.tbl    "table" -- table matter                                 -->
<!ENTITY % p.form   "formula|dformula|dformgrp" -- mathematical formulas    -->
<!ENTITY % p.zz     "(%p.el;)|(%p.tbl;)|(%p.lst.d;)|(%p.form;)"
                    -- paragraph subelements                                -->

<!ENTITY % p.zz.ph "q|pages|(%p.em.ph;)|(%p.rf.ph;)" -- phrases             -->
<!ENTITY % s.zz     "p|(%p.zz;)" -- section subelements                     -->


<!-- ++++++++++++++++++++++++++++++++++++++++++++++++++++++++++++++++++++++ -->
<!--    Models                                                              -->
<!-- ++++++++++++++++++++++++++++++++++++++++++++++++++++++++++++++++++++++ -->

<!ENTITY % m.addr   "(%ade.ph;)*" -- address (no name)                      -->
<!ENTITY % m.bib    "(no?, title, (%bib;)*)" -- bibliographic entry         -->
<!ENTITY % m.copy   "(date|cpyrtnme|cpyrtclr)+" -- copyright notice data    -->
<!ENTITY % m.date   "(#PCDATA)" -- date                                     -->
<!ENTITY % m.fig    "EMPTY" -- default FIG content                          -->
<!ENTITY % m.sec    "(title?, (%s.zz;)*, section*)" -- section              -->
```

```
<!ENTITY % m.name  "((fname? & surname), (degree|school)*, role*, (%ade.ph;)*,
                   aff?)" -- name components                              -->
<!ENTITY % m.org   "(orgname, orgdiv*, %m.addr;)" -- organization name     -->
<!ENTITY % m.ph    "(#PCDATA|(%p.zz.ph;)|(%p.form;))*" -- phrase model     -->
<!ENTITY % m.pseq  "(p, (p|(%p.zz;))*)" -- P with sequence                 -->
<!ENTITY % m.poem  "(stanza+|poemline+)" -- poetry sub-elements            -->


<!-- ++++++++++++++++++++++++++++++++++++++++++++++++++++++++++++++++++++++ -->
<!--     Attribute Definitions                                             -->
<!-- ++++++++++++++++++++++++++++++++++++++++++++++++++++++++++++++++++++++ -->

<!ENTITY % a.id     "id ID #IMPLIED" -- ID attribute definition             -->
<!ENTITY % a.rid    "rid IDREF #REQUIRED" -- IDREF attribute definition     -->
<!ENTITY % au.rid   "rids IDREFS #IMPLIED" -- to refer to a unique id of
                                              an affiliation               -->
<!ENTITY % a.sizes "sizex NUTOKEN #IMPLIED
                    sizey NUTOKEN #IMPLIED
                    unit CDATA #IMPLIED"
                    -- unit must be specified if sizex or sizey are.        -->
<!ENTITY % a.types "(latin|greek|cyrillic|hebrew|kanji) latin"
                    -- Indicates which alphabet is used in the
                    element (title, p, q). This may be changed to a notation
                    attribute, where the notation could describe a keyboard
                    mapping. Modify the set as necessary.                  -->
<!ENTITY % d.types "(1 | 2 | 3 | 4 | 5) #IMPLIED"
                    -- Suggestions for date types:
                    1=ISO 8601:1988, 2=mm-dd-yy, 3=mm/dd/yy, 4=dd-mm-yy,
                    5=month day year; if more needed (e.g. "day month year")
                    modify or extend this list as necessary.               -->

<!ENTITY % e.types "(1|2|3|4|5|6) #IMPLIED"
                    -- Suggestions for emphasis types:
                    1=bold, 2=italic, 3=bold italic, 4=underline,
                    5=non proportional, 6=smallcaps; if more needed
                    modify or extend this list as necessary.               -->

<!ENTITY % l.types "(1 | 2 | 3 | 4 | 5| 6) #IMPLIED"
                    -- Suggestions for list types:
                    1=arabic, 2=upper alpha, 3=roman, 4=bullet, 5=dash,
                    6=unlabelled; if more needed (e.g. lower alpha)
                    modify or extend this list as necessary.               -->


<!-- ++++++++++++++++++++++++++++++++++++++++++++++++++++++++++++++++++++++ -->
<!--     Accessible Document Parameter Entities                            -->
<!-- ++++++++++++++++++++++++++++++++++++++++++++++++++++++++++++++++++++++ -->

<!ENTITY % SDAFORM      "SDAFORM   CDATA    #FIXED"                         >
<!ENTITY % SDARULE      "SDARULE   CDATA    #FIXED"                         >
<!ENTITY % SDAPREF      "SDAPREF   CDATA    #FIXED"                         >
<!ENTITY % SDASUFF      "SDASUFF   CDATA    #FIXED"                         >
<!ENTITY % SDASUSP      "SDASUSP   NAME     #FIXED"                         >
```

```
<!-- ================================================================== -->
<!--     DATA CONTENT NOTATIONS                                          -->
<!-- ================================================================== -->

<!-- These are only some examples. Add other public notations as required. -->

<!NOTATION eps      PUBLIC
"+//ISBN 0-201-18127-4::Adobe//NOTATION PostScript Language Reference
Manual//EN"                                                              >
<!NOTATION tex      PUBLIC
"+//ISBN 0-201-13448-9::Knuth//NOTATION The TeXbook//EN"                 >
<!NOTATION cgmchar  PUBLIC     "ISO 8632/2//NOTATION Character encoding//EN" >
<!NOTATION cgmclear PUBLIC     "ISO 8632/4//NOTATION Clear text encoding//EN">
<!NOTATION tiff     PUBLIC     "ISO 12083:1993//NOTATION TIFF-1//EN"     >


<!-- ================================================================== -->
<!--     THE DOCUMENT STRUCTURE                                          -->
<!-- ================================================================== -->

<!--       ELEMENT              MIN  CONTENT              (EXCEPTIONS)   -->
<!ELEMENT (%doctype;)           - -  (front, body, appmat?, back?)
                                                          +(%i.float;)   >

<!-- ================================================================== -->
<!--     FRONT MATTER ELEMENTS                                           -->
<!-- ================================================================== -->

<!-- The following declaration is specific to Articles                   -->
<!ELEMENT front                 O O  (titlegrp, authgrp, date?, pubfront?,
                                     ((%fmsec.d;)|keyword|keyphras)*)    >

<!ELEMENT (%fmsec.d;)           - O  %m.sec;                             >


<!-- ++++++++++++++++++++++++++++++++++++++++++++++++++++++++++++++++++ -->
<!--   Title Group                                                       -->
<!-- ++++++++++++++++++++++++++++++++++++++++++++++++++++++++++++++++++ -->

<!ELEMENT titlegrp              O O  (title, subtitle*)                  >
<!ELEMENT (title|subtitle)      - O  %m.ph;                              >


<!-- ++++++++++++++++++++++++++++++++++++++++++++++++++++++++++++++++++ -->
<!--   Author Group                                                      -->
<!-- ++++++++++++++++++++++++++++++++++++++++++++++++++++++++++++++++++ -->

<!ELEMENT authgrp               O O  (author|corpauth|aff)*              >
<!ELEMENT author                - O  %m.name;                            >
<!ELEMENT (fname|surname|role|degree|orgname|orgdiv)
                                - O  (#PCDATA)                           >

<!ELEMENT (aff|corpauth|school)
                                - O  %m.org;                             >
```

```
<!ELEMENT (%ade.ph;)            - O  (#PCDATA)                                >

<!-- ++++++++++++++++++++++++++++++++++++++++++++++++++++++++++++++++++++++ -->
<!--    Publisher's Front Matter                                             -->
<!-- ++++++++++++++++++++++++++++++++++++++++++++++++++++++++++++++++++++++ -->

<!ELEMENT pubfront              - O  ((%pub;) | (%pub.ph;))*                  >
<!ELEMENT (%pub.ph;|contract)   - O  (#PCDATA)                                >
<!ELEMENT (pubname|avail|sponsor)
                                - O  %m.org;                                  >
<!ELEMENT reprint               - O  (%m.org;|%m.name;)                       >

<!-- ++++++++++++++++++++++++++++++++++++++++++++++++++++++++++++++++++++++ -->
<!--            Article's History                                            -->
<!-- ++++++++++++++++++++++++++++++++++++++++++++++++++++++++++++++++++++++ -->

<!-- The following 2 declarations are specific to Articles                  -->
<!ELEMENT history               - O  (received|accepted|revised|misc)*        >
<!ELEMENT (received|accepted|revised)
                                - O  (date)                                   >
<!ELEMENT misc                  - O  (p*, date)                               >

<!-- ++++++++++++++++++++++++++++++++++++++++++++++++++++++++++++++++++++++ -->
<!--    Copyright                                                            -->
<!-- ++++++++++++++++++++++++++++++++++++++++++++++++++++++++++++++++++++++ -->

<!ELEMENT cpyrt                 - -  %m.copy;                                 >
<!ELEMENT cpyrtclr              - -  %m.org;                                  >
<!ELEMENT cpyrtnme              - -  (%m.org;|%m.name;)                       >

<!-- ++++++++++++++++++++++++++++++++++++++++++++++++++++++++++++++++++++++ -->
<!--    Conference Group                                                     -->
<!-- ++++++++++++++++++++++++++++++++++++++++++++++++++++++++++++++++++++++ -->

<!ELEMENT confgrp               - -  (no?, confname, date?, location?,
                                     sponsor?)                                >
<!ELEMENT confname              - O  (#PCDATA)                                >

<!-- ++++++++++++++++++++++++++++++++++++++++++++++++++++++++++++++++++++++ -->
<!--    Date                                                                 -->
<!-- ++++++++++++++++++++++++++++++++++++++++++++++++++++++++++++++++++++++ -->

<!ELEMENT date                  - O  %m.date;                                 >
```

```
<!-- ===================================================================== -->
<!--    BODY ELEMENTS                                                       -->
<!-- ===================================================================== -->

<!-- +++++++++++++++++++++++++++++++++++++++++++++++++++++++++++++++++++++ -->
<!--    Body Structure                                                      -->
<!-- +++++++++++++++++++++++++++++++++++++++++++++++++++++++++++++++++++++ -->

<!ELEMENT body              O O  (part+|chapter+)                          >
<!ELEMENT part              - O  (no?, title?, (%s.zz;)*, chapter+)        >
<!ELEMENT chapter           - O  (no?, %m.sec;)                            >
<!ELEMENT section           - O  (no?, title?, (%s.zz;)*, subsect1*)       >
<!ELEMENT subsect1          - O  (no?, title?, (%s.zz;)*, subsect2*)       >
<!ELEMENT subsect2          - O  (no?, title?, (%s.zz;)*, subsect3*)       >
<!ELEMENT subsect3          - O  (no?, title?, (%s.zz;)*, subsect4*)       >
<!ELEMENT subsect4          - O  (no?, title?, (%s.zz;)*, subsect5*)       >
<!ELEMENT subsect5          - O  (no?, title?, (%s.zz;)*, subsect6*)       >
<!ELEMENT subsect6          - O  (no?, title?, (%s.zz;)*)                  >
<!ELEMENT no                - O  (#PCDATA)                                 >


<!-- +++++++++++++++++++++++++++++++++++++++++++++++++++++++++++++++++++++ -->
<!--    Section Subelements                                                 -->
<!-- +++++++++++++++++++++++++++++++++++++++++++++++++++++++++++++++++++++ -->

<!ELEMENT p                 - O  (#PCDATA|(%p.zz.ph;)|(%p.zz;))*           >

<!-- +++++++++++++++++++++++++++++++++++++++++++++++++++++++++++++++++++++ -->
<!--    Paragraph Subelements                                               -->
<!-- +++++++++++++++++++++++++++++++++++++++++++++++++++++++++++++++++++++ -->

<!ELEMENT bq                - -  %m.pseq;                                  >
<!ELEMENT indaddr           - O  %m.name; -- individual address           -->
<!ELEMENT orgaddr           - O  %m.org;  -- organization address         -->
<!ELEMENT artwork           - O  EMPTY                                     >

<!ELEMENT lit               - -  RCDATA                                    >

<!ELEMENT (%p.lst.d;)       - -  (head?, item)*                            >
<!ELEMENT item              - O  %m.pseq;                                  >

<!ELEMENT deflist           - -  ((head, ddhd)?, term, dd)*                >
<!ELEMENT (term|head|ddhd)  - O  %m.ph;                                    >
<!ELEMENT dd                - O  %m.pseq;                                  >

<!ELEMENT biblist           - O  (head?, citation)*                        >
<!ELEMENT citation          - O  %m.bib;                                   >
<!ELEMENT (othinfo|subject|sertitle)
                            - O  %m.ph;                                    >

<!ELEMENT location          - O  %m.addr;                                  >
<!ELEMENT (msn|pages)       - O  (#PCDATA)                                 >
<!ELEMENT keyword           - O  (#PCDATA)                                 >
<!ELEMENT keyphras          - O  (#PCDATA)                                 >
```

```
<!ELEMENT indxflag              - O  EMPTY                                >

<!-- ++++++++++++++++++++++++++++++++++++++++++++++++++++++++++++++++++++ -->
<!--    Poetry                                                            -->
<!-- ++++++++++++++++++++++++++++++++++++++++++++++++++++++++++++++++++++ -->

<!ELEMENT poem                  - O  %m.poem;                             >
<!ELEMENT stanza                - O  (poemline)+                          >
<!ELEMENT poemline              - O  (#PCDATA|cline|%p.em.ph;)*           >
<!ELEMENT cline                 - O  (#PCDATA|%p.em.ph;)*                 >

<!-- ++++++++++++++++++++++++++++++++++++++++++++++++++++++++++++++++++++ -->
<!--    Phrases                                                           -->
<!-- ++++++++++++++++++++++++++++++++++++++++++++++++++++++++++++++++++++ -->

<!ELEMENT q                     - -  %m.ph;                               >
<!ELEMENT (%p.em.ph;)           - -  %m.ph;                               >
<!ELEMENT (%p.rf.ph;)           - -  (#PCDATA)                            >

<!-- ++++++++++++++++++++++++++++++++++++++++++++++++++++++++++++++++++++ -->
<!--    For HyTime Links                                                  -->
<!-- ++++++++++++++++++++++++++++++++++++++++++++++++++++++++++++++++++++ -->

<!ELEMENT nameloc               - O (nmlist*) -- assigns a local ID to
                                   named objects                         -->
<!ELEMENT nmlist                - O (#PCDATA) -- list of local ID or entity
                                   names                                 -->

<!-- ++++++++++++++++++++++++++++++++++++++++++++++++++++++++++++++++++++ -->
<!--    Floating Elements                                                 -->
<!-- ++++++++++++++++++++++++++++++++++++++++++++++++++++++++++++++++++++ -->

<!ELEMENT figgrp                - -  (title? & fig*)                      >
<!ELEMENT fig                   - O  %m.fig;                              >
<!ELEMENT footnote              - -  (no?, %m.pseq;)        -(%i.float;)  >
<!ELEMENT note                  - -  (no?, %m.pseq;)                      >

<!-- ++++++++++++++++++++++++++++++++++++++++++++++++++++++++++++++++++++ -->
<!--    Tables                                                            -->
<!-- ++++++++++++++++++++++++++++++++++++++++++++++++++++++++++++++++++++ -->

<!ELEMENT table                 - -  (no?, title?, tbody)   -(%i.float;)  >
<!ELEMENT tbody                 - O  (head*, tsubhead*, row*)             >
<!ELEMENT row                   - O  (tstub?, cell*)                      >
<!ELEMENT tsubhead              - O  %m.ph;                               >
<!ELEMENT (tstub|cell)          - O  %m.pseq;                             >
```

```
<!-- ++++++++++++++++++++++++++++++++++++++++++++++++++++++++++++++++++++ -->
<!--    Mathematics                                                       -->
<!-- ++++++++++++++++++++++++++++++++++++++++++++++++++++++++++++++++++++ -->

<!ENTITY % maths PUBLIC "ISO 12083:1994//DTD Mathematics//EN"            >
%maths;

<!-- Remove these comments if the formulas follow a NOTATION rather than SGML.
<!ELEMENT dformgrp             - O  (dformula)+                           >
<!ELEMENT (formula|dformula)   - -  CDATA                                 >
-->

<!-- ==================================================================== -->
<!--    APPENDIX ELEMENTS                                                 -->
<!-- ==================================================================== -->

<!ELEMENT appmat               - O  (appendix+)                           >
<!ELEMENT appendix             - O  (no?, %m.sec;)                        >


<!-- ==================================================================== -->
<!--    BACK MATTER ELEMENTS                                              -->
<!-- ==================================================================== -->

<!-- The following declaration is specific to Articles                   -->
<!ELEMENT back                 - O  (%bmsec.d;|biblist)*                  >

<!ELEMENT (%bmsec.d;)          - O  %m.sec;                               >


<!-- ==================================================================== -->
<!--    ATTRIBUTE DEFINITION LISTS                                        -->
<!-- ==================================================================== -->

<!-- HyTime attributes were added to all references,
     the citation and doclink elements                                   -->

<!-- The SGML Document Access attributes for Braille, large print
and voice synthesis markup have been added to the attributes already
declared in this DTD in the first section following, and then for
all elements which have no attributes except for the SDA set.            -->

<!--      ELEMENT  NAME      VALUE        DEFAULT                        -->
<!ATTLIST abstract %a.id;
          %SDAPREF;                       "<h1>Abstract</h1>"             >

<!ATTLIST ack      %a.id;
          %SDAPREF;                       "<h1>Acknowledgements</h1>"     >

<!ATTLIST acqno
          %SDAFORM;                       "para"
          %SDAPREF;                       "Acquisition/order number: "    >

<!ATTLIST aff      %a.id;                                                 >
```

```
<!ATTLIST appendix  %a.id;
         %SDAPREF;                            "<h1>Appendix</h1>"        >

<!ATTLIST artwork   %a.id;
                    %a.sizes;
                    name        ENTITY        #IMPLIED
         %SDAFORM;                            "fig #attrib ID"           >

<!ATTLIST author    %au.rid;
         %SDAFORM;                            "au"                       >

<!ATTLIST biblist   file        ENTITY        #IMPLIED
         %SDAFORM;                            "list"
         %SDAPREF;                            "Bibliography"             >

<!ATTLIST chapter   %a.id;
         SDABDY     NAMES       #FIXED        "title h1"
         SDAPART    NAMES       #FIXED        "title h2"                 >

<!ATTLIST citation  id          ID            #REQUIRED
                    HyTime      NAME          #FIXED bibloc
         %SDARULE;                            "title it
                                              author para
                                              corpauth para
                                              sertitle it"               >

<!ATTLIST corpauth  %a.id;
         %SDAFORM;                            "au"                       >

<!ATTLIST country   cnycode     NAME          #IMPLIED
                                          -- name should follow ISO 3166 -->

<!ATTLIST date      type        %d.types;
         %SDAPREF;                            "Date:"                    >

<!ATTLIST dd        %a.id;
         %SDAFORM;                            "para"                     >

<!ATTLIST deflist   %a.id;
         %SDAFORM;                            "list"
         %SDAPREF;                            "<?SDATRANS>Definitions "  >

<!ATTLIST %doctype; %a.id;
                    HyTime      NAME          #FIXED HyDoc
                    %SDAFORM;                 "article"                  >

<!ATTLIST fig       %a.id;
                    %a.sizes;
                    name        ENTITY        #IMPLIED
                    scale       NUMBER        100
         %SDAPREF;                            "<?SDATRANS>Figure: "      >

<!ATTLIST figgrp   %a.id;
         %SDARULE;                            "title para"               >
```

```
<!ATTLIST footnote  %a.id;
          %SDAFORM;                            "fn"                  >

<!ATTLIST indxflag  ref1        CDATA          #IMPLIED
                    ref2        CDATA          #IMPLIED
                    ref3        CDATA          #IMPLIED
                    ref4        CDATA          #IMPLIED              >

<!ATTLIST item      %a.id;
          %SDAFORM;                            "litem"               >

<!ATTLIST nameloc   HyTime      NAME           nameloc
                    id          ID             #REQUIRED
                    -- multloc attributes --
                    ordering    (ordered|noorder)
                                               noorder
                    -- is ordering of locations significant? --
                    set         (set|notset)   notset
                    -- make multiple a set by ignoring duplicates --
                    aggloc      (aggloc|agglink|nagg)
                                               nagg
                    -- are multiple locations an aggregate? --
                    %SDAPREF;                "<?SDATRANS>Nameloc:"   >

<!ATTLIST nmlist    HyTime      NAME           nmlist
                    nametype    (entity|element)
                                               entity
                    -- entity names or IDs of elements --
                    obnames     (obnames|nobnames)
                                               nobnames
                    -- objects treated as names? --
                    docorsub    ENTITY         #IMPLIED
                    dtdorlpd    NAMES          #IMPLIED
                    %SDAPREF;                "<?SDATRANS>Namelist:"  >

<!ATTLIST note      %a.id;
          %SDAFORM;                            "note"                >

<!ATTLIST p         %a.id;
                    alphabet    %a.types;
          %SDAFORM;                            "para"                >

<!ATTLIST part      %a.id;
          %SDARULE;                            "chapter #use SDAPART"  >

<!ATTLIST %p.em.ph; type        %e.types;
          %SDARULE;                            "[emph type=1] b
                                                [emph type=2] it
                                                [emph type=(3|4|5|6)] other" >
```

```
<!ATTLIST %p.lst.d; %a.id;
          type              %l.types;
      %SDAFORM;                          "list"
      %SDAPREF;             "[list type=1]#set (item,#count(item,1))
                            [list type=2]#set (item,#count(item,A)
                            [list type=3]#set (item,#count(item,I))
                            [list type=4]#set (item,#count(item,'* ')
                            [list type=5]#set (item,#count(item,'- '))"  >

<!ATTLIST (%p.rf.ph;) %a.rid;
          %a.id;
          HyTime  NAME      #FIXED  clink
          HyNames CDATA     #FIXED  "rid linkend"
      %SDAFORM;                     "xref #attrib IDREF"               >

<!ATTLIST %p.tbl;  %a.id;
      %SDAFORM;                     "table"
      %SDARULE;                     "title h3
                                    head hdcell"
      %SDAPREF;                     "<?SDATRANS>"                      >

<!ATTLIST q         %a.id;
          alphabet      %a.types;
          %SDAPREF;                 "'"
          %SDASUFF;                 "'"                                >

<!ATTLIST section   %a.id;
      SDABDY    NAMES      #FIXED           "title h2"
      SDAPART   NAMES      #FIXED           "title h3"                 >

<!ATTLIST subsect1  %a.id;
      SDABDY    NAMES      #FIXED           "title h3"
      SDAPART   NAMES      #FIXED           "title h4"                 >

<!ATTLIST subsect2  %a.id;
      SDABDY    NAMES      #FIXED           "title h4"
      SDAPART   NAMES      #FIXED           "title h5"                 >

<!ATTLIST subsect3  %a.id;
      SDABDY    NAMES      #FIXED           "title h5"
      SDAPART   NAMES      #FIXED           "title h6"                 >

<!ATTLIST subsect4  %a.id;
      SDABDY    NAMES      #FIXED           "title h6"
      SDAPART   NAMES      #FIXED           "title b"                  >

<!ATTLIST (subsect5|subsect6)
                    %a.id;
      SDABDY    NAMES      #FIXED           "title b"
      SDAPART   NAMES      #FIXED           "title b"                  >

<!ATTLIST term      %a.id;
      %SDAFORM;                             "term"                     >
```

```
<!ATTLIST title      alphabet    %a.types;
                     purpose     (normal|run)    normal
          %SDAFORM;                              "ti"              >


<!-- ================================================================== -->
<!--     SDA ATTRIBUTES                                                 -->
<!-- ================================================================== -->

<!-- The following declarations support elements whose only attributes are
SDA attributes:                                                      -->

<!ATTLIST avail
          %SDAFORM;                              "para"
          %SDAPREF;                              "Available from: "   >

<!ATTLIST body
          %SDARULE;                              "chapter #use SDABDY "   >

<!ATTLIST bq
          %SDAFORM;                              "bq"                 >

<!ATTLIST cell
          %SDAFORM;                              "cell"               >

<!ATTLIST cpyrtclr
          %SDAFORM;                              "para"
          %SDAPREF;                              "Copyright clearance center: ">

<!ATTLIST coden
          %SDAFORM;                              "para"
          %SDAPREF;                              "CODEN: "            >

<!ATTLIST contract
          %SDAFORM;                              "para"
          %SDAPREF;                              "Contract or grant number: "  >

<!ATTLIST sponsor
          %SDAFORM;                              "para"
          %SDAPREF;                              "(Contract or grant) sponsor:">

<!ATTLIST confgrp
          %SDAFORM;                              "para"
          %SDAPREF;                              "Conference group: "  >

<!ATTLIST confname
          %SDAFORM;                              "para"
          %SDAPREF;                              "Conference name: "   >

<!ATTLIST cpyrt
          %SDAFORM;                              "para"
          %SDAPREF;                              "<?SDATRANS>Copyright notice:">

<!ATTLIST ddhd
          %SDAFORM;                              "lhead"              >
```

```
<!ATTLIST ded
          %SDAPREF;                    "<h1>Dedication</h1>"          >

<!ATTLIST email
          %SDAFORM;                    "para"
          %SDAPREF;                    "Electronic address: "         >

<!ATTLIST extent
          %SDAFORM;                    "para"
          %SDAPREF;                    "Number of pages: "            >

<!ATTLIST fax
          %SDAFORM;                    "para"
          %SDAPREF;                    "FAX number: "                 >

<!ATTLIST head
          %SDAFORM;                    "lhead"                        >

<!ATTLIST (indaddr|orgaddr)
          %SDAFORM;                    "para"
          %SDAPREF;                    "Address: "                    >

<!ATTLIST issn
          %SDAFORM;                    "para"
          %SDAPREF;                    "ISSN: "                       >

<!ATTLIST (keyphras|keyword)
          %SDAFORM;                    "term"                         >

<!ATTLIST lit
          %SDAFORM;                    "lit"                          >

<!ATTLIST location
          %SDAFORM;                    "para"
          %SDAPREF;                    "Location: "                   >

<!ATTLIST othinfo
          %SDAFORM;                    "para"                         >

<!ATTLIST acidfree
          %SDAFORM;                    "para"
          %SDAPREF;                    "Acid free paper indicator: " >

<!ATTLIST phone
          %SDAFORM;                    "para"
          %SDAPREF;                    "Phone: "                      >

<!ATTLIST pubid
          %SDAFORM;                    "para"
          %SDAPREF;                    "Publisher's ID number: "      >

<!ATTLIST pubname
          %SDAFORM;                    "para"
          %SDAPREF;                    "Publisher: "                  >
```

```
<!ATTLIST pages
          %SDAFORM;                          "pp"                          >

<!ATTLIST price
          %SDAFORM;                          "para"
          %SDAPREF;                          "Price: "                     >

<!ATTLIST row
          %SDAFORM;                          "row"                         >

<!ATTLIST reprint
          %SDAFORM;                          "para"
          %SDAPREF;                          "Reprint source: "            >

<!ATTLIST san
          %SDAFORM;                          "para"
          %SDAPREF;                          "Standard address number: "   >

<!ATTLIST subtitle
          %SDAFORM;                          "h1"                          >

<!ATTLIST subject
          %SDAFORM;                          "it"                          >

<!ATTLIST supmatl
          %SDAFORM;                          "para"
          %SDAPREF;                          "Supporting material: "       >

<!ATTLIST sertitle
          %SDAFORM;                          "ti"                          >

<!ATTLIST tbody
          %SDAFORM;                          "tbody"                       >

<!ATTLIST tstub
          %SDAFORM;                          "stubcell"                    >

<!ATTLIST tsubhead
          %SDAFORM;                          "hdcell"                      >

<!-- Remove this comment around the next three declarations if formulas
     follow a notation rather than SGML.
<!ATTLIST formula
          %a.id;
          notation NOTATION (tex)            #IMPLIED
          alphabet %a.types;
          %SDAPREF;                          "<?SDATRANS>Inline formula: "
          %SDASUSP;                          "SUSPEND"                     >
```

```
<!ATTLIST dformula
          %a.id;
          alphabet %a.types;
          notation NOTATION (tex)             #IMPLIED
          num      CDATA                      #IMPLIED
          align    (left|center|right)        center
          %SDAPREF;                           "<?SDATRANS>Display formula: "
          %SDASUSP;                           "SUSPEND"                      >

<!ATTLIST dformgrp
          %a.id;
          num      CDATA                      #IMPLIED
          align    (left|center|right) center
          %SDAPREF;                      "<?SDATRANS>Display formula group: ">
-->
```

8 The Serial DTD

```
<!-- This is the ISO12083:1994 document type definition for Serials.       -->
<!-- Copyright: (C) International Organization for Standardization 1994.
Permission to copy in any form is granted for use with conforming SGML
systems and applications as defined in ISO 8879:1986, provided this
notice is included in all copies.                                           -->
<!-- ==================================================================== -->
<!--     PUBLIC DOCUMENT TYPE DEFINITION SUBSET                             -->
<!-- ==================================================================== -->

<!-- Typical invocation:
<!DOCTYPE serial PUBLIC "ISO 12083:1994//DTD Serial//EN"
 [<!ENTITY % ISOnum PUBLIC "ISO 8879:1986//ENTITIES Numeric and
          Special Graphic//EN"                                  >
  <!ENTITY % ISOpub PUBLIC "ISO 8879:1986//ENTITIES
          Publishing//EN"                                       >
  <!ENTITY % ISOtech PUBLIC "ISO 8879:1986//ENTITIES
          General Technical//EN"                                >
  <!ENTITY % ISOdia PUBLIC "ISO 8879:1986//ENTITIES
          Diacritical Marks//EN"                                >
  <!ENTITY % ISOlat1 PUBLIC "ISO 8879:1986//ENTITIES
          Added Latin 1//EN"                                    >
  <!ENTITY % ISOlat2 PUBLIC "ISO 8879:1986//ENTITIES
          Added Latin 2//EN"                                    >
  <!ENTITY % ISOamso PUBLIC "ISO 8879:1986//ENTITIES
          Added Math Symbols: Ordinary//EN"                     >
  <!ENTITY % ISOgrk1 PUBLIC "ISO 8879:1986//ENTITIES
          Greek Letters//EN"                                    >
  <!ENTITY % ISOgrk3 PUBLIC "ISO 8879:1986//ENTITIES
          Greek Symbols//EN"                                    >
  %ISOnum;
  %ISOpub;
  %ISOtech;
  %ISOdia;
  %ISOlat1;
```

```
  %ISOlat2;
  %ISOamso;
  %ISOgrk1;
  %ISOgrk3;
  <!ENTITY % ereview PUBLIC "-//USA-DOD//DTD
          SUP MIL-M-28001 EREVIEW REV B//EN"                      >
  %ereview;
]>                                                                       -->

<!-- NOTES: 1. ISO/IEC TR 9573 Parts 12-16 are currently under review and will
              contain complete special character entity sets.
           2. MIL-M-28001 EREVIEW are the CALS facilities for electronic
              review.                                                    -->

<!-- This is the document type declaration subset for a Serial. Articles will
be embedded within this document type.                                   -->

<!-- Entity naming conventions are the same as for Books and Article     -->

<!ENTITY % serial "serial" -- default document type generic identifier   -->


<!-- +++++++++++++++++++++++++++++++++++++++++++++++++++++++++++++++++++ -->
<!--    Specialized Elements                                             -->
<!-- +++++++++++++++++++++++++++++++++++++++++++++++++++++++++++++++++++ -->

<!ENTITY % bmsec.i "glossary|index" -- indexes and glossary              -->
<!ENTITY % spub    "reprint|cpyrt|date|pubname|location|confgrp|avail|
                   issueid|coden|acqno|acidfree|price|extent"
                   -- serial pubfront                                    -->
<!ENTITY % spub.ph "lccardno|reportid|edition|volid|catalog|package|pubid"
                   -- serial publication related front matter material   -->
<!ENTITY % i.sflt  "aseqntl|advert" -- serial floats                     -->


<!-- +++++++++++++++++++++++++++++++++++++++++++++++++++++++++++++++++++ -->
<!--    Models                                                           -->
<!-- +++++++++++++++++++++++++++++++++++++++++++++++++++++++++++++++++++ -->

<!ENTITY % m.adv   "EMPTY" -- default advertisement content              -->
<!ENTITY % m.toc   "EMPTY" -- table of contents model                    -->

<!-- Article declaration subset is included here.                        -->
<!ENTITY % serart PUBLIC "ISO 12083:1994//DTD Article//EN"                >
%serart;

<!-- end article declaration subset                                      -->

<!ENTITY % m.idx   "(%m.sec;|((indxname|indxsubj)*,pages*))" -- model for
                   indexes and glossary                                  -->
```

```
<!-- ==================================================================== -->
<!--    THE DOCUMENT STRUCTURE                                            -->
<!-- ==================================================================== -->

<!--        ELEMENT             MIN  CONTENT                (EXCEPTIONS)  -->
<!ELEMENT  (%serial;)           - -  (serfront, serbody, serback?)
                                              +(%i.sflt;|%i.float;)>

<!-- ==================================================================== -->
<!--    FRONT MATTER ELEMENTS                                             -->
<!-- ==================================================================== -->

<!ELEMENT  serfront             O O  (title, stitle?, alttitle?, serpubfr?,
                                                            toc?)>

<!-- ++++++++++++++++++++++++++++++++++++++++++++++++++++++++++++++++++++ -->
<!--    Title Group                                                       -->
<!-- ++++++++++++++++++++++++++++++++++++++++++++++++++++++++++++++++++++ -->

<!ELEMENT  (stitle|alttitle) O O  %m.ph;                                  >

<!-- ++++++++++++++++++++++++++++++++++++++++++++++++++++++++++++++++++++ -->
<!--             Serial Publisher's Front Matter                          -->
<!-- ++++++++++++++++++++++++++++++++++++++++++++++++++++++++++++++++++++ -->

<!ELEMENT serpubfr              - O  ((%spub;)|(%spub.ph;))*               >
<!ELEMENT (%spub.ph;)           - O  (#PCDATA)                             >
<!ELEMENT issueid               - O  (issueno, issuept?, supplid?)         >
<!ELEMENT (issueno|issuept|supplid)
                                - O  (#PCDATA)                             >

<!-- ++++++++++++++++++++++++++++++++++++++++++++++++++++++++++++++++++++ -->
<!--    Table of Contents                                                 -->
<!-- ++++++++++++++++++++++++++++++++++++++++++++++++++++++++++++++++++++ -->

<!ELEMENT toc                   - O  %m.toc;                               >

<!-- ==================================================================== -->
<!--    BODY ELEMENTS                                                     -->
<!-- ==================================================================== -->

<!-- ++++++++++++++++++++++++++++++++++++++++++++++++++++++++++++++++++++ -->
<!--    Body Structure                                                    -->
<!-- ++++++++++++++++++++++++++++++++++++++++++++++++++++++++++++++++++++ -->

<!ELEMENT serbody               O O  (serpart+|sersec+)                    >
<!ELEMENT serpart               - O  (title?, (%s.zz;|sersec|article)*)
                                -- Department or Special Features         -->
<!ELEMENT sersec                - O  (title?, (%s.zz;|article)*)
                                -- Book Reviews, Engineering Notes, etc.  -->
```

```
<!-- ++++++++++++++++++++++++++++++++++++++++++++++++++++++++++++++++++++++ -->
<!--          Floating elements                                              -->
<!-- ++++++++++++++++++++++++++++++++++++++++++++++++++++++++++++++++++++++ -->

<!ELEMENT advert              - O  %m.adv;                                  >
<!ELEMENT aseqntl             - -  %m.sec;
          -- Asequential elements are intended to be used as filler items  -->


<!-- ====================================================================== -->
<!--     BACK MATTER ELEMENTS                                               -->
<!-- ====================================================================== -->

<!ELEMENT serback             - O  ((%bmsec.d;)|(%bmsec.i;))*               >
<!ELEMENT (%bmsec.i;)         - O  %m.idx;                                  >
<!ELEMENT (indxname|indxsubj)
                              - O  (#PCDATA)                                >


<!-- ====================================================================== -->
<!--     ATTRIBUTE DEFINITION LISTS                                         -->
<!-- ====================================================================== -->
<!-- The SGML Document Access attributes for Braille, large print
and voice synthesis markup have been added.                                 -->

<!--       ELEMENT    NAME       VALUE        DEFAULT                       -->

<!ATTLIST advert      %a.id;
                      %a.sizes;
                      name       ENTITY       #IMPLIED
                      %SDAFORM;               "fig"                         >

<!ATTLIST catalog     %SDAFORM;               "para"
                      %SDAPREF;               "<?SDATRANS>Cataloguing
                                              in publication information:"  >

<!ATTLIST %serial;    %a.id;
                      %SDAFORM;               "serial"                      >

<!ATTLIST edition     %SDAFORM;               "para"
                      %SDAPREF;               "<?SDATRANS>Edition:"         >

<!ATTLIST glossary    %a.id;
                      %SDAPREF;               "<h1>Glossary</h1>"           >

<!ATTLIST index       %a.id;
                      %SDAPREF;               "<h1>Index</h1>"              >

<!ATTLIST (indxname|indxsubj)
                      %SDAFORM;               "term"                        >

<!ATTLIST lccardno    %SDAFORM;               "para"
                      %SDAPREF;               "LC card number:"             >
```

```
<!ATTLIST package   %SDAFORM;                  "para"
                    %SDAPREF;                  "Packaging method:"          >

<!ATTLIST reportid  %SDAFORM;                  "para"
                    %SDAPREF;                  "Report identifier:"         >

<!ATTLIST (stitle|alttitle)
                    alphabet    %a.types;
                    %SDAFORM;                  "ti"                         >

<!ATTLIST toc       %SDAFORM;                  "list"
                    %SDAPREF;                  "<?SDATRANS>Contents"        >

<!ATTLIST volid     %SDAFORM;                  "para"
                    %SDAPREF;                  "Volume identifier:"         >
```

9 The Mathematics DTD

```
<!-- This is the ISO12083:1994 document type definition for Mathematics     -->

<!-- Copyright: (C) International Organization for Standardization 1994.
Permission to copy in any form is granted for use with conforming SGML
systems and applications as defined in ISO 8879:1986, provided this notice
is included in all copies.                                                  -->

<!-- ================================================================== -->
<!--     PUBLIC DOCUMENT TYPE DEFINITION SUBSET                             -->
<!-- ================================================================== -->

<!--
This DTD is included by the Book and Article DTDs of ISO12083:1994.
As it is a separate entity it may also be included by other DTDs.

Since there is no consensus on how to describe the semantics of formulas,
it only describes their presentational or visual structure. Since, however,
there is a strong need for such description (especially within the
print-disabled community), it is recommended that the following
declaration be added where there is a requirement for a consistent,
standardized mechanism to carry semantic meanings for the SGML
elements declared throughout this part of this International Standard:

<!ENTITY % SDAMAP "SDAMAP    NAME     #IMPLIED"             >

and that the attribute represented by %SDAMAP; be made available for
all elements which may require a semantic association, or, in the simpler
case, be added to all elements in this DTD.                                 -->
```

```
<!-- ==================================================================== -->
<!--  Parameter entities describing the possible contents of formulas.    -->
<!-- ==================================================================== -->

<!ENTITY % p.trans "bold|italic|sansser|typewrit|smallcap|roman"
                 -- character transformations                             -->
<!ENTITY % m.math "fraction|subform|sup|inf|top|bottom|middle|fence|mark|
   post|box|overline|undrline|radical|array|hspace|vspace|break|markref|
   #PCDATA" -- mathematical formula elements                              -->


<!-- ==================================================================== -->
<!-- Accessible Document and other Parameter Entities
     If this DTD is not imbedded by a ISO12083:1994 Book or Article,
     the comment delimiters should be removed.                            -->
<!-- ==================================================================== -->

<!--ENTITY % SDAFORM      "SDAFORM  CDATA   #FIXED"                       -->
<!--ENTITY % SDARULE      "SDARULE  CDATA   #FIXED"                       -->
<!--ENTITY % SDAPREF      "SDAPREF  CDATA   #FIXED"                       -->
<!--ENTITY % SDASUFF      "SDASUFF  CDATA   #FIXED"                       -->
<!--ENTITY % SDASUSP      "SDASUSP  NAME    #FIXED"                       -->


<!-- ==================================================================== -->
<!-- This entity is for an attribute to indicate which alphabet is
     used in the element (formula, dformula). This may be changed to
     a notation attribute, where the notation could describe a
     keyboard mapping. Modify the set as necessary.
     If this DTD is not imbedded by a ISO12083:1994 Book or Article,
     the comment delimiters should be removed.                            -->
<!-- ==================================================================== -->

<!--ENTITY % a.types "(latin|greek|cyrillic|hebrew|kanji) latin"          -->


<!-- ==================================================================== -->
<!--   Character transformations                                          -->
<!-- ==================================================================== -->

<!--       ELEMENT               MIN  CONTENT              EXPLANATIONS    -->
<!ELEMENT bold                   - -  (%p.trans;|#PCDATA)* -- bold         -->
<!ELEMENT italic                 - -  (%p.trans;|#PCDATA)* -- italic       -->
<!ELEMENT sansser                - -  (%p.trans;|#PCDATA)* -- sans serif   -->
<!ELEMENT typewrit               - -  (%p.trans;|#PCDATA)* -- typewriter   -->
<!ELEMENT smallcap               - -  (%p.trans;|#PCDATA)* -- small caps   -->
<!ELEMENT roman                  - -  (%p.trans;|#PCDATA)* -- roman        -->
```

```
<!-- ================================================================== -->
<!--   Fractions                                                        -->
<!-- ================================================================== -->

<!--        ELEMENT             MIN  CONTENT                EXPLANATIONS    -->
<!ELEMENT fraction              - -  (num, den)             -- fraction     -->
<!ELEMENT num                   - -  (%p.trans;|%m.math;)* -- numerator    -->
<!ELEMENT den                   - -  (%p.trans;|%m.math;)* -- denominator  -->
<!--        ELEMENT   NAME      VALUE            DEFAULT                    -->
<!ATTLIST fraction  shape       (built|case) #IMPLIED
                    align       (left|center|right)
                                                 center
                    style       (single|double|triple|dash|dot|bold|blank|none)
                                                 single                      >


<!-- ================================================================== -->
<!--   Superiors, inferiors, accents, over and under                    -->
<!-- ================================================================== -->

<!--        ELEMENT             MIN  CONTENT                EXPLANATIONS    -->
<!ELEMENT sup                   - -  (%p.trans;|%m.math;)* -- superior     -->
<!ELEMENT inf                   - -  (%p.trans;|%m.math;)* -- inferior     -->
<!--        ELEMENT   NAME      VALUE            DEFAULT                    -->
<!ATTLIST sup       location    (pre|post)       post
                    arrange     (compact|stagger)
                                                 compact                     >
<!ATTLIST inf       location    (pre|post) post
                    arrange     (compact|stagger) compact                    >


<!-- ================================================================== -->
<!--   Embellishments                                                   -->
<!-- ================================================================== -->

<!--        ELEMENT             MIN  CONTENT                EXPLANATIONS    -->
<!ELEMENT top                   - -  (%p.trans;|%m.math;)*
                                                      -- top embellishment   -->
<!ELEMENT middle                - -  (%p.trans;|%m.math;)*
                                                     -- middle, or "through" -->
<!ELEMENT bottom                - -  (%p.trans;|%m.math;)*
                                                     -- bottom embellishment -->
<!--        ELEMENT   NAME      VALUE            DEFAULT                    -->
<!ATTLIST top       align       (left|center|right)
                                                 center
                    sizeid      ID               #IMPLIED
                                                 -- to pass on the height    -->
<!ATTLIST middle    align       (left|center|right)
                                                 center
                    sizeid      ID               #IMPLIED
                                                 -- to pass on the height    -->
<!ATTLIST bottom    align       (left|center|right)
                                                 center
                    sizeid     ID              #IMPLIED
                                                 -- to pass on the height    -->
```

```
<!-- The subform element is defined later                                  -->


<!-- ================================================================== -->
<!--   Fences, boxes, overlines and underlines                             -->
<!-- ================================================================== -->

<!--      ELEMENT                 MIN  CONTENT                EXPLANATIONS    -->
<!ELEMENT mark                    - O  EMPTY                                   >
<!ELEMENT fence                   - -  (%p.trans;|%m.math;)* -- fence         -->
<!ELEMENT post                    - O  EMPTY                 -- post          -->
<!ELEMENT box                     - -  (%p.trans;|%m.math;)* -- box           -->
<!ELEMENT overline                - -  (%p.trans;|%m.math;)* -- overline      -->
<!ELEMENT undrline                - -  (%p.trans;|%m.math;)* -- underline     -->
<!--      ELEMENT       NAME      VALUE             DEFAULT                   -->
<!ATTLIST mark          id        ID                #REQUIRED                  >
<!ATTLIST fence         lpost     CDATA             "|" -- left post          --
                        rpost     CDATA             "|" -- right post         --
                        style     (single|double|triple|dash|dot|bold|blank|none)
                                                    single
                        sizeid    ID                #IMPLIED
                                                    -- to pass on the height  --
                        sizeref   IDREF             #IMPLIED
                                                    -- to pick up a height    -->
<!ATTLIST post          post      CDATA             "|"
                        style     (single|double|triple|dash|dot|bold|blank|none)
                                                    single
                        sizeid    ID                #IMPLIED
                                                    -- to pass on the height  --
                        sizeref   IDREF             #IMPLIED
                                                    -- to pick up a height    -->
<!ATTLIST box           style     (single|double|triple|dash|dot|bold|blank|none)
                                                    single                     >
<!ATTLIST overline      type      CDATA             "-" -- embellishment type --
                        style     (single|double|triple|dash|dot|bold|blank|none)
                                                    single
                        start     IDREF             #IMPLIED
                        end       IDREF             #IMPLIED                   >

<!ATTLIST undrline      type      CDATA             "_" -- embellishment type --
                        style     (single|double|triple|dash|dot|bold|blank|none)
                                                    single
                        start     IDREF             #IMPLIED
                        end       IDREF             #IMPLIED                   >


<!-- ================================================================== -->
<!--   Labelled arrows                                                     -->
<!-- ================================================================== -->

<!--      ELEMENT                 MIN  CONTENT                EXPLANATIONS    -->
<!ELEMENT subform                 - -  (%p.trans;|%m.math;)* -- base element  -->
```

```
<!--       ELEMENT   NAME       VALUE            DEFAULT                 -->
<!ATTLIST subform   sizeid     ID               #IMPLIED
                                                -- to pass on a width, or
                                                a height                --
                    sizeref    IDREF            #IMPLIED
                                                -- to pick up a width    -->


<!-- ==================================================================== -->
<!--    Roots                                                             -->
<!-- ==================================================================== -->

<!--       ELEMENT              MIN  CONTENT                EXPLANATIONS  -->
<!ELEMENT radical               - -  (radix?, radicand) -- root or radical -->
<!ELEMENT radix                 - -  (%p.trans;|%m.math;)* -- radix        -->
<!ELEMENT radicand              O O  (%p.trans;|%m.math;)* -- radicand     -->


<!-- ==================================================================== -->
<!--    Arrays                                                            -->
<!-- ==================================================================== -->

<!--       ELEMENT              MIN  CONTENT                EXPLANATIONS  -->
<!ELEMENT array                 - -  (arrayrow+|arraycol+) -- array        -->
<!ELEMENT arrayrow              - O  (arraycel+)       -- array row        -->
<!ELEMENT arraycol              - O  (arraycel+)       -- array column     -->
<!ELEMENT arraycel              - O  (%p.trans;|%m.math;)* -- array cell   -->

<!--       ELEMENT   NAME       VALUE            DEFAULT                 -->
<!ATTLIST array     rowalign   NMTOKENS         #IMPLIED -- row alignment  --
                    colalign   NMTOKENS         #IMPLIED -- column
                                                          alignment --
                    rowsep     NMTOKENS         #IMPLIED -- row separators --
                    colsep     NMTOKENS         #IMPLIED -- column
                                                          separators -->


<!-- ==================================================================== -->
<!--    Spacing                                                           -->
<!-- ==================================================================== -->

<!--       ELEMENT              MIN  CONTENT                EXPLANATIONS  -->
<!ELEMENT hspace                - O EMPTY           -- horizontal spacing -->
<!ELEMENT vspace                - O EMPTY           -- vertical spacing   -->
<!ELEMENT break                 - O EMPTY           -- turn line, break   -->
<!ELEMENT markref               - O EMPTY           -- hmark reference    -->

<!--       ELEMENT   NAME       VALUE            DEFAULT                 -->
<!ATTLIST hspace    space      CDATA            "1 mm"
                                                   -- units as required  -->
<!ATTLIST vspace    space      CDATA            "1 mm"
                                                   -- units as required  -->
<!ATTLIST markref   refid      IDREF            #REQUIRED
                    direct     (hor|ver)        hor
                                                 -- horizontal or vertical -->
```

```
<!-- ================================================================== -->
<!--   Formula elements                                                 -->
<!-- ================================================================== -->

<!--      ELEMENT              MIN  CONTENT                EXPLANATIONS    -->
<!ELEMENT formula              - -  (%p.trans;|%m.math;)*
                                                      -- in-line formula -->
<!ELEMENT dformula             - -  (%p.trans;|%m.math;)*
                                                      -- display formula -->
<!ELEMENT dformgrp             - -  (formula|dformula)+
                                                -- display formula group -->

<!--      ELEMENT   NAME       VALUE            DEFAULT                    -->
<!ATTLIST formula   id         ID               #IMPLIED
                    alphabet   %a.types;
                    %SDAPREF;      "<?SDATRANS>Inline formula"
                    %SDASUSP;       "SUSPEND"                              >
<!ATTLIST dformula  id         ID               #IMPLIED
                    num        CDATA            #IMPLIED
                    align      (left|center|right)
                                                center
                    alphabet   %a.types;
                    %SDAPREF;      "<?SDATRANS>Display formula"
                    %SDASUSP;       "SUSPEND"                              >
<!ATTLIST dformgrp  id         ID               #IMPLIED
                    num        CDATA            #IMPLIED
                    align      (left|center|right)
                                                center
                    %SDAPREF;      "<?SDATRANS>Display formula group"      >
```

Annex A

(informative)

Comments on the DTDs

A.1 Design philosophy

The Document Type Definitions comprising this International Standard are based on ANSI Z39.59-1988, Electronic Manuscript Preparation and Markup originally created by the Association of American Publishers (AAP). The structure of the original DTDs permit easy modification and extension. The present DTDs continue this philosophy.

ANSI Z39.59-1988 was designed before the SGML standard (ISO 8879:1986) was available. This International Standard draws on the experience gained with SGML since the completion of ANSI Z39.59-1988. All ambiguities, redundancies and formatting specific aspects were removed from ANSI Z39.59-1988. The short reference syntax is deprecated by this International Standard, but short references can be added by current users. The names of the generic identifiers were made longer and more meaningful. Five major groups influenced the modifications of ANSI Z39.59-1988:

a. The European Workgroup on SGML. The work of this group of European publishers was published in 1991, in the form of the Majour DTD for article headers. Elements and attributes which were required to make ANSI Z39.59-1988 compatible with Majour were added.

b. The European Physical Society. This professional organization submitted a set of comments which were all applied. The Society endorses the use of this International Standard by its members.

c. International Committee for Accessible Document Design (ICADD). These comments enable easy translation of SGML coded documents using ISO 12083 into Braille, large type and computer voice. ICADD endorses the use of this International Standard. (See Annex A.8)

d. ISO 10744:1992, HyTime. Several comments on the draft of this International Standard mentioned the lack of facilities for hypertext. Documents conforming to this International Standard are minimal hyperlinking HyTime documents.

e. The AAP Math Update Committee. The objective of this committee was to make a harmonized DTD for mathematics that would replace the mathematics DTD in ISO/IEC TR 9573:1988, the AAP mathematics DTD and the DTD in use by the Euromath project. Several comments on the draft of this International Standard proposed that this International Standard adopt the work of this committee.

A.2 Description of the structure

A.2.1 Overall structure of Books and Articles

Books and **Articles** consist of front matter (**front**), followed by the main body (**body**), followed by an appendix matter part (**appmat**) (optional), followed by back matter (**back**) (optional). Both the start- and the end-tag of the document type element are required. The start- and the end-tag of the front matter and main body may be omitted. The end-tags of the appendix matter and back matter may be omitted. "Floating elements" (**%i.float;**) (see figure A.33, figure groups, footnotes and notes) can be interspersed anywhere in the document. The overall structure of Books and Articles is shown in figures A.1 and A.2.

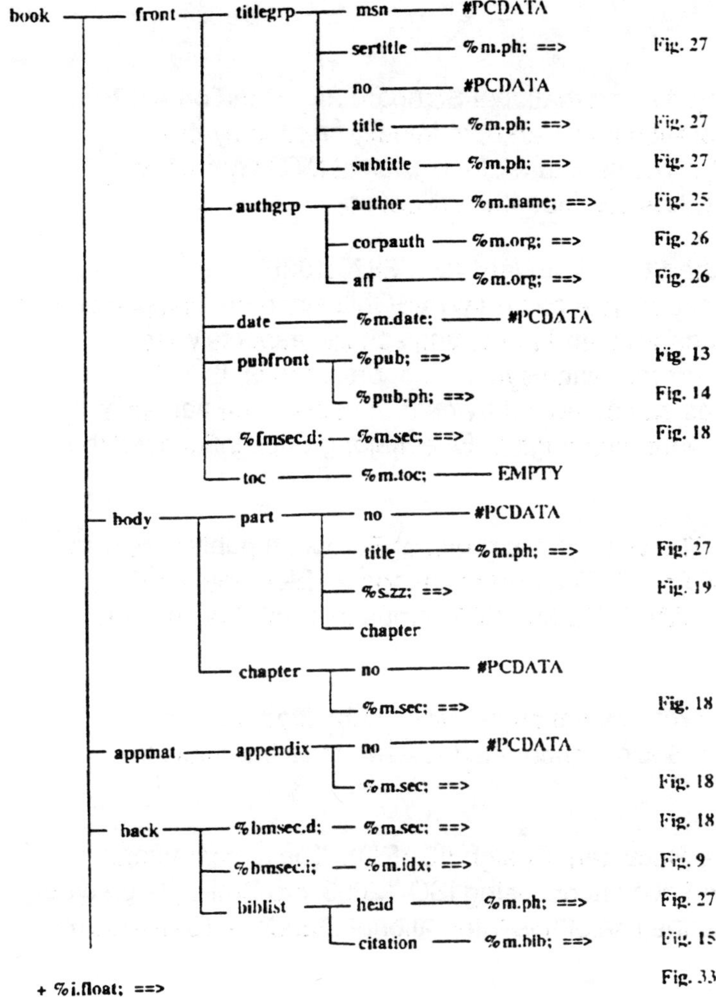

Figure A.1 Overall structure of Books

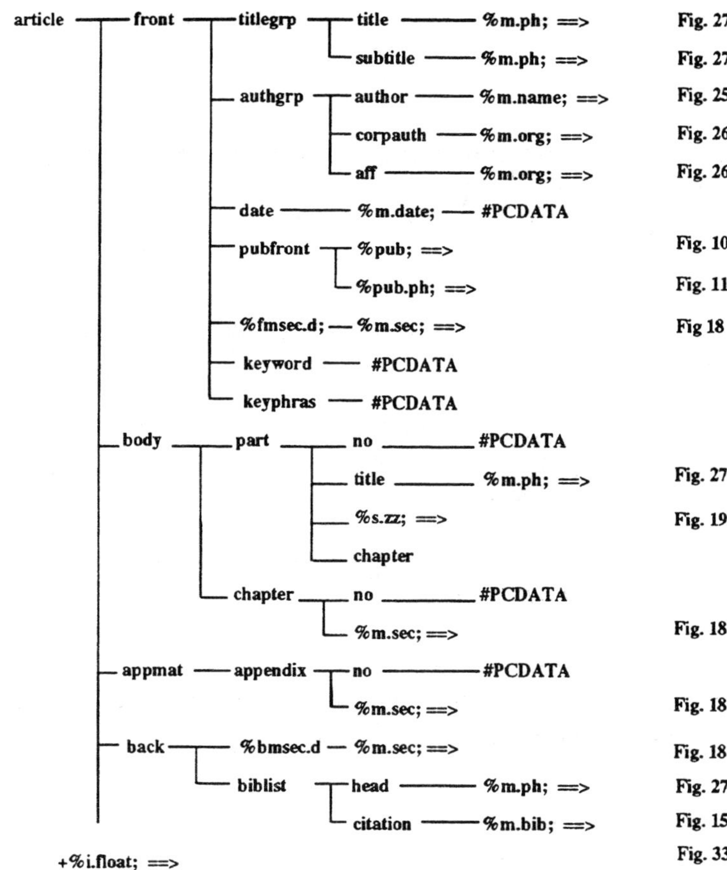

Figure A.2 Overall structure of Articles

A.2.2 Front matter, appendix matter and back matter structure of Books

A book front matter element (**front**) consists of a title group (**titlegrp**), followed by an author group (**authgrp**), followed by a date (**date**) (optional), followed by the publisher's front matter group (**pubfront**)(optional), followed by front matter sections (**%fmsec.d;**) (optional and repeatable)(see figure A.5), followed by a table of contents (**toc**)(optional). Both the start- and the end-tag of the front matter may be omitted.

The title group element (**titlegrp**) consists of a monographic series number (**msn**)(optional), followed by a (monographic) series title (**sertitle**)(optional), followed by a number (**no**)(optional), followed by a title (**title**) and a subtitle (**subtitle**)(optional). Both the start- and the end-tag of the title group may be omitted.

The monographic series number (**msn**) and number (**no**) elements are normally numbers, and therefore consist of parsed character data (**#PCDATA**). Their end-tags may be omitted.

The (monographic) series title (**sertitle**), the title (**title**) and subtitle (**subtitle**) elements consist of "phrase models" (**%m.ph;**)(see figure A.27). The end-tags of the series title, the title and subtitle elements may be omitted.

The author group element (**authgrp**) consists of an author element (**author**), a corporate body as an author element (**corpauth**) and an affiliation element (**aff**). All these are optional and repeatable and they may be entered in any order. The start- and the end-tag of the author group element may be omitted.

The author element (**author**) consists of "name subelements" (**%m.name;**)(see figure A.25). The end-tag of the author element may be omitted.

The corporate body as an author element (**corpauth**) and affiliation element (**aff**) consist of "organization name subelements" (**%m.org;**)(see figure A.26). The end-tags of the corporate body as an author and affiliation elements may be omitted.

The date element (**date**) consists of "date subelements" (**%m.date;**) which consist of #PCDATA. The end-tag of the date element may be omitted.

The publisher's front matter group element (**pubfront**) contains "publisher information subelements" (**%pub;**)(see figure A.3) or "publication information subelements" (**%pub.ph;**)(see figure A.4). These are in arbitrary order, optional and repeatable. The end-tag of the publisher's front matter group may be omitted.

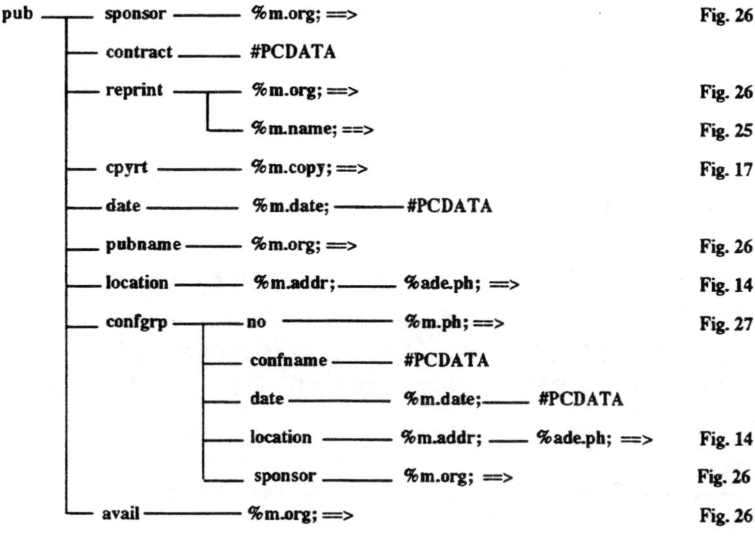

Figure A.3 Publisher information subelements for Books (%pub;)

"Publisher information subelements" (**%pub;**)(see figure A.3) are defined as a contract or grant sponsor (**sponsor**), or a contract number (**contract**), or a reprint source (**reprint**), or a copyright notice (**cpyrt**), or a date (**date**), or the publisher's name (**pubname**), or the location (**location**), or a conference information group (**confgrp**), or an availability notice (**avail**).

The sponsor (**sponsor**), publisher's name (**pubname**) and availability notice (**avail**) elements consist of "organization name subelements" (**%m.org;**)(see figure A.26). The end-tags of these elements may be omitted.

The contract (**contract**) element consists of parsed character data (**#PCDATA**). The end-tag of the contract element may be omitted.

The reprint source element (**reprint**) consists of "organization name subelements" (**%m.org;**)(see figure A.26), or of "name subelements" (**%m.name;**)(see figure A.25). The end-tag of the reprint element may be omitted.

The copyright notice element (**cpyrt**) consists of "copyright notice subelements" (**%m.copy;**)(see figure A.17). Neither the start-tag nor the end-tag of the copyright notice element may be omitted.

The date element (**date**) consists of "date subelements" (**%m.date;**) which consists of parsed character data (**#PCDATA**). The end-tag of the date element may be omitted.

The location element (**location**) consists of "address subelements" (**%m.addr;**)(see figure A.14). The end-tag of the location element may be omitted.

The conference group element (**confgrp**) consists of a number element (**no**)(optional), followed by a conference name element (**confname**), followed by a date element (**date**)(optional), followed by a location element (**location**)(optional), followed by a sponsor element (**sponsor**)(optional). Neither the start-tag nor the end-tag of the conference group element may be omitted.

The conference name element (**confname**) consists of parsed character data (**#PCDATA**). The end-tag of the conference name element may be omitted.

"Publication information subelements" (**%pub.ph;**)(see figure A.4) are defined as a coden number (**coden**) or an acquisition/order number (**acqno**) or an isbn number (**isbn**) or an lc card number (**lccardno**) or a report id number (**reportid**) or an edition number (**edition**) or a volume id number (**volid**) or a catalog number (**catalog**) or an acid free paper indicator (**acidfree**) or a price (**price**) or the extent of the work (**extent**) or the packaging (**package**) or the publisher's unique id number (**pubid**). All these elements consist of parsed character data (**#PCDATA**) and their end-tags may be omitted.

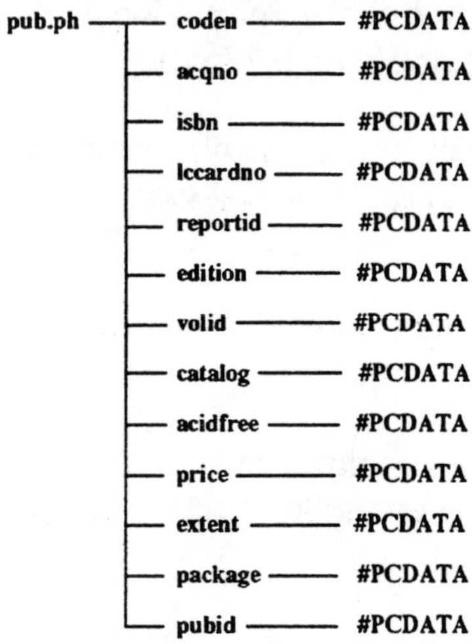

Figure A.4 Publication information subelements for Books (%pub.ph;)

"Front matter sections" (**%fmsec.d;**)(see figure A.5) are defined as a foreword (**foreword**), an introduction (**intro**), a preface (**preface**), an acknowledgment (**ack**), a dedication (**ded**), an abstract (**abstract**) or supporting material-availability (**supmtl**).

The foreword element (**foreword**), the introduction (**intro**), the preface element (**preface**), the acknowledgment element (**ack**), the dedication element (**ded**), the abstract element (**abstract**) and supporting material-availability element (**supmatl**) consist of "section elements" (**%m.sec;**)(see figure A.18). The end-tags of the foreword, preface and introduction, acknowledgment, dedication, abstract and supporting material-availability elements may be omitted.

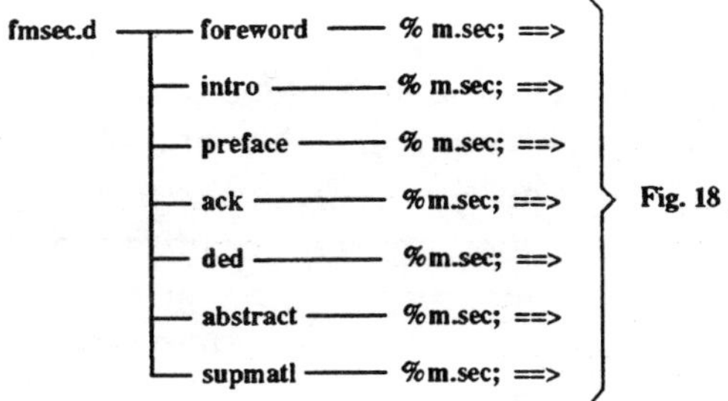

Figure A.5 Front matter sections for Books (%fmsec.d)

The table of contents element (**toc**) is defined as "table of contents subelements" (**%m.toc;**)(see figure A.6). "Table of contents subelements" (**%m.toc;**) are defined as EMPTY.

The content of a table of contents is generated by the application software. The end-tag of the table of contents element must be omitted, since it is an EMPTY element.

m.toc ——— EMPTY

Figure A.6 Table of contents subelements for Books (%m.toc;)

A book appendix matter element (**appmat**) is defined as one or more appendices (**appendix**). The end-tag of the appendix matter element may be omitted.

The appendix element (**appendix**) consists of a number (**no**)(optional), and "section subelements" (**%m.sec;**)(see figure A.18). The end-tag of the appendix element may be omitted.

A book back matter element (**back**) is defined as "back matter section subelements" (**%bmsec.d;**)(see figure A.7), "index and glossary elements" (**%bmsec.i;**)(see figure A.8) or a bibliography list (**biblist**). All these may appear in arbitrary order and are optional and repeatable. The end-tag of the back matter element may be omitted.

"Back matter section subelements" (**%bmsec.d;**)(see figure A.7) consist of afterwords (**afterwrd**) or notes (**notes**) or the vita element (**vita**). Afterwords (**afterwrd**), notes (**note**) and the vita (**vita**) element consist of "section subelements" (**%m.sec;**)(see figure A.18). The end-tags of afterwords, notes and vita may be omitted.

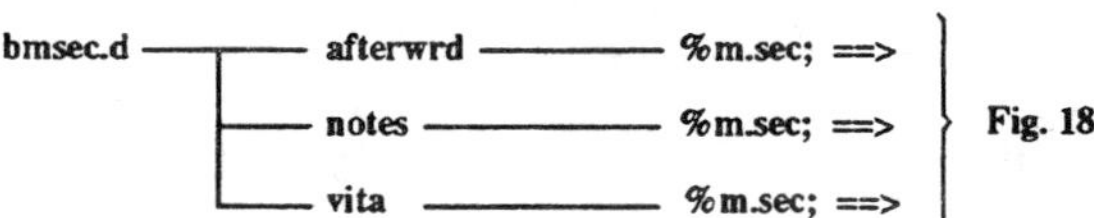

Figure A.7 Back matter section subelements for Books (%bmsec.d;)

"Index and glossary elements" (**%bmsec.i;**)(see figure A.8) consist of the glossary element (**glossary**) or the index element (**index**). The glossary and index elements consist of "index and glossary subelements" (**%m.idx;**)(see figure A.9). The end-tags of the glossary element and the index element may be omitted.

bmsec.i ─┬─ glossary ——— %m.idx; ==> Fig. 9
└─ index ——— %m.idx; ==> Fig. 9

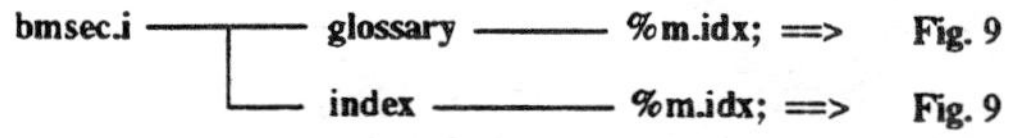

Figure A.8 Index and glossary elements for Books (%bmsec.i;)

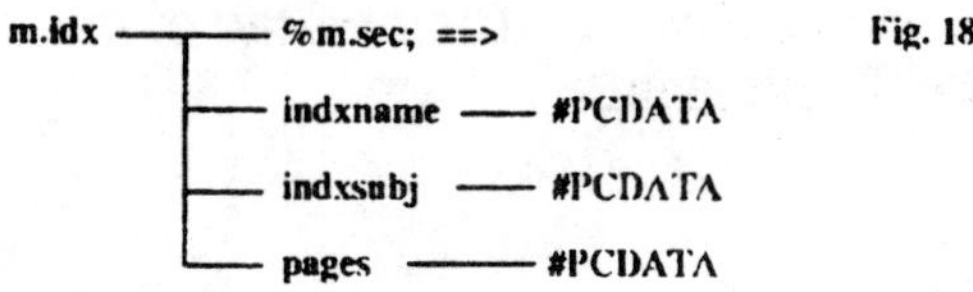

Figure A.9 Index and glossary subelements for Books (%m.idx;)

The bibliography list element (**biblist**)(see figure A.1) consists of a (list) header element (**head**)(optional) and a bibliographic entry, the citation element (**citation**). The header is optional and the citation element is mandatory. The pair (head, citation) is optional and repeatable. The end tag of the bibliography list element may be omitted.

The list header element (**head**) consists of "phrase model subelements" (**%m.ph;**)(see figure A.27). The end-tag of the list header element may be omitted.

The citation element (**citation**) consists of "bibliographic entry subelements" (**%m.bib;**)(see figure A.15). The end-tag of the bibliographic entry element may be omitted.

A.2.3 Front matter, appendix matter and back matter structure of Articles

An article front matter element (**front**) consists of a title group (**titlegrp**), followed by an author group (**authgrp**), followed by a date (**date**)(optional), followed by the publisher's front matter group (**pubfront**)(optional), followed by front matter sections (**%fmsec.d;**)(see figure A.12) or a keyword (**keyword**) or a key phrase (**keyphras**)(the last three form an optional and repeatable "or" group). Both the start- and the end-tag of the front matter may be omitted.

The title group element (**titlegrp**) consists of a title (**title**) and a subtitle (**subtitle**)(optional and repeatable). Both the start- and the end-tag of the title group may be omitted.

The title (**title**) and subtitle (**subtitle**) elements consist of "phrase models" (**%m.ph;**)(see figure A.27). The end-tags of the title and subtitle elements may be omitted.

The author group element (**authgrp**) consists of an author element (**author**), a corporate body as an author element (**corpauth**) and an affiliation element (**aff**). All these are optional and repeatable and they may be entered in any order. The start- and the end-tag of the author group element may be omitted.

The author element (**author**) consists of "name subelements" (**%m.name;**)(see figure A.25). The end-tag of the author element may be omitted.

The corporate body as an author element (**corpauth**) and affiliation element (**aff**) consist of "organization name subelements" (**%m.org;**)(see figure A.26). The end-tags of the corporate body as an author and affiliation elements may be omitted.

The publisher's front matter group element (**pubfront**) contains "publisher information subelements" (**%pub;**)(see figure A.10) or "publication information subelements" (**%pub.ph;**)(see figure A.11). These are in arbitrary order, optional and repeatable. The end-tag of the publisher's front matter group may be omitted.

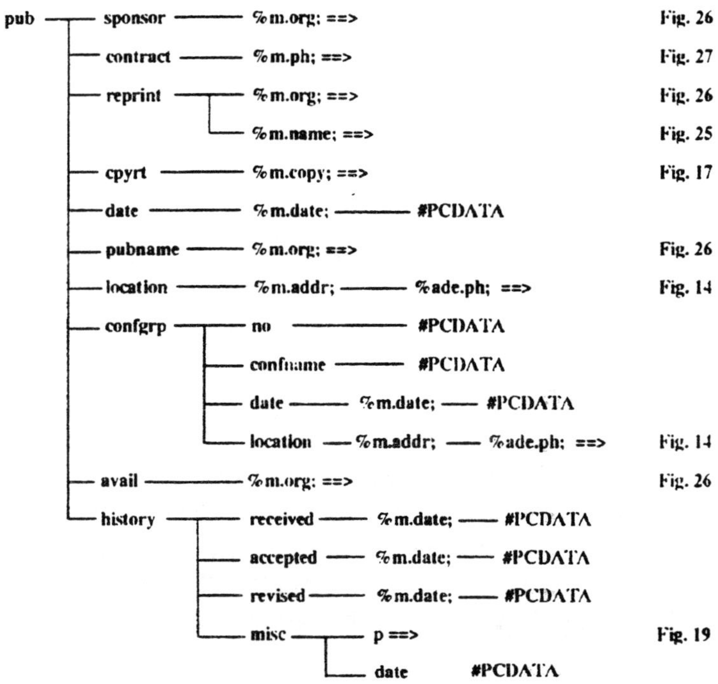

Figure A.10 Publisher information subelements for Articles (%pub;)

"Publisher information subelements" (**%pub;**)(see figure A.10) are defined as a contract or grant sponsor (**sponsor**), or a contract number (**contract**), or a reprint source (**reprint**), or a copyright notice (**cpyrt**), or a date (**date**), or the publisher's name (**pubname**), or the location (**location**), or a conference information group (**confgrp**), or an availability notice (**avail**), or the article's publication history (**history**). The contents of all these elements is the same as for Books, except the history element.

The article's publication history (**history**) consists of the received date (**received**), or the accepted date (**accepted**) or the revised date (**revised**) or a miscellaneous date (**misc**). The end-tag of the history element may be omitted.

The article's publication history element (**history**), the article's received date element (**received**), the article's date of acceptance for publication (**accepted**) consist of a date (**date**) element. The miscellaneous date element (**misc**) all consist of paragraphs (**p**) followed by a date (**date**). Paragraphs (**p**) have mixed content consisting of parsed character data (#PCDATA) or "paragraph subelements" (**%p.zz.ph;**)(see figure A.28) or "phrases" (**%p.zz;**)(see figure A.20). The end-tags of all these elements may be omitted.

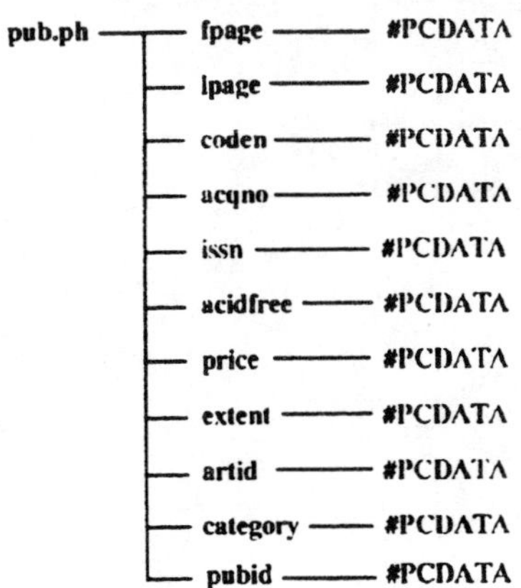

Figure A.11 Publication information subelements for Articles (%pub.ph;)

"Publication information subelements" (**%pub.ph;**)(see figure A.11) are defined as a coden number (**coden**) or an acquisition/order number (**acqno**) or an issn number (**issn**) or an acid free paper indicator (**acidfree**) or a price (**price**) or the extent of the work (**extent**) or the article id (**artid**) or the article's category (**category**), or the publisher's unique identifier (**pubid**). These elements all consist of parsed character data (**#PCDATA**), and the end-tags of all these elements may be omitted.

"Front matter sections" (**%fmsec.d;**)(see figure A.12) are defined as a dedication (**ded**), an abstract (**abstract**) or supporting material-availability (**supmatl**).

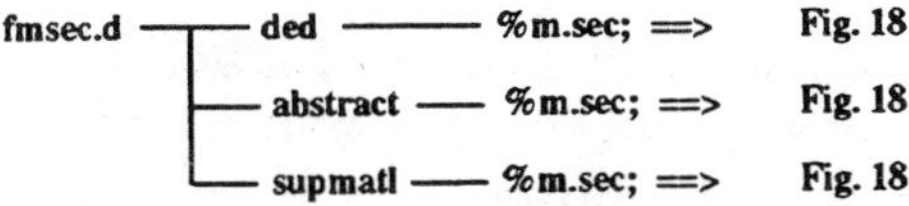

Figure A.12 Front matter sections for Articles (%fmsec.d;)

The dedication element (**ded**), the abstract element (**abstract**) and supporting material-availability element (**supmatl**) consist of "section elements" (**%m.sec;**)(see figure A.18). The end-tags of the acknowledgment, dedication, abstract and supporting material-availability elements may be omitted.

An article appendix matter element (**appmat**) is defined as one or more appendices (**appendix**). The end-tag of the appendix matter element may be omitted.

The keyword element (**keyword**) and the keyphrase element (**keyphras**) are defined as parsed character data (**#PCDATA**). The end-tags of the keyword and keyphrase elements may be omitted.

The article appendix element (**appendix**) is identical to that of the book document type. It consists of a number (**no**)(optional), followed by "section elements" (**%m.sec;**)(see figure A.18). The end-tag of the appendix element may be omitted.

An article back matter element (**back**) is defined as "back matter sections" (**%bmsec.d;**)(see figure A.13) or a bibliography list (**biblist**). All these may appear in arbitrary order and are optional and repeatable. The end-tag of the back matter element may be omitted.

```
bmsec.d ──┬── ack ──── %m.sec; ==>   Fig. 18
          └── vita ─── %m.sec; ==>   Fig. 18
```

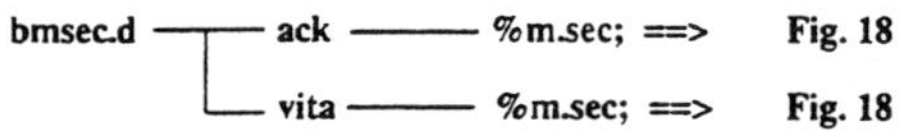

Figure A.13 Back matter sections for Articles (%bmsec.d;)

"Back matter sections" (**%bmsec.d;**)(see figure A.13) consist of the acknowledgment element (**ack**) or the vita element (**vita**). The acknowledgment element (**ack**) and the vita (**vita**) element consists of "section elements" (**%m.sec**)(see figure A.18). The end-tag of the acknowledgment and vita elements may be omitted.

The bibliography list element (**biblist**) consists of a (list) header element (**head**)(optional) and a bibliographic entry, a citation element (**citation**). The header is optional and the citation is mandatory. The pair (header, citation) is optional and repeatable. The end tag of the bibliography list element may be omitted.

The list header element (**head**) consists of "phrase model subelements" (**%m.ph;**)(see figure A.27). The end-tag of the list header element may be omitted.

The citation element (**citation**) consists of "bibliographic entry subelements" (**%m.bib;**)(see figure A.15). The end-tag of the citation element may be omitted.

A.2.4 The main body DTD

A body element (**body**) consists of one or more part elements (**part**) or one or more chapter elements (**chapter**). Both the start- and the end-tag of the body element may be omitted.

A part element (**part**) consists of a number element (**no**)(optional), a title element (**title**), "section subelements" (**%s.zz;**)(see figure A.19)(optional and repeatable), followed by at least one chapter element (**chapter**). The end-tag of the part element may be omitted.

A chapter element (**chapter**) consists of a number element (**no**)(optional), followed by "section elements" (**%m.sec;**)(see figure A.18). The end-tag of the chapter element may be omitted.

A.2.5 Common parameter entities of Books and Articles

A.2.5.1 The address model

The "address model" (**%m.addr;**) consists of "address elements" (**%ade.ph;**) (see figure A.14).

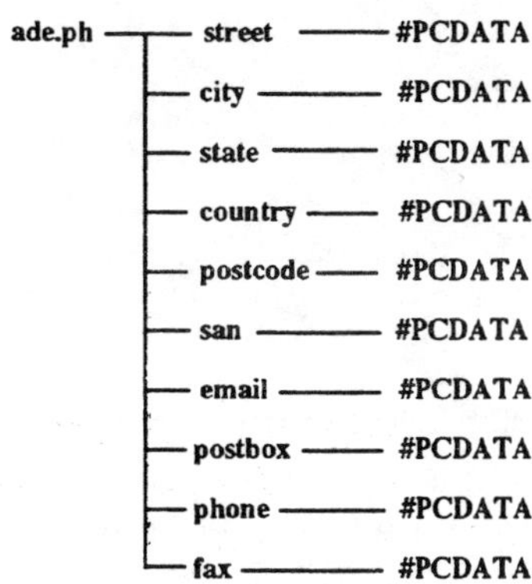

Figure A.14 The address elements (%ade.ph;)

The "address elements" (**%ade.ph;**)(see figure A.14) consist of a street name (**street**), or a city name (**city**), or a state name (**state**), or a country name (**country**), or a postal code (**postcode**), or a standard address number (**san**), or an electronic mail address (**email**), or a post box number (**postbox**), or a telephone number (**phone**), or a fax number (**fax**). These elements consist of (#PCDATA). The end-tags of all the address elements may be omitted.

A.2.5.2 The bibliographic entry model

The "bibliographic entry model" (**%m.bib;**) (see figure A.15) consists of a number (**no**), followed by a title (**title**), followed by "bibliographic data components" (**%bib;**)(see figure A.16). The number is optional, the title is mandatory and the bibliographic data components are optional and repeatable.

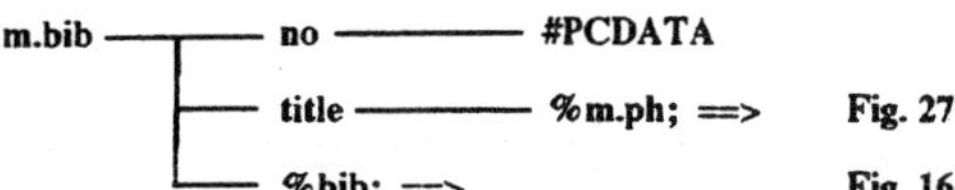

Figure A.15 The bibliographic entry model (%m.bib;)

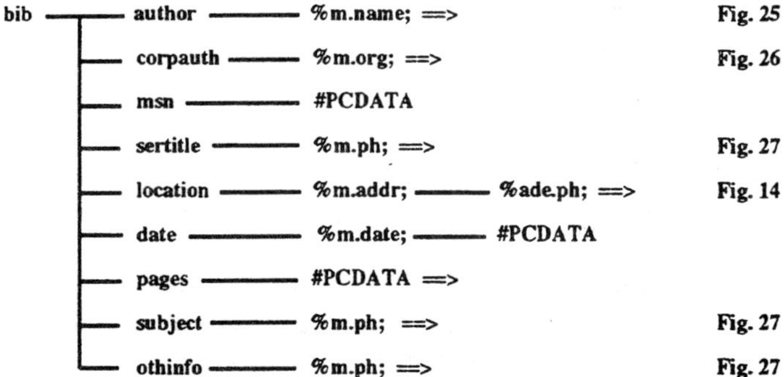

Figure A.16 Bibliographic data components (%bib;)

"Bibliographic data components" (**%bib;**) (see figure A.16) are an author (**author**), or a corporate body as an author (**corpauth**), or a monographic series number (**msn**), or a monographic series title (**sertitle**), or the publisher's location (**location**), or the publication date (**date**), or the page numbers of the work (**pages**), or the subject (**subject**), or other bibliographic information (**othinfo**).

The author element (**author**) consists of "name model elements" (**%m.name;**)(see figure A.25). The end-tag of the author element may be omitted.

The corporate body as an author element (**corpauth**) consists of "organization name model elements" (**%m.org;**)(see figure A.26). The end-tag of the corpauth element may be omitted.

The monographic series number element (**msn**) and the page numbers of the work (**pages**) consist of parsed character data (**#PCDATA**). The end-tag of the monographic series number element may be omitted.

The monographic series title (**sertitle**), the subject (**subject**) and other bibliographic information (**othinfo**) elements all consist of "phrase model" subelements (**%m.ph;**)(see figure A.27). The end-tags of these four elements may be omitted.

The publisher's location element (**location**) consists of "address model" subelements (**%m.addr;**)(see figure A.14). The end-tag of the location element may be omitted.

A.2.5.3 The copyright notice data model

The "copyright notice data model" (**%m.copy;**)(see figure A.17) consists of a copyright date (**date**), the name of the copyright owner (**cpyrtnme**), the name of the copyright clearance center (**cpyrtclr**). One of these three elements must appear at least once, but all may be repeated.

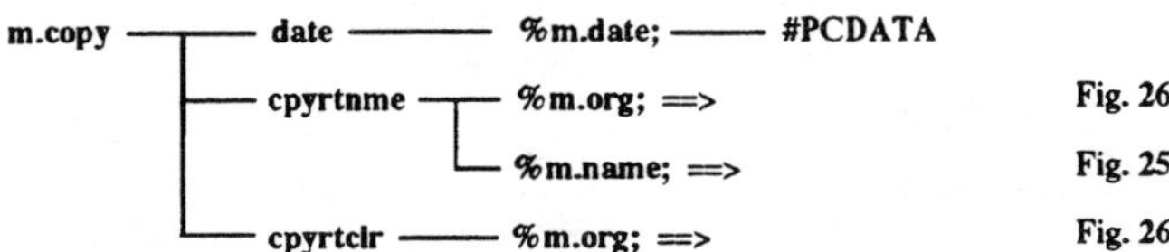

Figure A.17 The copyright notice data model (%m.copy;)

The name of the copyright owner element (**cpyrtnme**) has "organization name model" subelements (**%m.org;**)(see figure A.26) or "name model" subelements (**%m.name;**)(see figure A.25). The name of the copyright clearance center element (**cpyrtclr**) has "name model" subelements (**%m.name;**)(see figure A.25). Neither the start-tag nor the end-tag of the copyright owner or copyright clearance center elements may be omitted.

A.2.5.4 The date model

The date element (**date**) consists of the "date model" (**%m.date;**) which consists of parsed character data (**#PCDATA**). The end-tag of the date element may be omitted.

A.2.5.5 The figure model

The "figure model" (**%m.fig;**) is EMPTY.

A.2.5.6 The section model

The "section model" (**%m.sec;**)(see figure A.18) consists of a title element (**title**)(optional), section subelements (**%s.zz;**)(see figure A.19)(optional and repeatable) and a subsection level 1 element (**subsect1**)(optional and repeatable).

The subsection level 1 element (**subsect1**) consists of a number element (**no**)(optional), a title element (**title**)(optional), section subelements (**%s.zz;**)(see figure A.19)(optional and repeatable) and a subsection level 2 element (**subsect2**)(optional and repeatable). The subsections nest down to level 6 and all have the same structure.

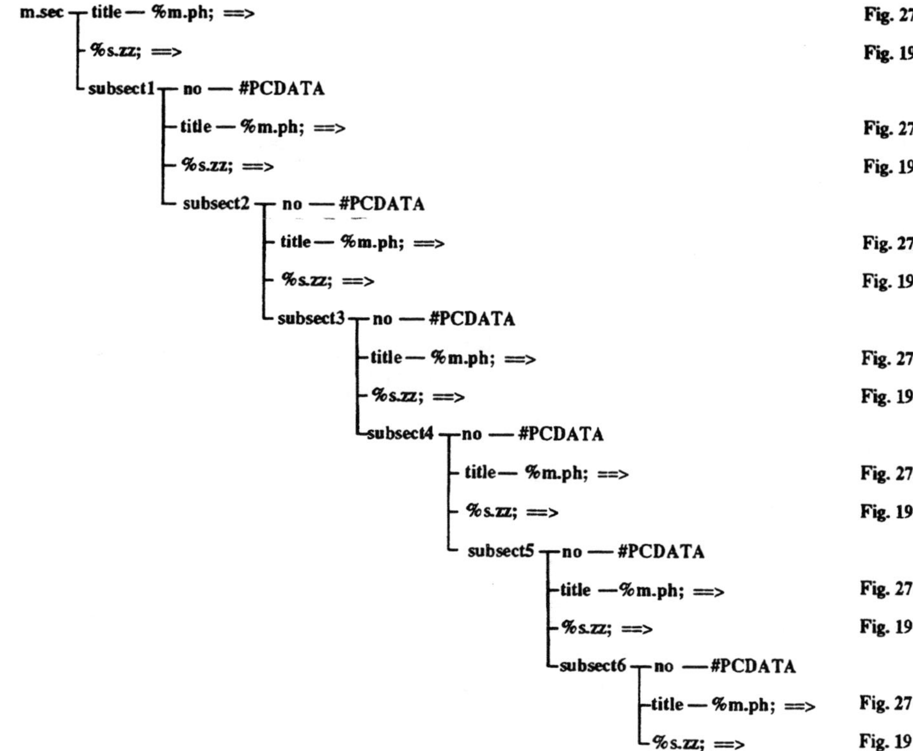

Figure A.18 The section model (%m.sec;)

"Section subelements" (**%s.zz**)(see figure A.19) consist of paragraphs (**p**) or "paragraph subelements" (**%p.zz;**)(see figure A.20).

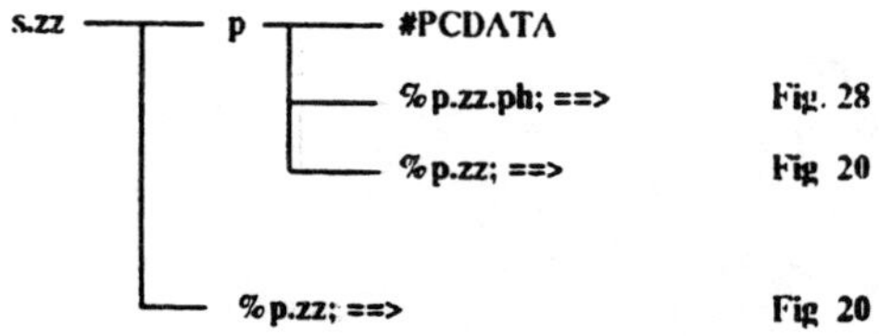

Figure A.19 Section subelements (%s.zz;)

Paragraphs (**p**) have mixed content consisting of parsed character data (**#PCDATA**) or "paragraph subelements" (**%p.zz.ph;**) (see figure A.28) or "phrases" (**%p.zz;**)(see figure A.20). The content of a paragraph is optional and repeatable. The end-tag of a paragraph may be omitted.

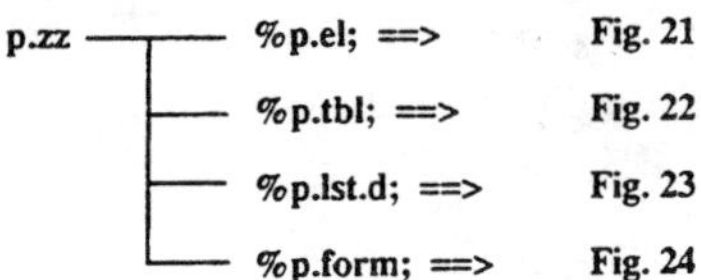

Figure A.20 Paragraph subelements (%p.zz;)

"Paragraph subelements" (**%p.zz;**) (see figure A.20) consist of "general paragraph elements" (**%p.el;**)(see figure A.21), or "table matter" (**%p.tbl;**)(see figure A.22), or a "list" (**%p.lst.d;**)(see figure A.23) or "mathematical formula elements" (**%p.form;**)(see figure A.24).

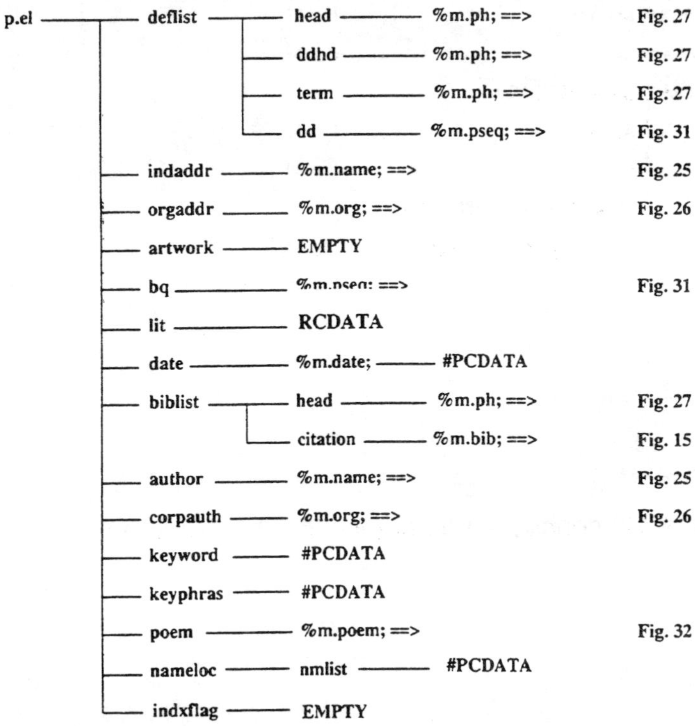

Figure A.21 General paragraph elements (%p.el;)

"General paragraph elements" (**%p.el;**)(see figure A.21) consist of a definition list element (**deflist**), or an organizational address element (**orgaddr**), or an individual's address element (**indaddr**), or an artwork element (**artwork**), or a block quotation element (**bq**), or a literal string element (**lit**), or a date element (**date**), or a bibliography list element (**biblist**), or an author element (**author**), or a corporate body as an author element (**corpauth**), or a keyword element (**keyword**), or a keyphrases element (**keyphras**), or a poem (**poem**) element, or a named location address (**nameloc**) or a flag to an index entry (**indxflag**).

The definition list element (**deflist**) consists of a heading element (**head**), a definition description heading (**ddhd**), a definition term (**term**) followed by a definition description (**dd**). The pair (**head,ddhd**) is optional and the complete group is optional and repeatable. The heading (**head**), definition description heading (**ddhd**) and definition term (**term**) elements consist of "phrase model subelements" (**%m.ph;**) (see figure A.27). The definition description (**dd**) element consists of "paragraph with sequence model subelements" (**%m.pseq;**)(see figure A.31). Neither the start- or the end-tag of the definition list element may be omitted. The end-tags of the heading, definition description heading, definition term and definition description elements may all be omitted.

The organizational address element (**orgaddr**) consists of "organization address subset model elements" (**%m.org;**)(see figure A.26). The end-tag of the organizational address element may be omitted.

The individual's address element (**indaddr**) consists of "name model elements" (**%m.name;**)(see figure A.25). The end-tag of the individual's address element may be omitted.

The artwork element (**artwork**) is an EMPTY element. The end-tag of the artwork element must be omitted.

The block quotation element (**bq**) consists of "paragraph with sequence model subelements" (**%m.pseq;**)(see figure A.31). Neither the start- or the end-tag may be omitted from the block quotation element.

The literal string element (**lit**) consists of replaceable character data (**RCDATA**). Neither the start- or the end-tag may be omitted from the literal string element.

The keyword (**keyword**) and keyphrase (**keyphras**) elements consist of parsed character data (**#PCDATA**). The end-tags of both the keyword and keyphrase elements may be omitted.

The poem element (**poem**) consists of the "poem model elements" (**%m.poem;**)(see figure A.32). The end-tag of the poem element may be omitted.

The named location address element (**nameloc**) consists of a name list element (**nmlist**)(optional and repeatable). The end-tag of the named location address element may be omitted. The name list element (**nmlist**) consists of parsed character data (**#PCDATA**). The end-tag of the name list element may be omitted.

The flag to an index entry element (**indxflag**) is an EMPTY element. Its end-tag must be omitted.

The "table matter elements" (**%p.tbl;**) (see figure A.22) consist of the table element (**table**).

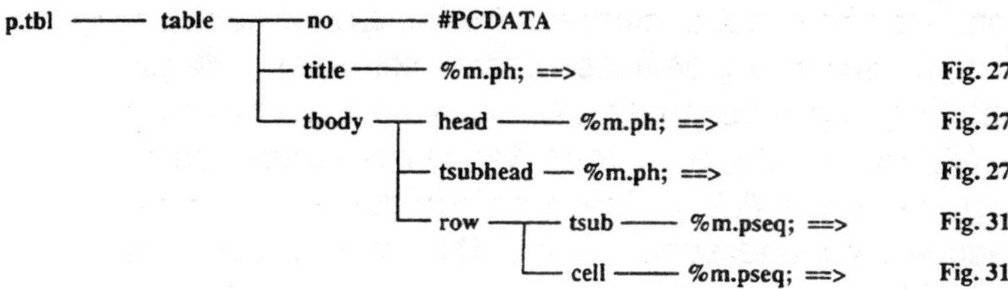

Figure A.22 Table matter elements (%p.tbl;)

The table element (**table**) consists of a number element (**no**), a title element (**title**), a table body element (**tbody**). Table matter elements (**%p.tbl;**)(see figure A.22) and general floating elements (**%i.float;**)(see figure A.33) are excluded from appearing inside the table element. The number element is optional. Neither the start- or the end-tag may be omitted from the table element.

The table body element (**tbody**) consists of a table header element (**head**), a table column subordinate header element (**tsubhead**), and a row element (**row**). The header, table column subordinate header and row elements are all optional and repeatable. The end-tag of the table body element may be omitted.

The table column subordinate header element (**tsubhead**) consists of "phrase model elements" (**%m.ph;**)(see figure A.27). The end-tag of the table column subordinate header element may be omitted.

The row element (**row**) consists of a table stub line element (**tstub**) and a cell element (**cell**). The table stub line element is optional and the cell element is optional and repeatable. The end-tag of the row element may be omitted.

Table stub line elements (**tstub**) and cell elements (**cell**) may both consist of "paragraph with sequence model elements" (**%m.pseq;**)(see figure A.31). The "list elements" (**%p.lst.d;**)(see figure A.23) consist of the list element (**list**).

Figure A.23 The list elements (%p.lst.d;)

The list element (**list**) consists of a list header element (**head**) followed by a list item element (**item**). The list header element is optional, and the list item element is mandatory. The pair (**head, item**) is optional and repeatable. Neither the start- or the end-tag of the list element may be omitted.

The list item element (**item**) consists of "p with sequence model elements" (**%m.pseq;**)(see figure A.31).

The "mathematical formula elements" (**%p.form;**) (see figure A.24) consist of the inline formula element (**formula**), or the display formula element (**dformula**), or the display formula group (**dformgrp**).

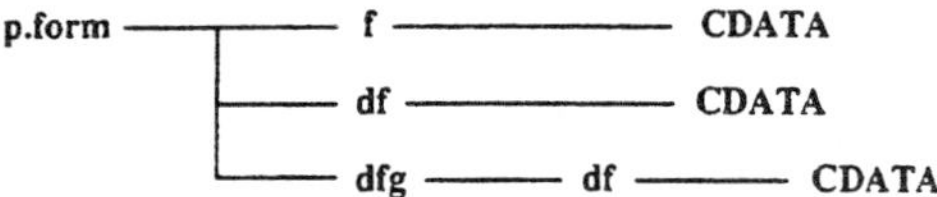

Figure A.24 Mathematical formula elements (%p.form;)

The display formula group element (**dformgrp**) consists of one or more display formula elements (**dformula**). The end-tag of the display formula group element may be omitted.

The formula (**formula**) element and the display formula element (**dformula**) have a structure which is defined by a separate DTD. See Annex A.6 for a description of the ISO12083 Mathematics DTD.

Figure A.24 shows the case where display formula element (**dformula**) and the inline formula element (**formula**) may consist of CDATA. In situations where the complete implementation of the mathematics DTD would be too complex, this can be a reasonable compromise. The end tag of both tags may not be omitted.

A.2.5.7 The name model

The "name model elements" (**%m.name;**)(see figure A.25) consist of a first name element (**fname**), a surname element (**surname**) (in either order), a degree element (**degree**) or a school element (**school**), a role element (**role**), "address elements" (**%ade.ph;**)(see figure A.14), and an affiliation element (**aff**). The first name element is optional, the surname element is mandatory, the degree and school elements are optional and repeatable, the role element is optional and repeatable, the "address elements" are optional and repeatable, and the affiliation element is optional.

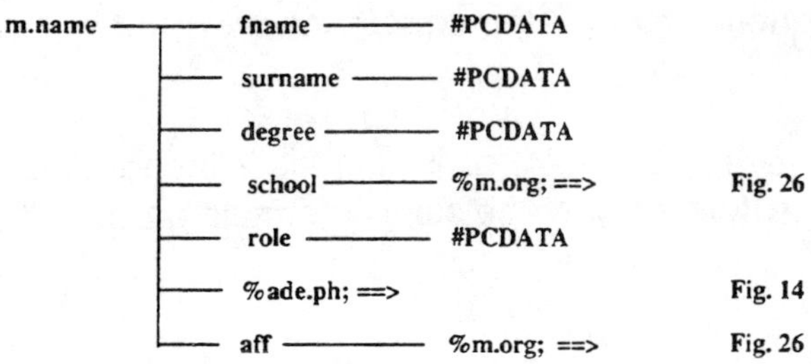

Figure A.25 The name model elements (%m.name;)

The first name element (**fname**), the surname element (**surname**), the degree element (**degree**) and the role element (**role**) consist of (**#PCDATA**). The end-tags of the first name element, the degree element and the role element may be omitted. The end-tag of the surname element may be omitted.

The school element (**school**) and the affiliation element (**aff**) consist of "organization name model elements" (**%m.org;**)(see figure A.26). The end-tag of the school and affiliation element may be omitted.

A.2.5.8 The organization name model

The "organization name model" (**%m.org;**) (see figure A.26) consists of an organization name element (**orgname**), an organization division (**orgdiv**) and "address model elements" (**%m.addr;**) (see figure A.14). The organization name element is mandatory, the organization division element is optional and repeatable.

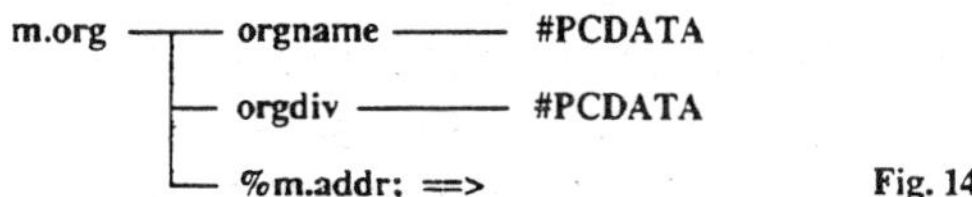

Figure A.26 The organization name model (%m.org;)

The organization name element (**orgname**) and the organization division element (**orgdiv**) consist of (**#PCDATA**). The start- and the end-tag of the organization name element may be omitted. The end-tag of the organization division element may be omitted.

A.2.5.9 The phrase model

The "phrase model" (**%m.ph;**)(see figure A.27) has mixed content consisting of parsed character data (**#PCDATA**), or "phrase elements" (**%p.zz.ph;**)(see figure A.28), or "mathematical formula elements" (**%p.form;**)(see figure A.24). The "phrase model" group is optional and repeatable.

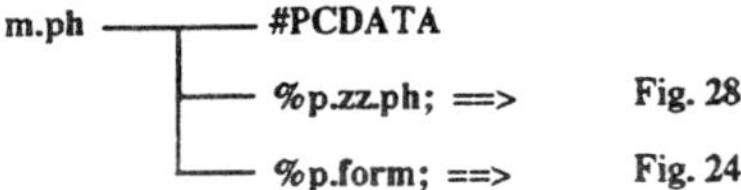

Figure A.27 The phrase model (%m.ph;)

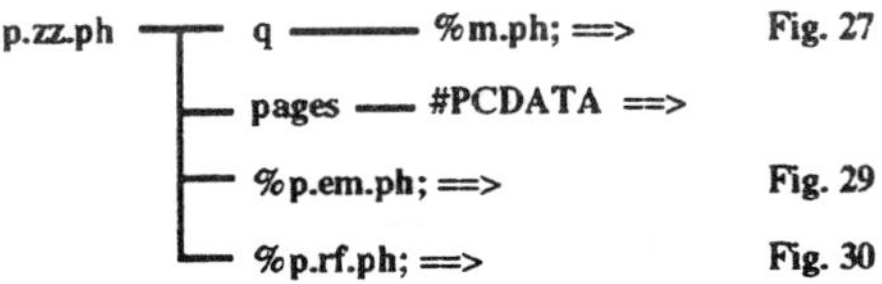

Figure A.28 Phrase elements (%p.zz.ph;)

The "phrase elements" (**%p.zz.ph;**)(see figure A.28) consist of a quotation element (**q**), or a pages element (**pages**), or "emphasis elements" (**%p.em.ph;**)(see figure A.29), or "reference elements" (**%p.rf.ph;**)(see figure A.30).

The quotation element (**q**) consists of "phrase model elements"(**%m.ph;**)(see figure A.27). Neither the start- or the end-tag of the quotation element may be omitted.

The "emphasis element" (**%p.em.ph;**)(see figure A.29) consist of an emphasis (**emph**) element that denotes 6 levels of emphasis using an attribute (**type**). The emphasis element consists of "phrase model elements" (**%m.ph;**)(see figure A.27). Neither the start- or the end-tag may be omitted on the emphasis element.

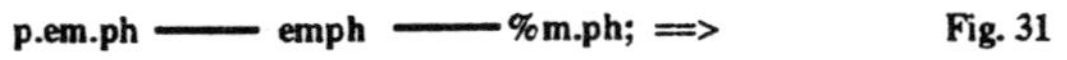

p.em.ph —— emph ——%m.ph; ==> Fig. 31

Figure A.29 Emphasis elements (%p.em.ph;)

The "reference elements" (**%p.rf.ph;**)(see figure A.30) consist of a note reference element (**noteref**), or a footnote reference element (**fnoteref**), or a figure reference element (**figref**), or a table reference element (**tableref**), or an artwork reference element (**artref**), or an appendix reference element (**appref**), or a citation reference (**citeref**), or a section reference (**secref**), or a formula reference (**formref**). These reference elements are available for Books and Articles.

For Books, a glossary reference element (**glosref**) or an index reference element (**indexref**) are also available, in addition to the reference elements above.

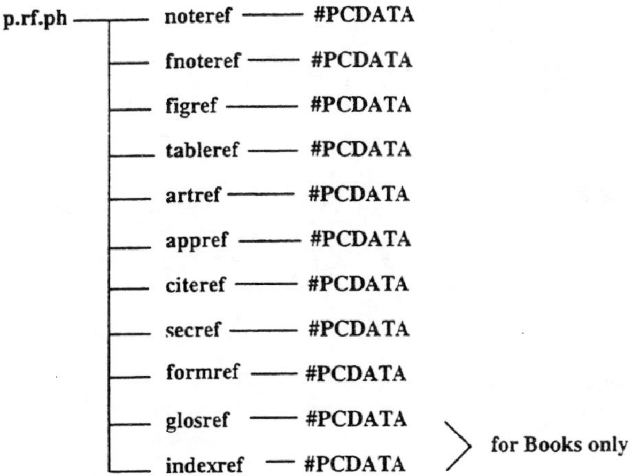

Figure A.30 Reference elements (%p.rf.ph;)

All reference elements consist of #PCDATA and their end-tags may not be omitted.

A.2.5.10 The paragraph with sequence model

The "paragraph with sequence model" (**%m.pseq;**)(see figure A.31) consists of a paragraph (**p**), followed by either a paragraph (**p**) or "paragraph subelements" (**%p.zz;**)(see figure A.20). The pair (paragraph or paragraph subelements) is optional and repeatable.

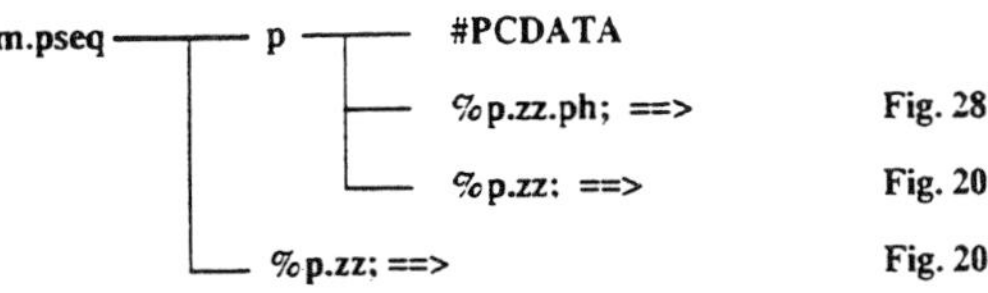

Figure A.31 The paragraph with sequence model (%m.pseq;)

A.2.5.11 The poem model

The "poem model" (**%m.poem;**)(see figure A.32) consists of a stanza element (**stanza**) followed by a poem line (**poemline**). A stanza or poemline element must appear at least once and is repeatable.

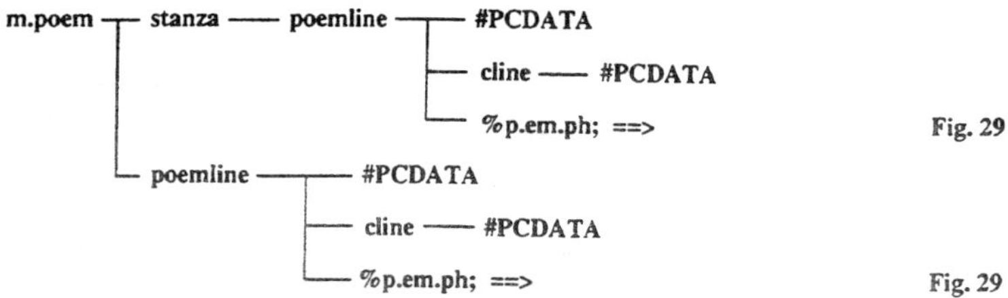

Figure A.32 The poem model (%m.poem;)

The stanza element (**stanza**) consists of at least one poem line element (**poemline**) which is repeatable. The end-tag of the stanza element may be omitted.

The poem line element (**poemline**) is a mixed content element consisting of parsed character data (**#PCDATA**) or a continuation line element (**cline**) or "emphasis elements" (%**p.em.ph;**)(see figure A.29). All these elements are optional and repeatable. The end-tag of the poemline element may be omitted.

The continuation line element (**cline**) consists of parsed character data (**#PCDATA**) or emphasis elements (%**p.em.ph;**). The end-tag of the continuation line may be omitted.

A.2.5.12 Floating elements

"Floating elements" (%**i.float;**)(see figure A.33) consist of the figure grouping element (**figgrp**) or a footnote element (**footnote**) or a note element (**note**). These elements may appear at all levels in Books and Articles.

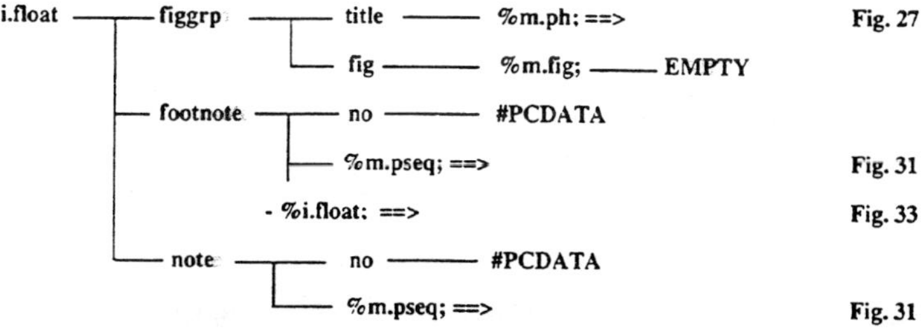

Figure A.33 Floating elements (%i.float;)

The figure grouping element (**figgrp**) consists of a title element (**title**) followed by a figure element (**fig**). The title element is optional and the figure element is optional and repeatable. Neither the start- or the end-tag of the figure grouping element may be omitted.

The footnote element (**footnote**) consists of a number element (**no**) followed by "paragraph with sequence model elements" (**%m.pseq;**)(see figure A.31). The number element is optional. Neither the start- or the end-tag of the footnote element may be omitted. Any floating element (**%i.float;**) is excluded from a footnote.

The note element (**note**) consists of a number element (**no**) followed by "paragraph with sequence model elements" (**%m.pseq;**)(see figure A.31). The number element is optional. Neither the start- or the end-tag of the note in text element may be omitted.

A.2.6 Structure of Serials

The overall structure of Serials is shown in figure A.34.

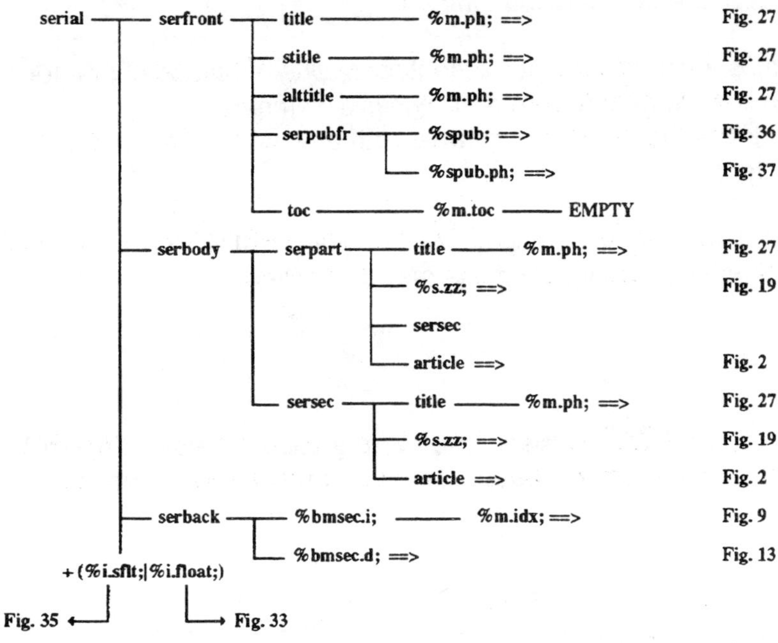

Figure A.34 Overall structure of Serials

The serial element (**serial**) consists of a serial front matter element (**serfront**), a serial body element (**serbody**), followed by a serial back matter element (**serback**). The serial back matter element (**serback**) is optional; the others are obligatory. Neither the start- or the end-tag of the serial element may be omitted.

"Serial float elements" (**%i.sflt;**)(see figure A.35) and "floating elements"(**%i.float;**)(see figure A.33) may appear at any level of the serial document.

"Serial float elements" (**%i.sflt**)(see figure A.35) consist of an asequential material element (**asqntl**), or an advertisement element (**advert**). The asequential material element (**asqntl**) consists of "section model elements" (**%m.sec;**)(see figure A.18). Neither the start- or the end-tag of the asequential material element may be omitted. The advertisement element (**advert**) consists of "advertisement model elements" (**%m.adv;**). This model is EMPTY.

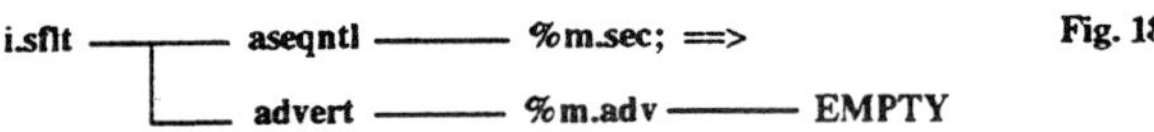

Figure A.35 Serial float elements (%i.sflt;)

A.2.6.1 Serial front matter elements

The serial front matter element (**serfront**) consists of a title element (**title**), followed by a short title element (**stitle**), followed by an alternative title element (**alttitle**), followed by a serial publisher's front matter element (**serpubfr**), followed by a table of contents element (**toc**). All elements are optional except for the title element. Both the start- and the end-tag of the serfront element may be omitted.

The short title element (**stitle**) and the alternative title element (**alttitle**) all consist of phrase model elements (**%m.ph;**)(see figure A.27).

The serial publisher's front matter element (**serpubfr**) consists of "serial publisher front matter elements" (**%spub;**)(see figure A.36) or "serial publisher front matter phrase elements" (**%spub.ph;**)(see figure A.37). These are optional and repeatable. The end tag of the serial publisher's front matter element may be omitted.

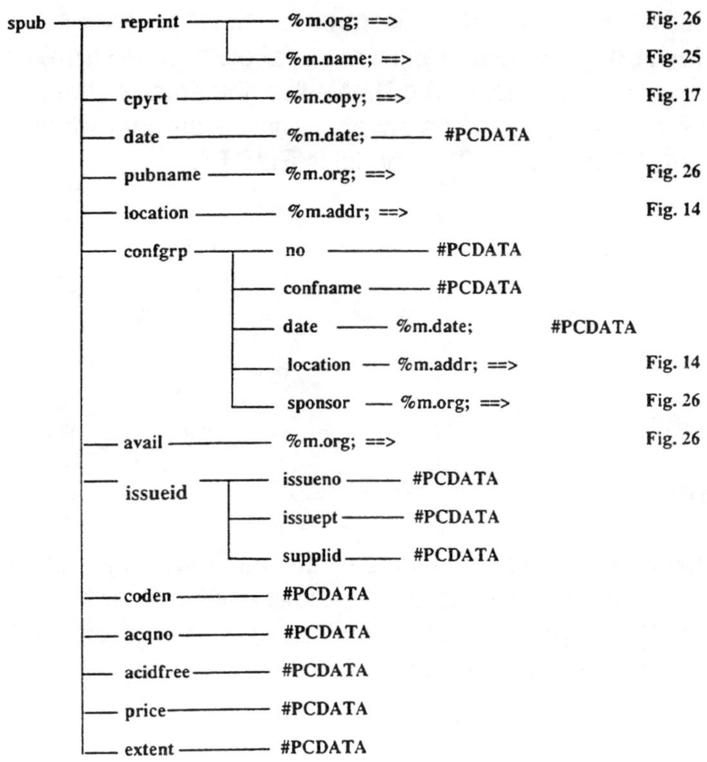

Figure A.36 Serial publisher's front matter elements (%spub;)

"Serial publisher's front matter elements" (**%spub;**)(see figure A.36) consist of a reprint source element (**reprint**), or a copyright element (**cpyrt**), or a date element (**date**), or a publisher's name element (**pubname**), or a publisher's location element (**location**), or a conference group element (**confgrp**), or an availability notice element (**avail**), or an issue identifier element (**issueid**), or a coden number element (**coden**), or an acquisition/order number element (**acqno**), or an acid free paper indicator element (**acidfree**), or a price element (**price**), or an extent of the work element (**extent**). All these elements have the same content as defined above for Books and Articles, except for the issue identifier element (**issueid**). The end-tags of all these elements may be omitted.

The issue identifier element (**issueid**) consists of an issue number element (**issueno**), an issue part element (**issuept**), a supplement to issue identifier element (**supplid**). The issue number element is obligatory, the others are optional. They all consist of "parsed character data" (**#PCDATA**). The end-tags of all these elements may be omitted.

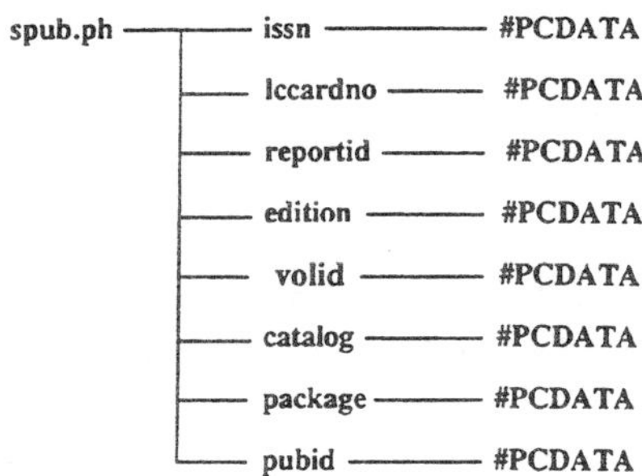

Figure A.37 Serial publisher front matter phrase elements (%spub.ph;)

"Serial publisher front matter phrase elements"(**%spub.ph;**)(see figure A.37) consist of an issn number element (**issn**), or an lc card number element (**lccardno**), or a report identifier number (**reportid**), or an edition element (**edition**), or a volume identifier element (**volid**), or a catalog element (**catalog**), or a package element (**package**), or a publisher's identifier element (**pubid**). All these elements consist of "parsed character data" (**#PCDATA**). The end-tags of all these elements may be omitted.

The table of contents element consists of "table of contents model elements" (**%m.toc**), which is EMPTY and which may be re-declared, if needed, to support a more complex structure.

A.2.6.2 Serial body elements

The serial body element (**serbody**) consists of one or more part elements (**serpart**) or one or more serial sections (**sersec**). Both the start- and the end-tag of the serial body element may be omitted.

The part element (**serpart**) consists of a title element (**title**), followed by "section subelements" (**%s.zz;**)(see figure A.19), or a serial section element (**sersec**), or an article element (**article**). The title element is optional, the group of the three following elements is optional and repeatable. The end-tag of the part element may be omitted.

The serial section element (**sersec**) consists of a title element (**title**), followed by "section subelements" (**%s.zz;**), or an article element (**article**). The title element is optional, the group of the two following elements is optional and repeatable. The end-tag of the serial section element may be omitted.

A.2.6.3 Serial back matter elements

The serial back matter element (**serback**) consists of "back matter sections" (**%bmsec.d;**)(see figure A.13) or "index and glossary" (**%bmsec.i;**)(see figure A.8). This group is optional and repeatable. The end-tag of the serial back matter element may be omitted.

A.3 Inclusion of special characters

A.3.1 Use of (public) entity sets

Characters which are not part of ISO/IEC 646 may be used in documents conforming to this International Standard by using entity references to any of the entities defined in ISO 8879, or to those defined in ISO/IEC TR 9573 parts 12-16, which is currently under review.

Users who need to include characters which are not provided by the above public entity sets, should to refer to their own public entity sets in the document type declaration subset of any conforming document.

Use of entity references is recommended for incidental use of a few special symbols. Where long sequences of symbols from another alphabet are required, different techniques are recommended as described below.

A.3.2 Use of the alphabet attribute

In documents containing a mixture of text portions which use different alphabets (such as Latin and greek), the use of entity references is not practical. Here we recommend the use of the alphabet attribute on the title, p and q elements. The data of the element is still entered using the Latin alphabet (the letters of which are found in the document's character set, ISO/IEC 646), but specifying for example alphabet=greek would imply a mapping between the Latin letters keyed in and equivalent Greek symbols. The Latin letter a, for example, could be translated into the Greek letter alpha.

This mapping can be formalized by introducing a notation in the DTD:

```
<!NOTATION greek PUBLIC "+//ISBN 1-88124::NISO//NOTATION GREEK-1//EN">
```

and by changing the alphabet attribute into a notation attribute:

```
<!ATTLIST p alphabet NOTATION (latin|greek) #IMPLIED                >
```

A.3.3 Modifying the SGML declaration

Documents which are entirely in other alphabets (greek, kanji, hebrew,...) should indicate their use of a different document character set by modifying the SGML declaration in the way described by ISO.

A.4 Electronic review and annotation

If the application is to support interchange between authors and publishers, a review mechanism should be added to the document type declaration subset. This International Standard suggests the adoption of the U.S. Department of Defense MIL-M-28001 electronic review fragment using the following public identifier:

```
<!ENTITY % ereview PUBLIC "-//USA-DOD//DTD SUP MIL-M-28001 EREVIEW REVB//EN">
```

The electronic review declaration set provides the required SGML structures for the review of SGML text documents electronically using SGML for the comments. The capability supported by these structures enables reviewers located in diverse environments to make and exchange comments to multiple copies of a document file over a network. The comments may then be sorted, processed, and incorporated into the document by the "owner" system.

The electronic review declaration set consists of a portable electronic review "toolkit" suitable for incorporation into any document type declaration, for use in review of any document instance of that type. This set consists of a standalone "toolkit" that may be referenced as a public entity for use with a given document type declaration, with little or no change to that document type declaration.

Use of the toolkit requires:

a) unique identifiers on elements (at least to the level of granularity included in the review);

b) redefinition of the document level element via parameterization to include a "modreq" (modification request) floating element.

An example of referencing the electronic review toolkit for use with the Book DTD, without change to the publicly registered DTD, is as follows:

```
<!DOCTYPE book PUBLIC "ISO 12083:1994//DTD Book//EN"
[

<!-- The following parameter entity replaces
<!ENTITY % i.float "modreq | figgrp | footnote | note" --floating elements-->

<!ENTITY % ereview PUBLIC "-//USA-DOD//DTD SUP MIL-M-28001 EREVIEW REVB//EN">
%ereview;

<!-- Note that the % i.float parameter entity must replace that declared
elsewhere in this DTD.  Using this technique, one may create a file which
includes modreq elements anywhere in the current instance or a review
document which would consist only of modreq elements. -->
]>
```

Some examples of functionality that can be supported by these additional structures are sorting comments by basis of comment ID information (reviewer, date, organization, etc.), sorting comments related to a particular user-defined topic, tracking the comments by basis of configuration/version information, tracking the disposition of the comments, tracking the status of the owner organization's response to the comment. Refer to MIL-M-28001 for more detailed information.

A.5 Short references

The use of short references is deprecated by this International Standard. Users who need them for reasons of backward compatibility with ANSI/NISO Z39.59-1988 should add the corresponding markup declarations to their DTD.

A.6 Mathematics

The Association of American Publishers (AAP) *Standard for Electronic Manuscript Preparation and Markup* has a companion guide called *Markup of Mathematical Formulas* which contains a DTD for mathematical formulas. ISO/IEC TR 9573 also contains a DTD for mathematical formulas. The AAP Math Update committee was formed with the objective to unify these DTDs. Since several comments on the draft form of this International Standard made explicit reference to the work of this committee, it was decided to include it.

The following text is an explanation of the Mathematics DTD.

A.6.1 Introduction and notation

The Mathematics DTD is included by the Book and Article DTDs of this International Standard. As it is a separate entity it may also be included by other DTDs. It only describes the presentational or visual structure of formulas, since there is no consensus on how to describe their semantics.

The Mathematics DTD defines the structure of in-line formulas (**formula**) and display formulas (**dformula**). An important design principle is that the formulas encoded as suggested need never be read or typed by human beings, although an attempt was made to keep the markup transparent.

For every element X that has an ID attribute there is an element XREF with an IDREF attribute, that indicates a reference to an element X. Attribute names that start with "l" ("r") usually relate to something on the left (right).

Neither start- or end-tags of any of the elements (except EMPTY ones) may be omitted, unless explicitly mentioned in the following sections.

A.6.2 Parameter entities

The parameter entities describing the possible contents of formulas are: **p.trans** and **m.math**. The character transformations bold, italic etc. are described by p.trans while m.math contains general mathematical elements.

If the DTD is not used with the Article or Book DTD from this International Standard, but with another DTD, the comments surrounding the accessible document (SDA) parameter entities should be removed.

The smallest units of a formula are letters and symbols. The letters may be from five alphabets: Latin, Greek, Cyrillic, Hebrew and Kanji; the default alphabet is Latin. For incidental use of letters from other alphabets, entity references should be used. For more extensive use the **alphabet** attribute on the <formula> or <dformula> tag, which may have one of the five values listed above, is recommended. A mapping between the characters typed into the document and the special alphabet may be achieved by defining a notation.

A.6.3 Character transformations

To the five standard alphabets one may apply the transformation elements bold (**bold**), italic (**italic**), sans-serif (**sansser**), typewriter or non-proportional (**typewrit**), small caps (**smallcap**) or roman (**roman**). These transformations change the appearance (weight, shape, ...) of the characters and symbols. This makes entity sets such as ISOgrk4 (bold Greek) obsolete – at least for the purpose of this International Standard.

The transformations can be combined. For example a bold italic X is obtained by <b><it>X</it></b>. Obviously, some combinations are meaningless, but the decision what to do with such combinations can be left to the processing application.

Some transformations are only ever applied to individual characters, such as blackboard bold, script and german (fraktur). They should therefore be marked up as entity references, rather than individual elements. Although one can apply the six transformations for which elements are defined also to individual characters. For cases where, however, many bold or italic characters are required together, elements are more practical.

If large portions of text are required inside a formula, the formula element should be closed and the appropriate text element used from the imbedding DTD.

A.6.4 Fractions

A formula is seen as a linear, that is one-dimensional, sequence of atoms (letters, symbols) and built-up constructions. Basic operations such as +, - and / are just typed as a linear sequence. One of the first obvious deviations from this one-dimensional "flow" is the fraction, which is a two-dimensional object. (Other exceptions are radicals and arrays.)

Fractions need hardly be discussed, since there is no lower-level markup possible for a fraction. One could look upon a built-up or case fraction as a horizontal bar with top and bottom embellishments, but this type of markup has no obvious advantage.

The fraction element (**fraction**) consists of a numerator (**num**) followed by a denominator (**den**). The width of the fraction bar is determined by the widest of the two constituent elements, i.e. numerator and denominator. The **shape** attribute indicates whether the fraction is built-up (**built**) or case (**case**). The **align** attribute tells what the horizontal alignment is (**left**, **center** or **right**) of the narrowest constituent with respect to the fraction bar. The **style** attribute indicates the style of the fraction bar (**single, double, triple, dash, dot, bold, blank, none**).

Inline fractions, where the numerator is separated from the denominator by a solidus should be marked up using the fence construct. For these cases, the sizing is with respect to the height, not the width of the constituents.

A.6.5 Embellishments

Superiors, inferiors, accents, overlines and underlines can be regarded as instances of a more general "embellishment" construct, where elements are placed at a certain position with respect to a central, or base element. The base element, which is in fact a subformula element (**subform),** does not change in size or position because of the embellishments; the position of the embellishments is determined by the size of the base element, and their size may be reduced.

The subformula element is either the preceding single symbol, e.g. φ, or the preceding tagged construction, e.g. <fen>...</fen>. The following positions can be discriminated:

```
tl        t        tr
 l  subformula     r
bl        b        br
```

The correspondence between these positions and elements is as follows: subformula= <**subform**>, tl, tr = <**sup**>, bl, br = <**inf**>, t = <**top**>, b = <**bot**>. The subform element can be required to solve ambiguities resulting from nesting.

An embellishment that goes "through" the base element is coded with the middle element (**mid**). The positions "l" and "r" have no markup at present. Superiors and inferiors have attributes **location** and **arrange**; location can be **pre** or **post**, arrange can be either **compact** (the default way of placing inferiors and superiors) or **stagger**. For example:

```
 1 3
H
  2
```

is encoded as

```
<subform>H</subform><sup>1</sup><inf stagger>2</inf><sup stagger>3</sup>
```

The stagger attribute is a way to get rid of the meaningless, and undesirable, zero-width element <zw> (which probably originates from TeX's {}, which is used to code the above example as H^1{}_2{}^3).

Multiple inferiors or superiors are specified from left to right. For example:

```
ij kl
  H
```

is encoded as

```
<subform>H</subform><sup pre>ij</sup><sup>kl</sup>
```

Multiple top and bottom embellishment are specified from the inside to the outside, from the top to the bottom. This is not an elegant solution, but specifying multiple <sup pre> from the inside to the outside as well, means reading from right to left, which is equally or even more undesirable!

Notice that

```
     l
ij k
  H
```

can be encoded as

```
<subform>H</subform><sup pre>ij</sup><sup>k<sup>l</sup></sup>
```

or as

```
<subform>H<sup pre>ij</sup><sup>k</sup></subform><sup>l</sup>
```

depending on whether l is a superscript to k (resulting in a typographically smaller l), or to the rest of the expression (in which case the l would have the same size as the k).

Top, middle and bottom embellishments have an **align** attribute that specifies the horizontal alignment (**left**, **center**, **right**) with respect to the center of the base element. The **sizeid** attribute has a declared value of a unique identifier (ID). This allows the height or width of the embellishment to be passed on to another element.

A.6.6 Fences, boxes, overlines and underlines

Another category of embellishments is formed by the fences, boxes, overlines and underlines. The property of this category is: the size of the embellishment, i.e. the width of overlines and underlines, and the height of fences, is determined by the dimensions of the base element. That is: the height of a fence is determined by the height of the enclosed sub-formula, and the width of overlines and underlines is determined by the width of the enclosed sub-formula.

The fence element (**fence**), the box element (**box**), the overline element (**overline**) and the underline element (**undrline**) all have the general mathematical elements (%p.trans;|%m.trans;) as content.

In some cases a mechanism is needed to have the height of a fence fixed by that of another fence, for example in

```
        a+b   a-b
(a+b) (--- + ---)
        2     2
```

This is solved using an attribute **sizeid** which has the declared value ID, see below. The fence element has separate attributes for both the left and the right post. It would be better to have post-type and post-style attributes on both the fence open tag and the fence close tag, as in

```
<fence posttype=(>a+b</fence posttype=)>
```

However, this is impossible in SGML. Left and right posts must have their own attributes, since it must be possible to type (a+b]. Thus the **lpost** and **rpost** attributes, which have declared value CDATA, may be used to indicate the symbol of the fence. Default is the vertical bar (|). The **style** attribute indicates the style of the fence (**single, double, triple, dash, dot, bold, blank, none**). The **sizeid** and **sizeref** attributes allow sizes to be picked up or defined.

The empty post element (**post**) can be placed inside (or outside) a fence if this is required. The size of each post is determined by the innermost enclosing fence construction. The **style** attribute indicates the style of the post (**single, double, triple, dash, dot, bold, blank, none**). The **sizeid** and **sizeref** attributes allow sizes to be picked up or defined.

The box element (**box**) has a **style** attribute indicating the style of the box (**single, double, triple, dash, dot, bold, blank, none**).

There is one problem with the use of elements for overlines (**overline**) and underlines (**undrline**), namely a formula with partially overlapping overline and underline, for example

```
    _______
U V W X Y Z
    -------
```

This problem is solved with an EMPTY marker element (**mark**) which has an ID attribute. The mark element points at a specific place inside a string. Underline and overline run from start-tag to end-tag, unless start point or end point is overridden by references to marks, which are given by the IDREF attributes **start** and **end**:

```
<undrline start="x"><overline>UV<mark id="x">WX</overline>YZ</undrline>
```

A.6.7 Labelled arrows

A third kind of embellishment is what can be called "labelled arrows". Here, the width of a base element, in most cases a horizontal arrow, is determined by the width of the embellishment, precisely the other way around from overlines and underlines. It is unknown if any application exists of a similar mechanism for adjusting the height of a base element to fit an embellishment on the left or the right. There is no final solution for this kind of embellishment, although it can be achieved as follows. Suppose you want to encode

```
            2  2
           x +y -->0
f(x, y) -----------> 0
```

This could be done like this

```
f(x, y) <subform sizeref="x">&larr;</subform>
<top size="x">x<sup>2</sup>+y<sup>2</sup>&larr;0</top> 0
```

The base element (**subform**) allows to determine its size by referring to the embellishment. The subform element has **sizeid** and **sizeref** atributes. This is a case where omission of tags could cause ambiguities.

In the case of multiple embellishments, the largest one should be given the sizeid attribute.

A.6.8 Radicals

For radicals (roots) the mechanism in the AAP DTD was taken over. The radical element (**radical**) is composed of an optional radix element (**radix**) and a mandatory radicand element (**radicand**). The difference with the AAP DTD is that the radix is specified before the radicand. The reasons for this change are that the radix comes before the radicand (a) in the presentation on paper, (b) in the markup of systems such as TeX, and (c) when spoken aloud. Both the start-tag and the end-tag of the radicand element may be omitted.

A.6.9 Arrays

Arrays are in fact (simple) tables. The markup schemes for arrays resemble those of simple tables. Since there are no convincing arguments to differentiate piles or stacks on the one hand from matrices or arrays on the other hand, it is suggested to use the array construction for all of these.

A serious problem is the inability of SGML to markup a matrix as more than a horizontal sequence of columns, or as a vertical sequence of rows. In fact, a matrix is both simultaneously, and much more! The best one can do in SGML to give the user a choice: a matrix can be marked up as either a sequence of rows, or a sequence of cells. Another thing that cannot be expressed in SGML – and therefore cannot be checked by a parser – is the fact that all rows and columns have equal length.

The array element (**array**) consists of one or more array rows (**arrayrow**) or one or more array columns (**arraycol**). Each array row and column consists of one or more array cells (**arraycel**). The end-tags of array rows, columns and cells may be omitted.

The array element has attributes **rowalign** and **colalign** (to indicate the row and column alignment) and **rowsep** and **colsep** to indicate the row and column separators. These attributes have declared value NMTOKEN.

The separator values are constructed as follows. Specify from 1 to F+1 style tokens, where F is the number of columns or rows. A style token can have the value (single, double, triple, dash, dot, bold, blank or none). Each style token is preceded by a column or row number from 0 through F. 0 applies to the separator before the 1st column or row, and 1 through F to separators after corresponding columns or rows; unspecified separators are blank. Special "numbers" F (for final) and A (for all others) can be used. Examples (colsep):

```
"0 double F double" gives double rules as borders
"1 bold" gives bold rule after the first column
```

The alignment values are constructed as follows. Specify from 1 to F alignment tokens (left, center or right), where F is the number of columns or rows, to indicate the alignment of cells within the corresponding row or column. Default is center. Tokens are paired with column or row numbers, as with colsep and rowsep. Examples:

```
"1 left A right" gives left aligned first column, all others right
"1 left" gives left aligned first column, all others center
```

A.6.10 Commutative diagrams

No attempt was made to cover commutative diagrams. They describe their own logical structure far better than anything else can and, as can be seen by looking at them, that structure is rarely anything as simple as a tree.

A.6.11 Spacing and alignment

It is not clear how to handle markup spacing, breaking and alignment of formulas. For lack of something better the ideas from the AAP DTD have been used.

The break element (**break**) indicates the locations in a formula where a line break should occur. This element was maintained, although it is probably superfluous in many circumstances.

The mark element (**mark**) identifies a point somewhere in a formula; it was described earlier, under fences. A mark reference element (**markref**) enables the alignment of (parts of) a formula to the point indicated by the mark element. The **direction** attribute has values horizontal (**hor**) and vertical (**ver**) to show in which direction the alignment should take place.

Horizontal and vertical space can be obtained by using the elements **hspace** and **vspace**. The amount of space is given by the **space** attribute. As units of measurements the ones proposed by TeX can be used (pt for point, pc for pica, in for inch, bp for big point, cm for centimeter, mm for millimeter, dd for didot point, cc for cicero and sp for scaled point), but users may define their own as required.

A.7 Complex tables

A base set of tags for complex tabular material is contained in the AAP's *Standard for Electronic Manuscript Preparation and Markup* series: *Markup of Tabular Material.* There are many other public and proprietary table DTDs available. The AAP tables update committee will try to unify these DTDs.

A.8 Facilities for Braille, large print and computer voice

A.8.1 Introduction

The International Committee for Accessible Document Design d ("ICADD") has published guidelines for designing SGML applications which enable the preparation of texts for near-automatic conversion to Grade 2 Braille and for publication both in large print and computer voice editions. This International Standard follows these guidelines.

By introducing fixed "SGML Document Access" (SDA) attributes, users of any DTDs, including those which comprise this International Standard, will create documents which can be easily mapped into documents conforming to the ICADD DTD. Documents that conform to the ICADD DTD can be readily translated into Braille. Each element has an SDA attribute which indicates how and onto which elements of the ICADD tagset it should be mapped.

A.8.2 Mapping to the base tag set

A small set of "canonical" elements has been created to support the basic output formats available in Braille. They are:

ANCHOR	Mark Spot on a Page
AU	Author(s)
B	Bold Emphasized Text
BOOK	Highest Level Element for Document
BOX	Boxed or Sidebar Information
BQ	Block Quotation
FIG	Figure Title and Description
FN	Footnote
H1	Major Level Heading within Book
H2	Second Level Heading

H3	Third Level Heading or BOX Heading
H4	Fourth Level Heading
H5	Fifth Level Heading
H6	Sixth Level Heading
IPP	Page Number of Ink Print Page
IT	Italic Emphasized Text
LANG	Language Indicator
LHEAD	List Heading
LIST	List of Items
LIT	Literal or Computer Text
LITEM	List Item
NOTE	Note in Text
OTHER	Other Emphasized Text
PARA	Paragraph
PP	Print Page Reference
TERM	Term or Keyword
TI	Title of the Book
XREF	Cross Reference

An optional set of canonical elements has been created to support the creation of tables which may be used for Braille, large type and computer voice. They are:

TABLE	The highest level element, which will include at least one TGROUP
TGROUP	Allows repeated combinations of the next three elements to appear within one table
THEAD	Table Header
TBODY	Table Body
TFOOT	Table Footer
COLDEF	Column Definition (which carries necessary attributes for the column information)
HDROW	Row in a Header
HDCELL	Cell in a Header
ROW	Row in the Table Body
STUBCELL	The Non-Data Carrying Stub Cell of a Row
SSTCELL	A Sub-Stub Cell in a Row (usually with different indent)
CELL	Table Cell
SHORTXT	Short Text Element provides alternative text for a stub cell or head cell for voice representation or for a cell reference to longer text carried in the NOTE in a Braille table
NOTE	Text extracted from Braille table cells in order to allow the narrowest possible column widths in the table body

A.8.2.1 One-to-one mappings

In the Book DTD of this International Standard, a chapter is defined as follows:

```
<!ELEMENT  chapter            (no?, title?, (%s.zz;)*, section*) >
```

Neither the chapter element, nor any of its subelements, appear in the ICADD DTD. By using the SGML keyword "FIXED", a specific attribute value is associated with every appearance of the related element.

Take the title element as an example. Depending on where this element appears, it may mean different things. In the book's front material, it will be used to indicate the book's title. We "fix" the SDAFORM attribute for title so that it cannot be changed in the document instance.

```
<!ATTLIST title      SDAFORM        CDATA     #FIXED  "ti">
```

This indicates that wherever it is used, <title> stands for a <ti> in the SDA tagset.

A.8.2.2 Simple context-sensitive mappings

The ICADD technique includes both a simple mechanism for simple contextual mappings, and a more complex one for those situations in which the mapping may be dependent on the fulfillment of more than one condition in the element's ancestry.

```
<!ATTLIST  chap      SDARULE  CDATA      #FIXED    "title h2" >
<!ATTLIST  sec       SDARULE  CDATA      #FIXED    "title h3" >
```

The attribute SDARULE always takes an even number of arguments. In this example, we are defining the rules which apply while we are in chap and sec elements. Within each ATTLIST, one can declare any number of pairs of arguments. That is, within a chap, title maps to h2, and within a sec, title maps to h3.

Any element may have no declared mapping (that is, no fixed SDAFORM or SDARULE attributes). For each such element, the transformation process must discard both its start- and end-tags. A typical case where this must occur is with "containing elements", those which do not contain character content of their own, but which mark structural boundaries, and contain only other elements.

Note that very useful mappings can be constructed using only the SDAFORM and simple SDARULE attributes described above.

A.8.2.3 Complex context-sensitive mappings

A more complex example allows one to set a stack of open rules, where the rule closest to the current context overrides rules higher in the element ancestry (or previous in the stack). For example, in a content model where chapter could occur at multiple levels in the document, we need to be able to specify different mappings for title depending on whether chapter is in a part or not:

```
<!ELEMENT    body       (part+ | chapter+)  >
<!ELEMENT    part       (no?, title?, (%s.zz;)*, chapter+ )     >
<!ELEMENT    chapter    (no?, title?, (%s.zz;)*, section*)      >
```

We must recognize that if a title appears in a part it maps to h1, if it appears in a chapter within a part, it maps to an h2, but if the chapter is not in a part, the title maps to an h1. We do this by establishing rules within CHAPTER that set the two mapping conditions carried in attributes associated with the element immediately affected by the rules of its context:

```
<!ATTLIST chapter        SDABDY       NAMES       #FIXED      "title h1"
                         SDAPART      NAMES       #FIXED      "title h2" >
```

Use of the rules is established in the attributes of the elements which may appear in the stack:

```
<!ATTLIST body    SDARULE    CDATA     #FIXED    "chapter #use SDABDY ">
<!ATTLIST part    SDARULE    CDATA     #FIXED    "title h1
                                            chapter #use SDAPART">
```

As the transformation software encounters the attributes it sets the stack: Chapter will use the SDABDY rule unless the part start-tag appears first and resets the stack to SDAPART.

A.8.2.4 Generated text

A.8.2.4.1 Character text

The third type of ICADD attribute covers situations in which the name of an SGML element (its generic identifier) carries useful information which would be lost if the original element were transformed into a SDAFORM which carries only the information needed for presentation. (Often this is the kind of content that would be generated by a formatter or typesetting program.)

```
<!ATTLIST abstract    SDAPREF    CDATA      #FIXED   "<h1>Abstract</h1>">
```

The SDAPREF attribute carries "generated text," words to be produced by the translator software as a string to be substituted for the <abstract> start-tag. Generated text can also be associated with the end-tag and appears immediately before it. Note that generated text may contain markup.

When SDAPREF or SDASUFF attributes are used without an SDAFORM attribute, the result is effectively the simple replacement of both or either the source start- and end-tags by generated text. A basic example:

```
<!ATTLIST q     SDAPREF    CDATA    #FIXED         '"'
                SDASUFF    CDATA    #FIXED         '"'>
```

A.8.2.4.2 Consecutive numbering

Two types of numbering are needed in a typical document.

In the first type, elements are numbered consecutively throughout. This is supported by the following technique:

The SDAPREF attributes also allow the specification of automatic numbering. One may associate an automatically incremented value with an element and may also access that value with a SDAPREF attribute for one of that element's subelements.

The keyword #count causes the expression following to be interpreted. The expression itself appears within parentheses and may be mixed in with fixed text to be generated. The expression follows the form:

```
#COUNT(element, format)
```

and specifies both element which is being established as a counter and the format of the counter. One needs to specify the affected element since counters are sometimes associated with a specific element, and sometimes with its parent or child elements.

I specifies uppercase Roman numerals: I, II, III, IV, ...
i specifies lowercase Roman numerals: i, ii, iii, iv, ...
1 specifies Arabic numbers: 1, 2, 3, 4, ...
A specifies uppercase alphabetic: A, B, C, D, ...
a specifies lowercase alphabetic: a, b, c, d, ...

By default, the numbering starts at "1" (or the equivalent in the other formats). A counter can be initialized with an expression of the form:

```
1=3
```

as in

```
<!ATTLIST app      SDAPREF CDATA #FIXED "#count (app, A=3)" >
```

which indicates that the appendix numbering (where app is the element name for appendix) is upper case alphabetic and starts with the letter C. Note that this example includes no other generated text and would simply print the letter C in place of the app start-tag.

A.8.2.4.3 Numbering with reset

The second type of numbering is one whose counter needs to be reset under various conditions, particularly when a higher-level element changes. Often the value of a counter will be used in the SDAPREF attribute of any of an element's subelements. For example:

```
<!ATTLIST sec       SDAPREF CDATA #FIXED "Section #count (sec, A)" >
<!ATTLIST subsec    SDAPREF CDATA #FIXED "Subsection #count (sec,
    A).#count(subsec,a)" >
```

When the counter for a parent element changes (in this case SEC), the counter for the subelement is automatically reset to "1".

The example above would generate

Section A

when a SEC element first appeared, and

Subsection A.a

when the first SUBSEC element appears.

The following variation allows the format of the counter to be different from that of a parent element:

```
<!ATTLIST figure   SDAPREF   CDATA   #FIXED
     "Figure #count(sec, 1).#count(figure, 1))"    >
```

which will generate:

Figure 1.1, 1.2, 1.3 ...

and so on, until the next section, even if the sections are numbered A, B, C.

An exclamation mark in the counter format supports the case in which the counter should not be reset when the parent changes. A typical example might be figure numbers which are consecutive throughout a book but which incorporate the chapter or section number as well:

```
<!ATTLIST figure   SDAPREF   CDATA   #FIXED
     "Figure #count(sec, 1!).#count(figure, 1)"    >
```

which will generate:

Figure 1.1, 1.2, 1.3

in section A, and

Figure 2.4, 2.5, 2.6 in section B.

Under certain conditions, a counter needs to be reset even though the parent has no counter or its counter doesn't appear in the current element's generated text. The tilde character is the non-printing indicator:

A typical example:

```
<!ATTLIST listitem  SDAPREF  CDATA  #FIXED
     "#count(list ~)#count(listitem, 1). "   >
```

which will generate:

1.
2. and so on

and ensures that the listitems will be reset each time a new list starts.

A.8.2.4.4 Assigning SDAPREF values in a parent element

The final situation covered allows one to make numbering decisions based on a parent element even when an element may have a variety of parents:

```
<!ATTLIST orderedlist  SDAPREF  CDATA  #FIXED
     "#set(listitem, #count(listitem, 1)'. ')Generated text for
orderedlist."   >
<!ATTLIST bulletlist  SDAPREF  CDATA  #FIXED
     "#set(listitem,'&bullet; ')"   >
<!ATTLIST listitem  SDAPREF CDATA  #FIXED
     "#use(listitem, 1). "   >
```

#set always takes two arguments. The first is the name of the element in the source DTD which governs the counter. The second argument is either the format of the counter or the content of the prefix or suffix that will be referenced and picked up by the sub-element that needs it. Content other than counter formats must be set off using single quotes. In the example, the orderedlist element establishes that a listitem is prefaced with a numeric counter followed by a period and a space. When the same listitem element appears within a bulletlist, however, its prefix is a bullet followed by a space.

The #use function may take only one argument which is the name of the counter it should use. If there is a second argument, it is a format for a counter which overrides that which may have been set in the parent's attribute.

The #set function never appears in text generated by the element in which it is declared. It may, therefore, appear with other content which is to be generated, as in the example above where "Generated text for orderedlist." appears in place of the orderedlist start-tag.

The #set function is implied for any #count which is not explicitly set. That is, #set is used only for complex situations in which you wish to establish multiple possible prefix or suffix strings.

A.8.2.4.5 Notes:

To use actual angle brackets, hash marks, tildes, exclamation marks and quotation marks – both single and double – in all the SDAPREF and SDASUFF values, one should use SGML entity references, even when the special characters are used in a place where the context might inform their correct usage.

Note that all the capabilities available in SDAPREF are also available in SDASUFF attributes although they are not normally used there.

A.8.2.5 Attribute Handling

On occasion it will be necessary to carry the names and/or values of attributes through the SDA transformation process. This is accomplished with the use of three keywords which may be employed in association with any of the other SDA attributes.

#attlist brings forward the entire attribute list of the base element, excluding any attribute whose name begins with SDA (or its replacement as established by APPINFO; see below). This capability is used with SDAFORM or SDAPREF attributes.

#attrib (xxxxx) brings forward the attribute xxxxx and its value (complete with the equals sign and the quotation marks). This is used to isolate one or more specific attributes from a longer list and may be used with SDAFORM or SDAFORM attributes. That is: #attrib (xxxxx yyyyy) picks up both.

#attval (xxxxx) brings forward the value only of the attribute xxxxx. This may be used with generated text in an SDAPREF attribute to rename an attribute. This keyword may also be used with more than one argument.

Two examples:

```
<!ATTLIST graphic     SDAFORM   CDATA    #FIXED   "fig #attlist">
<!ATTLIST abstract    SDAPREF   CDATA    #FIXED
                   "<h1 #attrib (ID)>Abstract</h1>">
```

A.8.2.6 A basic location model

There are several classes of source DTD hierarchical structures which are not well served by the techniques described earlier in this booklet. Most important of those, by virtue of its use in a variety of existing DTDs, is the requirement to allow for the mapping of elements within a recursively nesting element.

For example, the following case

```
<!ELEMENT sec   -o   (title, (sec+|para+))    >

<sec><title>Level One Title</title>
```

```
<sec><title>Level Two Title</title>
    <sec><title>Level Three Title</title>
```

can easily create a structure in which the first title element must be mapped to the SDA h1, the second title must be mapped to an h2, and the third title element must be mapped to the SDA h3.

The #use construct described above deals with a variety of structures, but not with placement of an element within its tree or with respect to its subelements. For that reason, the committee has developed a small "location model" language to describe a set of standard conditions.

The syntax for these conditions involves use of ">", square brackets and parentheses. This was adopted because ">" is very unlikely to be a character allowed in an element name. Except for the use of the rare SGML feature CONCUR, the same is true of "(" and ")". The square brackets group together the location model in order to allow non-significant white space to occur.

The location model works exactly the same way as SDARULE except that the first argument, which occurs within square brackets, may represent a complex set of conditions which must be fulfilled for the mapping to occur. The location model may also appear within SDAPREF and SDASUFF to create context-sensitive generated text.

[chap>>p>>emph] means "the current element and its ancestry matches the pattern chap containing a p containing a emph". It is not necessary to put the current element into this pattern if emph is to contain it, but not necessarily immediately. You can put in the current element either by name or, sometimes more usefully, by the special symbol #CE.

[chap>p>emph>#CE] means "the current element and its ancestry matches the pattern chap immediately containing p immediately containing emph immediately containing the current element". ">>" and ">" can be mixed as needed.

[(chap|sec)>>p] means "either a chap or a sec containing a p".

[chap >> p ID=AC555 >> emph] indicates that the transformation is to take place only if the specified attribute value matches. The simpler case of [emph type=2] or [#CE type=2] demonstrates the checking of an attribute value for the current element.

Alternative values are allowed for attributes in location models. Thus: [chap>> p ID=(A|B|C) >> emph] means match a chap containing a p with ID attribute equal to an A OR a B OR C containing an emph.

Accordingly, for the nested sec example described above, the following attribute declarations would handle the mappings:

```
<!ATTLIST sec SDARULE #FIXED
            "title h1
            [sec>>title] h2
            [sec>>sec>>title] h3
            [sec>>sec>>sec>>title] h4"
```

A.8.2.7 Braille transcriber's notes

Certain transformations will always require the intervention of an experienced Braille transcriber. Often these can be predicted: One knows that in a DTD with the potential for complex tables, or one which supports the inclusion of graphics, that the Braillist should be alerted to either proofread or create the required content and markup.

In the case of graphics, for example, a sighted person will have to describe the image. It would be useful to have the transformation process place a marker in the text at each point where one knows in advance that such work will be necessary.

The ICADD technique recommends the consistent use of a processing instruction as just such a marker. The marker is placed by declaring an SDAPREF attribute at the highest level of the relevant element/sub-element group. For example, a marker should be put on a deflist element rather than on a dd or ddhd:

```
<!ATTLIST deflist SDAFORM    CDATA     #FIXED    "list"
                  SDAPREF    CDATA     #FIXED    "<?SDATRANS>Definitions" >
```

There is one other special processing instruction, intended to allow the suspension of the ICADD transformation process. <?SDASUSPEND> may appear in an SDAPREF attribute value and terminate transformation for the entire contents of the current element, allowing the source markup to survive the transformation and appear in the output file. For example, in this International Standard, this technique is used to preserve mathematical markup.

A.8.2.8 Support for mathematics and other special SGML notations

Documents encoded in SGML and containing specialized markup for fields such as mathematics and chemistry need particular, non-automatable handling for presentation to the visually impaired.

For production of Braille, large print and synthesized voice, there is one simple rule: The specialized markup in the original file must be preserved as it represents the greatest likely source of information for the domain expert who will prepare the files for production. (Note that the ICADD transformation techniques normally discard all source markup for which there is no mapping declared in the SDA attributes.)

Two ICADD techniques apply to this work.

A.8.2.8.1 Suspending the transformation process

A rarely used special attribute SDASUSP, intended to allow the suspension of the ICADD transformation process, may appear in the attribute list of any element.

With the argument "SUSPEND", it will terminate the normal ICADD transformation for the entire contents of the current element, allowing the source markup to survive the transformation and appear in the output file. For example, in this International Standard, this technique is used to preserve mathematical markup.

The argument "RESUME" resumes transformation for the contents of the current element. This argument, which is used only within an element within which transformation has been suspended, allows the nested element to be transformed while the parent is not.

The argument "DISCARD" allows the transformation process to take input from any DTD and remove it – including both markup and content – from the output file. This allows material which is included in the document instance but does not appear in print to be discarded rather than turned into Braille, large print or voice content.

A.8.2.8.2 Attribute to carry semantic markup

Since there is no consensus on how to describe the semantics of formulas, the mathematics DTD included with this Interational Standard describes only their presentational or visual structure. Since, however, there is a strong need for such description (especially within the print-disabled community), the following declaration should be added where there is a requirement for a consistent, standardized mechanism to carry semantic meanings for the SGML elements:

```
<!ENTITY % SDAMAP "SDAMAP   NAME    #IMPLIED"           >
```

The attribute represented by %SDAMAP; is to be used for all elements which may require a semantic association, or, in the simpler case, be added to all elements in a mathematical or similar DTD with requirements for specialized handling.

A.8.2.9 Support for multiple languages

The techniques described above for SDAPREF and SDASUFF are based on the premise that it makes sense to incorporate text directly into the DTD that will become part of the input stream to a Braille translation process. This, in turn, assumes that the text of the marked-up file and the text of the DTD will be the same – and more importantly, will remain the same.

In fact, this cannot be safely assumed. SGML is part of an active, international community in the forefront of reusing information across many borders and boundaries. An additional technique is needed to ensure the separability of the generated text from the remaining work that goes into making a DTD ICADD-enabled.

The ICADD committee suggests removing the specific contents of all generated text from the attribute declarations and defining them indirectly as SGML entities which are gathered in a set of declarations, which may exist either in an external file or within the DTD. Both mechanisms allow users to switch easily between different languages.

The following example illustrates the use of the external file. In the DTD is a reference to a local (system) or public entity set:

```
<!ENTITY % SDAGEN PUBLIC "-//EC-USA-CDA/ICADD//ENTITIES//EN">
%SDAGEN;
```

Wherever SDAPREF and SDASUFF attributes were used, instead of the form described elsewhere in this document, one would include:

```
<!ATTLIST email SDAPREF ENTITY #FIXED "sdaemail" >
```

Notice that the SDAPREF value is defined as having FIXED ENTITY attribute values instead of the CDATA attribute values as elsewhere in this Annex.

In the SDAGEN entities file, we might find for instance:

```
<!ENTITY sdaemail SDATA "Electronic Mail Address: ">
```

When it becomes appropriate to re-run the transformation process for a second language, the entity reference should be re-declared to refer to a second SDAGEN file, in the desired second language, edited locally by a translator (and not necessarily the DTD creator). This process is repeated for as many languages as are needed.

(Note that one could do some fancy renaming of the external entity files so that multiple files exist but, as needed, a copy is made which is temporarily called by the name embedded within the DTD. That way the DTD doesn't have to have the file name re-declared each time it is used to establish the mapping transformations for the new language.)

For any DTD which would be used in a variety of countries, this approach means that one defines one common entity file (presumably in the base language of the DTD) for the generated text which appears in all the SDAPREF and SDASUFF attributes declared throughout the DTD.

There is a disadvantage to this approach in that the person creating the ICADD-enabled DTD always needs to include (at least) one separate entity file. Accordingly, there is a slight risk of the two files becoming separated or out-of-synchronization. However, in the committee's opinion, this solution is better than the most obvious alternative: having to deal with multiple versions of the same DTD whose only differences are that they contain generated text attribute values in different languages.

There is a second approach which has the advantage of maintaining all the content in one file and the disadvantage of creating a slightly more cluttered DTD. One would decide which approach to use primarily based on whether one wants to have the DTD seem to be unchanging – only the external file changes – or whether one is more concerned about keeping everything needed for the transformation in one file.

The second technique involves the use, within the DTD, of marked section parameter entities for each language.

The example shows the principle:

```
<!ATTLIST email SDAPREF   ENTITY #FIXED              "sdaemail"
              COLOR            (brown|green|blue)    #IMPLIED
               TYPE       CDATA                   #REQUIRED     >

<!ENTITY % dutch         "IGNORE" >
<!ENTITY % french        "IGNORE" >
<!ENTITY % english       "INCLUDE" >

<![%dutch; [
<!ENTITY sdaemail CDATA "<para>Adres voor elektronische post:</para> "> ]]>

<![%english; [
<!ENTITY sdaemail CDATA "<para>Electronic Mail Address:</para> "> ]]>

<![%french; [
<!ENTITY sdaemail CDATA "<para>Adresse electronique:</para> "> ]]>
```

Here one declares a marked section parameter entity in the DTD for each relevant language and sets all languages to IGNORE except for the current one. The text – as well as anything else which may appear in the generated text attribute values, including context and markup – appears within the appropriately marked up marked section once for each language. Notice that non-ICADD declarations appear intermingled with the SDA attributes but that only the SDA declarations must use the declared entities.

From a practical point of view, the technique is quite easy to administer. All SDAPREF and SDASUFF values are declared as entities and given a unique name. Each is declared within a set of entity declarations gathered together for convenience, perhaps at the end of the DTD, within the appropriate marked section. That entire list is copied over and over, once for each language, and only the language-sensitive words are translated. The additional characters are left precisely as they are to ensure identical handling by the transformation process.

Note that either of these mechanisms result in a set of declared entities that will also now be valid elsewhere in documents conforming to the DTD. This means that if users attempt to declare entities which, by coincidence, have the same name, they will over-ride the declarations in the DTD's entity set. The committee recommends naming all such entities so that they begin with the letters "sda".

These techniques also mean that authors working with any of a number of common SGML editing tools will likely be offered dialog box pick lists of entity references – and these lists will include the entity references that are intended only for internal use within the DTD. In theory, an author could insert them anywhere in the document.

A.8.3 SDA Parameter Entities

The DTDs in this International Standard contain the following parameter entities (whose use is encouraged by others implementing the ICADD accessible document techniques):

```
<!--    Accessible Document Parameter Entities     -->
<!ENTITY % SDAFORM      "SDAFORM   CDATA     #FIXED" >
<!ENTITY % SDARULE      "SDARULE   CDATA     #FIXED" >
```

```
<!ENTITY % SDAPREF        "SDAPREF    CDATA     #FIXED" >
<!ENTITY % SDASUFF        "SDASUFF    CDATA     #FIXED" >
<!ENTITY % SDASUSP        "SDASUFF    NAME      #FIXED" >
```

A.8.4 Handling of special characters as entity references

Under most circumstances, an SGML parser will be used to transform a source SGML file into one marked up for Braille, large print or computer voice. That parser will normally transform all entity references into the content that has been defined for them. At that point, their value to the ongoing process vanishes; they will have been converted to machine specific or software specific codes.

For ICADD purposes, it is critical that they remain "unexpanded" so they are still computer and software independent when they reach Braille or other ICADD software.

Accordingly, all entity references used with the ICADD-enabling techniques must be declared as being of the type CDATA or SDATA. This will ensure they pass through the SGML parser unchanged.

The ICADD-enabled version of a typical SGML entity declaration:

```
<!ENTITY ntilde SDATA "&ntilde;">
```

A.8.5 Indicating ICADD usage in the SGML declaration

A document indicates conformance to the ICADD SGML Document Accessibility architecture in the APPINFO parameter of the SGML declaration, which specifies the characters in the "SDA prefix" that identifies attributes that represent "SDA declarations".

SDA declaration facilities are provided by attributes described in this document.

Conformance of a document to SDA is indicated by a parameter of the APPINFO parameter of the SGML declaration. Its format is:

```
APPINFO   "SDA"
```

The parameter can also specify the name of the "SDA prefix" if it is other than "SDA".

The format is:

```
APPINFO   "SDA=SDA"
```

where the second "SDA" is replaced by the new prefix name. A new name must be a valid name in the concrete syntax of the SGML declaration.

A.9 Facilities for HyTime (hypertext)

In the late 80's, a movement occurred in the hypertext world to combine descriptive markup with hypertext. A standard way of describing hyperdocuments was required, and SGML seemed to be a good tool for the job. At the same time, a project was started to create the Standard Music Description Language (SMDL), an attempt to describe musical, time-based, structures with SGML. Not much later, the two efforts were joined in a new ISO project which resulted in HyTime (ISO 10744).

HyTime is the ISO standard language for hypermedia and time-based documents. It is based on SGML and describes not only the logical structure of documents, but also of multi media objects which a document may include or point to. HyTime uses SGML as the syntax for representing links. The data which is being linked, however, may exist in any format desired.

HyTime does not specify a single "HyTime document type definition" or a "HyTime document architecture". HyTime is defined as a set of rules, called **architectural forms**, that application designers can apply in their DTDs.

HyTime consists of several "modules" which may be used more or less arbitrarily depending on the facilities that are required. For example, there are modules which specify how to define HyTime compatible elements in a DTD (via architectural forms), how to indicate the position of an object (**coordinates** and **markers**) and how to link various parts of a HyTime structure (**location address**). HyTime also has a query language, which permits creation of dynamic links to objects that change in time.

A.9.1 APPINFO parameter of SGML declaration

The starting point of an interconnected system must be an SGML document using HyTime constructs, called the **hub** document. Conformance of a document to HyTime, and thus the ability of a document to become a hub, is indicated by a parameter of the APPINFO parameter of the SGML declaration. Its format is:

```
APPINFO "HyTime"
```

All documents created with the Book or Article DTD can become a hub by setting the APPINFO parameter to HyTime in the SGML declaration.

A.9.2 Architectural forms

HyTime facilities are integrated into SGML DTDs via the technique of architectural forms. An architectural form describes in abstract terms what an element should do, without specifically giving the element a name. It defines the rules for creating and processing elements (just as document architectures are rules for creating and processing documents). By giving the element an attribute with the name **HyTime**, with values that are proposed by the HyTime standard, a HyTime system knows what action it should take.

In the Book and Article DTD of this International Standard, four types of architectural forms were used, to indicate what the highest level in the element structure of a HyTime document is; to create links to internal parts of the document, links to external (non-machine readable) bibliography references and links to external documents:

a) The elements Article and Book are the highest level elements in the element structure of a HyTime article or book, and so they conform to the **HyDoc** form. This was done by giving the HyTime attribute a fixed value HyDoc on the article and book elements. This requires the presence of the base module of HyTime.

b) For internal links, we used the existing elements defined by the parameter entity %p.rf.ph;. All references in %p.rf.ph; conform to the **clink** (contextual link) form. This was done by giving the HyTime attribute the fixed value **clink** and by changing the name of the **linkend** attribute to **rid** (which is easier to type and already existed). Unique identifier attributes (ID) were added to all elements which could be used as the end of a link (internal or external). These links require the presence of the base module and the hyperlinks module of HyTime.

c) The citation element, which describes a bibliographic entry, conforms to the **bibloc** form. This was done by giving the HyTime attribute the fixed value **bibloc**. The references that they present are not expected to be accessed automatically, since they probably do not exist on a computer which is accessible. This requires the presence of the location address module of HyTime.

d) HyTime provides a way of linking to anything that can be named as an entity or via an ID. This is accomplished by using the **nameloc** form. Again, this requires the presence of the location address module of HyTime.

A.9.3 Location addresses and the nameloc architectural form

There are three broad ways in which objects can be addressed by a HyTime document:

a) By the name of an entity or a unique identifier (a "name"). These are **name space locations.**

b) By a coordinate position. These are **coordinate locations**. These positions require the presence of the measurement module, which is not the case for the applications that are in accordance with this International Standard.

c) By a semantic construct. These are **semantic locations**. These are for the description of information objects to which access can not be automated (the citation element uses the bibliographic location address).

To come back to point 1, name space locations are locations addressed by a name. They can consist of the following:

a) entities;

b) elements in another document with an ID;

c) elements in this document which are not a location address, but which have an ID (for this purpose IDs were added to many elements in the DTDs of this International Standard).

The **nameloc** element type form associates a local ID with the objects in the list above (entities, elements in other documents with IDs, elements without IDs). The content of the nameloc element is an unlimited number of **namelist** elements. The nameloc element has an ID attribute which is required. The content of a namelist element is #PCDATA, and it may contain entity or element names.

Imagine an SGML document called "manual.sgm" which you wish to refer to in an article marked up in accordance with this International Standard. You would add the following entity definition to your article:

```
<!ENTITY manual SYSTEM "manual.sgm" >
```

Defining the named location address for this entity would be achieved as follows:

```
<nameloc id=manlink>
   <nmlist>
      manual
   </nmlist>
</nameloc>
```

Linking to this object is then achieved via any element of form clink, e.g. **citeref**:

```
<citeref rid=manlink>
```

If you want to define a named location address for elements which have a unique identifier, you can do this by giving the **nametype** attribute on the nmlist element the value "element". The following example defines a location name address for an element which has unique identifier ID=chap1 in the same document:

```
<nameloc id=chaplink>
   <nmlist nametype=element>
      chap1
   </nmlist>
</nameloc>
```

Again, linking to this element would be achieved via any element of form clink, such as the **secref** element:

```
<secref rid=chaplink>
```

By giving the attribute **obnames** on the nmlist element the value "obnames" the addressed objects are treated as names, and the object of the nameloc is the entire element with ID=chap1. The default value is "nobnames", which means that the content of the nameloc is the string "chap1".

You can go a step further and define location name addresses for objects that have unique identifiers inside manual.sgm. Suppose that the element with ID=chap1 exists inside manual.sgm, and you want to define a named location address for it. This is done by using the **docorsub** attribute on the nmlist element as follows:

```
<nameloc id=chaplink>
   <nmlist nametype=element obnames=obnames docorsub=source>
       chap1
   </nmlist>
</nameloc>
```

This named location address can be linked to by a clink element such as citeref:

```
<citeref rid=chaplink>
```

The link will be established as follows. The IDREF with value chaplink defines the end of the link to be the location address with unique id chaplink. This one, in turn, has its source in the entity manual specified by the docorsub attribute. The address is defined as the element with id chap1, which is found in the document manual.sgm. Since obnames is given, the entire chapter is returned to the citeref element for further processing.

A.9.4 HyTime conformance

To create hyperlinking HyTime documents, the HyTime declarations corresponding to a minimal hyperlinking HyTime document (plus support for anydtd and mixspace) must be added before the DOCTYPE declaration in any document using the Book and Article DTD:

```
<?HyTime VERSION "ISO/IEC 10744:1992" HYQNT=32>
<?HyTime MODULE base>
<?HyTime MODULE locs multloc anydtd mixspace>
<?HyTime MODULE links>
<!DOCTYPE book PUBLIC "ISO 12083:1994//DTD Book//EN">
<book>
```

Annex B

(informative)

Description of the Elements

ABSTRACT

Short Description: **Abstract**

How to Use: Begins an abstract within the front matter.

Example of Usage:

```
<abstract><title>Myocardial Infarct
<p>Of 708 myocardial infarctions. . .</abstract>
```

Content Type: element

Contained in: FRONT

Contains: TITLE, DATE, P, DEFLIST, ORGADDR, INDADDR, ARTWORK, BQ, LIT, BIBLIST, AUTHOR, CORPAUTH, KEYWORD, KEYPHRAS, POEM, NAMELOC, INDXFLAG, TABLE, LIST, FORMULA, DFORMULA, SECTION

Attributes:

Name: ID
Content: id
Default: #IMPLIED

How to Use: Uniquely identifies the abstract. May be used to cross-reference to within the document.

Name: SDAPREF
Content: cdata
Default: <h1>Abstract</h1>

How to Use: This is an Accessible Document Design Attribute which, if used, will prepare electronic text for Braille, large print and computer voice capability. This attribute contains generated fixed text strings or counters for prefixed text. It may specify a processing instruction calling for intervention by a Braille specialist.

ACCEPTED

Short Description: **Accepted date of article**

How to Use: Specifies when the article was accepted by the publisher. This is specified in the history statement.

Content Type: element

Contained in: HISTORY

Contains: DATE

ACIDFREE

Short Description: **Acid-free paper indicator**

How to Use: Specifies the acid free paper indicator.

Content Type: mixed

Contained in: PUBFRONT

Contains: #PCDATA

Attributes:

Name: SDAFORM
Content: cdata
Default: para

How to Use: This is an Accessible Document Design Attribute which, if used, will prepare electronic text for braille, large print and computer voice capability. This attribute provides a one-to-one mapping between an element in the source DTD and an element in the ICADD tagset.

Name: SDAPREF
Content: cdata
Default: Acid free paper indicator:

How to Use: This is an Accessible Document Design Attribute which, if used, will prepare electronic text for Braille, large print and computer voice capability. This attribute contains generated fixed text strings or counters for prefixed text. It may specify a processing instruction calling for intervention by a Braille specialist.

ACK

Short Description: **Acknowledgments**

How to Use: Begins the acknowledgment(s) within the front matter.

Example of Usage:

```
<ack><title>Acknowledgments
<p>The following people have been most helpful . . . </ack>
```

Content Type: element

Contained in: FRONT

Contains: TITLE, DATE, P, DEFLIST, ORGADDR, INDADDR, ARTWORK, BQ, LIT, BIBLIST, AUTHOR, CORPAUTH, KEYWORD, KEYPHRAS, POEM, NAMELOC, INDXFLAG, TABLE, LIST, FORMULA, DFORMULA, SECTION

Attributes:

Name: ID
Content: id
Default: #IMPLIED

How to Use: Uniquely identifies the acknowledgements. May be used to cross-reference to within the document.

Name: SDAPREF
Content: cdata
Default: <h1>Acknowledgements</h1>

How to Use: This is an Accessible Document Design Attribute which, if used, will prepare electronic text for Braille, large print and computer voice capability. This attribute contains generated fixed text strings or counters for prefixed text. It may specify a processing instruction calling for intervention by a Braille specialist.

ACQNO

Short Description: **Acquisition number**

How to Use: Specifies the acquisition or order number within the publisher's front matter. It is a string of characters used to acquire an item from a source (distributor, publisher, etc.), e.g., GPO or NTIS Order Number.

Content Type: mixed

Contained in: PUBFRONT

Contains: #PCDATA

Attributes:

Name: SDAFORM
Content: cdata
Default: para

How to Use: This is an Accessible Document Design Attribute which, if used, will prepare electronic text for braille, large print and computer voice capability. This attribute provides a one-to-one mapping between an element in the source DTD and an element in the ICADD tagset.

Name: SDAPREF
Content: cdata
Default: Acquisition/order number:

How to Use: This is an Accessible Document Design Attribute which, if used, will prepare electronic text for Braille, large print and computer voice capability. This attribute contains generated fixed text strings or counters for prefixed text. It may specify a processing instruction calling for intervention by a Braille specialist.

ADVERT

Short Description: **Advertisement**

How to Use: Specifies an advertisement or public notice within the serial publication. They may occur anywhere within a serial. The size attributes may be used to specify the size of the graphic or the space designated for the paste-in of a graphic. The content of the advert element is empty by default.

Content Type: empty

Contained in:

Contains:

Attributes:

Name: ID
Content: id
Default: #IMPLIED

How to Use: Uniquely identifies the advertisement. May be used to cross-reference to within the document.

Name: SIZEX
Content: nutoken
Default: #IMPLIED

How to Use: Specifies the width of the figure.

Name: SIZEY
Content: nutoken
Default: #IMPLIED

How to Use: Specifies the height of the figure.

Name: UNIT
Content: cdata
Default: #IMPLIED

How to Use: Specifies the type of sizes, such as points or picas.

Name: NAME
Content: entity
Default: #IMPLIED

How to Use: Specifies the actual figure advertisement to be placed. The named figure must be declared as an entity declaration in either the DTD or the document type declaration subset.

Name: SDAFORM
Content: cdata
Default: fig

How to Use: This is an Accessible Document Design Attribute which, if used, will prepare electronic text for braille, large print and computer voice capability. This attribute provides a one-to-one mapping between an element in the source DTD and an element in the ICADD tagset.

AFF

Short Description: **Author's affiliation**

How to Use: Specifies a grouping tag for the affiliation of an author or a group of author's, e.g. to a hospital or university.

Example of Usage:

```
<author><fname>Terence F.<surname>Moore
<role>President
<aff>Mid-Michigan Health Care Systems, Inc.
```

Content Type: element

Contained in: INDADDR, CPYRTNME, REPRINT, AUTHOR, AUTHGRP

Contains: ORGNAME, ORGDIV, STREET, CITY, STATE, COUNTRY, POSTCODE, SAN, EMAIL, POSTBOX, PHONE

Attributes:

Name: ID
Content: id
Default: #IMPLIED

How to Use: Uniquely identifies the affiliation. May be used to cross-reference to within the document.

AFTERWRD

Short Description: **Afterword**

How to Use: Specifies the afterword within the back matter of the document.

Content Type: element

Contained in: BACK

Contains: TITLE, DATE, P, DEFLIST, ORGADDR, INDADDR, ARTWORK, BQ, LIT, BIBLIST, AUTHOR, CORPAUTH, KEYWORD, KEYPHRAS, POEM, NAMELOC, INDXFLAG, TABLE, LIST, FORMULA, DFORMULA, SECTION

Attributes:

Name: ID
Content: id

Default: #IMPLIED

How to Use: Uniquely identifies the afterword. May be used to cross-reference to within the document.

Name: SDAPREF
Content: cdata
Default: <h1>Afterword</h1>

How to Use: This is an Accessible Document Design Attribute which, if used, will prepare electronic text for Braille, large print and computer voice capability. This attribute contains generated fixed text strings or counters for prefixed text. It may specify a processing instruction calling for intervention by a Braille specialist.

ALTTITLE

Short Description: **Alternate Title**

How to Use: Begins an alternate title in the front matter of the serial.

Content Type: mixed

Contained in: SERFRONT

Contains: #PCDATA, FORMULA, DFORMULA, DFORMGRP, Q, PAGES, EMPH, NOTEREF, FNOTEREF, FIGREF, TABLEREF, ARTREF, APPREF, CITEREF, SECREF

Attributes:

Name: ALPHABET
Content: (LATIN | GREEK | CYRILLIC | HEBREW | KANJI)
Default: LATIN

How to Use: Specifies the character set or alphabet used for this element. Modify the DTD as necessary to add new alphabets.

Name: SDAFORM
Content: cdata
Default: ti

How to Use: This is an Accessible Document Design Attribute which, if used, will prepare electronic text for braille, large print and computer voice capability. This attribute provides a one-to-one mapping between an element in the source DTD and an element in the ICADD tagset.

APPENDIX

Short Description: **Appendix**

How to Use: Begins an appendix within the back matter which is a complementary part of a written work that is not essential to the completeness of the text.

Example of Usage:

```
<appendix><no>Appendix A
<title>Math Declaration Set
```

Content Type: element

Contained in: APPMAT

Contains: NO, SECTION, DATE, TITLE, P, DEFLIST, ORGADDR, INDADDR, ARTWORK, BQ, LIT, BIBLIST, AUTHOR, CORPAUTH, KEYWORD, KEYPHRAS, POEM, NAMELOC, INDXFLAG, TABLE, LIST, FORMULA, DFORMULA

Attributes:

Name: ID
Content: id

Default: #IMPLIED

How to Use: Uniquely identifies the appendix. May be used to cross-reference to within the document.

Name: SDAPREF
Content: cdata
Default: <h1>Appendix</h1>

How to Use: This is an Accessible Document Design Attribute which, if used, will prepare electronic text for Braille, large print and computer voice capability. This attribute contains generated fixed text strings or counters for prefixed text. It may specify a processing instruction calling for intervention by a Braille specialist.

APPMAT

Short Description: **Appendix matter**

How to Use: Begins a group of appendices in a document.

Content Type: element

Contained in: BOOK

Contains: APPENDIX

APPREF

Short Description: **Appendix, reference to**

How to Use: Specifies a reference to an appendix. This tag is used with the rid attribute when the appendices and references to them will be numbered automatically.

Example of Usage:

```
Refer to Appendix <appref rid="ap1">
```

Content Type: mixed

Contained in: TSUBHEAD, EMPH, Q, SERTITLE, SUBJECT, OTHINFO, HEAD, DDHD, TERM, P, TITLE, SUBTITLE

Contains: #PCDATA

Attributes:

Name: ID
Content: id
Default: #IMPLIED

How to Use: Uniquely identifies the appendix reference. May be used to cross-reference to within the document.

Name: RID
Content: idref
Default: #REQUIRED

How to Use: This attribute is used to reference an appendix. The rid attribute references an id attribute on an appendix element.

Name: HYTIME
Content: name
Default: CLINK

How to Use: This indicates a contextual link.

Name: HYNAMES
Content: cdata
Default: rid linkends

How to Use: This indicates a contextual link. Unique identifier attributes are on all elements which may be used as the end of an external or internal link.

Name: SDAFORM
Content: cdata
Default: xref #attrib IDREF

How to Use: This is an Accessible Document Design Attribute which, if used, will prepare electronic text for braille, large print and computer voice capability. This attribute provides a one-to-one mapping between an element in the source DTD and an element in the ICADD tagset.

ARTICLE

Short Description: **Article**

How to Use: Begins an article. Identifies a manuscript that follows the structure of the article document type. This element is the first tag in an article document. It may also be used in a serial document structure.

Inclusion Elements: FIGGRP, FOOTNOTE, NOTE

Content Type: element

Contained in: SERSEC, SERPART

Contains: FRONT, BODY, APPMAT, BACK

Attributes:

Name: ID
Content: id
Default: #IMPLIED

How to Use: Uniquely identifies the article. May be used to cross-reference to within the document.

Name: HYTIME
Content: name
Default: HYDOC

How to Use: This indicates a contextual link.

Name: SDAFORM
Content: cdata
Default: article

How to Use: This is an Accessible Document Design Attribute which, if used, will prepare electronic text for braille, large print and computer voice capability. This attribute provides a one-to-one mapping between an element in the source DTD and an element in the ICADD tagset.

ARTID

Short Description: **Article unique ID**

How to Use: Specifies a unique identification number assigned by a publisher to an article.

Content Type: mixed

Contained in: PUBFRONT

Contains: #PCDATA

ARTREF

Short Description: **Reference to artwork**

How to Use: Specifies a reference to a piece of artwork. This tag is used with the rid attribute when the artwork and references to them will be numbered automatically.

Example of Usage:

```
See the reprint of da Vinci's Mona Lisa (Exhibit <artref rid="art1">)
for comparison.
```

Content Type: mixed

Contained in: TSUBHEAD, EMPH, Q, SERTITLE, SUBJECT, OTHINFO, HEAD, DDHD, TERM, P, TITLE, SUBTITLE

Contains: #PCDATA

Attributes:

Name: ID
Content: id
Default: #IMPLIED

How to Use: Uniquely identifies the artwork reference. May be used to cross-reference to within the document.

Name: RID
Content: idref
Default: #REQUIRED

How to Use: This attribute is used to reference artwork. The rid attribute references an id attribute on an artwork element.

Name: HYTIME
Content: name
Default: CLINK

How to Use: This indicates a contextual link.

Name: HYNAMES
Content: cdata
Default: rid linkends

How to Use: This indicates a contextual link. Unique identifier attributes are on all elements which may be used as the end of an external or internal link.

Name: SDAFORM
Content: cdata
Default: xref #attrib IDREF

How to Use: This is an Accessible Document Design Attribute which, if used, will prepare electronic text for braille, large print and computer voice capability. This attribute provides a one-to-one mapping between an element in the source DTD and an element in the ICADD tagset.

ARTWORK

Short Description: **Artwork**

How to Use: Specifies the artwork to be included in the document. It is similar to the figure element. The tag may be used to either reserve space or to specify the artwork. Size and identity of the artwork is specified using the attributes.

Example of Usage:

```
<artwork id="art1" name="ocean" sizex="134" sizey="110">
```

Content Type: empty

Contained in: GLOSSARY, INDEX, AFTERWRD, NOTES, VITA, APPENDIX, TSTUB, CELL, NOTE, FOOTNOTE, DD, ITEM, BQ, P, SUBSECT6, SUBSECT5, SUBSECT4, SUBSECT3, SUBSECT2, SUBSECT1, SECTION, CHAPTER, PART, FOREWORD, INTRO, PREFACE, ACK, DED, ABSTRACT, SUPMATL

Contains:

Attributes:

Name: ID
Content: id
Default: #IMPLIED

How to Use: Used to uniquely identify the artwork. May be used to cross-reference to within the document.

Name: SIZEX
Content: nutoken
Default: #IMPLIED

How to Use: Specifies the width.

Name: SIZEY
Content: nutoken
Default: #IMPLIED

How to Use: Specifies the height.

Name: UNIT
Content: cdata
Default: #IMPLIED

How to Use: Specifies the type of sizes, such as points or picas.

Name: NAME
Content: entity
Default: #IMPLIED

How to Use: Used to identify the name of the entity that contains the artwork file that should be set.

Name: SDAFORM
Content: cdata
Default: fig #attrib ID

How to Use: This is an Accessible Document Design Attribute which, if used, will prepare electronic text for braille, large print and computer voice capability. This attribute provides a one-to-one mapping between an element in the source DTD and an element in the ICADD tagset.

ASEQNTL

Short Description: **Asequential serial item**

How to Use: Specifies filler items to be used within the serial. It is a structured element with the same content as a section. It may be used anywhere within the structure of a serial.

Content Type: element

Contained in:

Contains: TITLE, DATE, KEYWORD, KEYPHRAS, P, DEFLIST, ORGADDR, INDADDR, ARTWORK, BQ, LIT, BIBLIST, AUTHOR, CORPAUTH, POEM, NAMELOC, INDXFLAG, TABLE, LIST, FORMULA, DFORMULA, SECTION

AUTHGRP

Short Description: **Author group**

How to Use: Groups the information about the author.

Content Type: element

Contained in: FRONT

Contains: AUTHOR, CORPAUTH

AUTHOR

Short Description: **Author**

How to Use: Specifies the information about an author such as first name, last name, degree, address, etc.

Example of Usage:

```
<author><fname>Judith D. <surname>Alvarez
```

Content Type: element

Contained in: GLOSSARY, INDEX, AFTERWRD, NOTES, VITA, APPENDIX, TSTUB, CELL, NOTE, FOOTNOTE, CITATION, DD, ITEM, BQ, P, SUBSECT6, SUBSECT5, SUBSECT4, SUBSECT3, SUBSECT2, SUBSECT1, SECTION, CHAPTER, PART, AUTHGRP, FOREWORD, INTRO, PREFACE, ACK, DED, ABSTRACT, SUPMATL

Contains: SURNAME, FNAME, DEGREE, ROLE, STREET, CITY, STATE, COUNTRY, POSTCODE, SAN, EMAIL, POSTBOX, PHONE, AFF

Attributes:

Name: RIDS
Content: idrefs
Default: #IMPLIED

How to Use: Specifies a cross-reference to one or more elements with unique identifiers used within the document.

Name: SDAFORM
Content: cdata
Default: au

How to Use: This is an Accessible Document Design Attribute which, if used, will prepare electronic text for braille, large print and computer voice capability. This attribute provides a one-to-one mapping between an element in the source DTD and an element in the ICADD tagset.

AVAIL

Short Description: **Distributor/available from**

How to Use: Specifies the source from which a work can be acquired or a location at which a work can be consulted if the work is not distributed by the named publisher.

Content Type: element

Contained in: PUBFRONT

Contains: ORGNAME, ORGDIV, STREET, CITY, STATE, COUNTRY, POSTCODE, SAN, EMAIL, POSTBOX, PHONE

Attributes:

Name: SDAFORM
Content: cdata
Default: para

How to Use: This is an Accessible Document Design Attribute which, if used, will prepare electronic text for braille, large print and computer voice capability. This attribute provides a one-to-one mapping between an element in the source DTD and an element in the ICADD tagset.

Name: SDAPREF
Content: cdata

Default: Available from:

How to Use: This is an Accessible Document Design Attribute which, if used, will prepare electronic text for Braille, large print and computer voice capability. This attribute contains generated fixed text strings or counters for prefixed text. It may specify a processing instruction calling for intervention by a Braille specialist.

BACK

Short Description: **Back matter**

How to Use: Begins the back matter of the document.

Content Type: element

Contained in: BOOK

Contains: BIBLIST, AFTERWRD, NOTES, VITA, GLOSSARY

BIBLIST

Short Description: **Bibliographic list**

How to Use: Groups a list of bibliographic references.

Content Type: element

Contained in: GLOSSARY, INDEX, AFTERWRD, NOTES, VITA, BACK, APPENDIX, TSTUB, CELL, NOTE, FOOTNOTE, DD, ITEM, BQ, P, SUBSECT6, SUBSECT5, SUBSECT4, SUBSECT3, SUBSECT2, SUBSECT1, SECTION, CHAPTER, PART, FOREWORD, INTRO, PREFACE, ACK, DED, ABSTRACT, SUPMATL

Contains: HEAD, CITATION

Attributes:

Name: FILE
Content: entity
Default: #IMPLIED

How to Use: May be used to specify an external file that contains a biliographic list of references.

Name: SDAFORM
Content: cdata
Default: list

How to Use: This is an Accessible Document Design Attribute which, if used, will prepare electronic text for braille, large print and computer voice capability. This attribute provides a one-to-one mapping between an element in the source DTD and an element in the ICADD tagset.

Name: SDAPREF
Content: cdata
Default: Bibliography

How to Use: This is an Accessible Document Design Attribute which, if used, will prepare electronic text for Braille, large print and computer voice capability. This attribute contains generated fixed text strings or counters for prefixed text. It may specify a processing instruction calling for intervention by a Braille specialist.

BODY

Short Description: **Body matter**

How to Use: Begins the body matter of the document. The body consists of either multiple parts or multiple chapters.

Content Type: element

Contained in: BOOK

Contains: PART, CHAPTER

Attributes:

Name: SDARULE
Content: cdata
Default: chapter #use SDABDY

How to Use: This is an Accessible Document Design Attribute which, if used, will prepare electronic text for braille, large print and computer voice capability. This attribute provides a mechanism to apply more complex mappings based on the ancestry of the current element.

BOOK

Short Description: **Book document type**

How to Use: Begins a book. Identifies a manuscript that follows the structure of a Book document type. This element is at the top of the hierarchy of a book or manuscript document. This element is the first tag in a book document.

Inclusion Elements: FIGGRP, FOOTNOTE, NOTE

Content Type: element

Contained in:

Contains: FRONT, BODY, APPMAT, BACK

Attributes:

Name: ID
Content: id
Default: #IMPLIED

How to Use: Uniquely identifies the book. May be used to cross-reference to within the document.

Name: HYTIME
Content: name
Default: HYDOC

How to Use: This indicates a contextual link.

Name: SDAFORM
Content: cdata
Default: book

How to Use: This is an Accessible Document Design Attribute which, if used, will prepare electronic text for braille, large print and computer voice capability. This attribute provides a one-to-one mapping between an element in the source DTD and an element in the ICADD tagset.

BQ

Short Description: **Quotation, block style**

How to Use: Specifies a block style quotation. This is normally used to identify a quotation of 50 or more words; e.g., an extract.

Content Type: element

Contained in: GLOSSARY, INDEX, AFTERWRD, NOTES, VITA, APPENDIX, TSTUB, CELL, NOTE, FOOTNOTE, DD, ITEM, BQ, P, SUBSECT6, SUBSECT5, SUBSECT4, SUBSECT3, SUBSECT2, SUBSECT1, SECTION, CHAPTER, PART, FOREWORD, INTRO, PREFACE, ACK, DED, ABSTRACT, SUPMATL

Contains: DATE, P, DEFLIST, ORGADDR, INDADDR, ARTWORK, BQ, LIT, BIBLIST, AUTHOR, CORPAUTH, KEYWORD, KEYPHRAS, POEM, NAMELOC, INDXFLAG, TABLE, LIST, FORMULA, DFORMULA

Attributes:

Name: SDAFORM
Content: cdata
Default: bq

How to Use: This is an Accessible Document Design Attribute which, if used, will prepare electronic text for braille, large print and computer voice capability. This attribute provides a one-to-one mapping between an element in the source DTD and an element in the ICADD tagset.

CATALOG

Short Description: **Catalog**

How to Use: Specifies the cataloging-in-publication (CIP) data. This information is supplied to the publisher by the Library of Congress or other national cataloging agency. The specific subelements and their content are determined by the cataloging agency.

Content Type: mixed

Contained in: PUBFRONT

Contains: #PCDATA

Attributes:

Name: SDAFORM
Content: cdata
Default: para

How to Use: This is an Accessible Document Design Attribute which, if used, will prepare electronic text for braille, large print and computer voice capability. This attribute provides a one-to-one mapping between an element in the source DTD and an element in the ICADD tagset.

Name: SDAPREF
Content: cdata
Default: <?SDATRANS>Cataloging in publication information:

How to Use: This is an Accessible Document Design Attribute which, if used, will prepare electronic text for Braille, large print and computer voice capability. This attribute contains generated fixed text strings or counters for prefixed text. It may specify a processing instruction calling for intervention by a Braille specialist.

CATEGORY

Short Description: **Category of article**

How to Use: Specifies the category that the article belongs to.

Content Type: mixed

Contained in: PUBFRONT

Contains: #PCDATA

CELL

Short Description: **Table cell entry**

How to Use: Specifies a cell within a table row.

Content Type: element

Contained in: ROW

Contains: DATE, P, DEFLIST, ORGADDR, INDADDR, ARTWORK, BQ, LIT, BIBLIST, AUTHOR, CORPAUTH, KEYWORD, KEYPHRAS, POEM, NAMELOC, INDXFLAG, TABLE, LIST, FORMULA, DFORMULA

Attributes:

Name: SDAFORM
Content: cdata
Default: cell

How to Use: This is an Accessible Document Design Attribute which, if used, will prepare electronic text for braille, large print and computer voice capability. This attribute provides a one-to-one mapping between an element in the source DTD and an element in the ICADD tagset.

CHAPTER

Short Description: **Chapter**

How to Use: Specifies the beginning of a chapter. A chapter consists of all the subelements that comprise a chapter of information.

Example of Usage:

```
<chapter><title>The Promise of Democracy
```

Content Type: element

Contained in: PART, BODY

Contains: NO, SECTION, DATE, TITLE, P, DEFLIST, ORGADDR, INDADDR, ARTWORK, BQ, LIT, BIBLIST, AUTHOR, CORPAUTH, KEYWORD, KEYPHRAS, POEM, NAMELOC, INDXFLAG, TABLE, LIST, FORMULA, DFORMULA

Attributes:

Name: ID
Content: id
Default: #IMPLIED

How to Use: Uniquely identifies the chapter. May be used to cross-reference to within the document.

Name: SDABDY
Content: names
Default: TITLE H1

How to Use: This is an Accessible Document Design Attribute which, if used, will prepare electronic text for braille, large print and computer voice capability. This attribute provides a mapping depending on the use of the element in context.

Name: SDAPART
Content: names
Default: TITLE H2

How to Use: This is an Accessible Document Design Attribute which, if used, will prepare electronic text for braille, large print and computer voice capability. This attribute provides a mapping depending on the use of the element in context.

CITATION

Short Description: **Citation**

How to Use: Specifies a citation within a bibliographic list.

Content Type: element

Contained in: BIBLIST

Contains: NO, DATE, AUTHOR, CORPAUTH, MSN, SERTITLE, PAGES, LOCATION, SUBJECT, TITLE

Attributes:

Name: ID
Content: id
Default: #REQUIRED

How to Use: Uniquely identifies the citation. May be used to cross-reference to within the document.

Name: HYTIME
Content: name
Default: BIBLOC

How to Use: This indicates a contextual link.

Name: SDARULE
Content: cdata
Default: title it author para corpauth para sertitle it

How to Use: This is an Accessible Document Design Attribute which, if used, will prepare electronic text for braille, large print and computer voice capability. This attribute provides a mechanism to apply more complex mappings based on the ancestry of the current element.

CITEREF

Short Description: **Reference to a citation**

How to Use: Specifies a citation reference. This tag is used with the rid attribute when the citation and references to them will be numbered automatically.

Content Type: mixed

Contained in: TSUBHEAD, EMPH, Q, SERTITLE, SUBJECT, OTHINFO, HEAD, DDHD, TERM, P, TITLE, SUBTITLE

Contains: #PCDATA

Attributes:

Name: ID
Content: id
Default: #IMPLIED

How to Use: Uniquely identifies the citation reference. May be used to cross-reference to within the document.

Name: RID
Content: idref
Default: #REQUIRED

How to Use: This attribute is used to reference a citation. The rid attribute references an id attribute on a citation element.

Name: HYTIME
Content: name
Default: CLINK

How to Use: This indicates a contextual link.

Name: HYNAMES
Content: cdata
Default: rid linkends

How to Use: This indicates a contextual link. Unique identifier attributes are on all elements which may be used as the end of an external or internal link.

Name: SDAFORM
Content: cdata
Default: xref #attrib IDREF

How to Use: This is an Accessible Document Design Attribute which, if used, will prepare electronic text for braille, large print and computer voice capability. This attribute provides a one-to-one mapping between an element in the source DTD and an element in the ICADD tagset.

CITY

Short Description: **City**

How to Use: Specifies the name of the city.

Example of Usage:

```
<city>Rockville
```

Content Type: mixed

Contained in: LOCATION, ORGADDR, INDADDR, CPYRTNME, CPYRTCLR, REPRINT, SPONSOR, PUBNAME, AVAIL, CORPAUTH, AFF, SCHOOL, AUTHOR

Contains: #PCDATA

CLINE

Short Description: **Poem continued line**

How to Use: Specifies a continued line within the poemline.

Content Type: mixed

Contained in: POEMLINE

Contains: #PCDATA

CODEN

Short Description: **Coden**

How to Use: Specifies the CODEN.

Content Type: mixed

Contained in: PUBFRONT

Contains: #PCDATA

Attributes:

Name: SDAFORM
Content: cdata
Default: para

How to Use: This is an Accessible Document Design Attribute which, if used, will prepare electronic text for braille, large print and computer voice capability. This attribute provides a one-to-one mapping between an element in the source DTD and an element in the ICADD tagset.

Name: SDAPREF
Content: cdata
Default: CODEN:

How to Use: This is an Accessible Document Design Attribute which, if used, will prepare electronic text for Braille, large print and computer voice capability. This attribute contains generated fixed text strings or counters for prefixed text. It may specify a processing instruction calling for intervention by a Braille specialist.

CONFGRP

Short Description: **Conference group**

How to Use: Identifies the information comprising the conference information for a conference proceeding.

Content Type: element

Contained in: PUBFRONT

Contains: NO, CONFNAME, DATE, LOCATION, SPONSOR

Attributes:

Name: SDAFORM
Content: cdata
Default: para

How to Use: This is an Accessible Document Design Attribute which, if used, will prepare electronic text for braille, large print and computer voice capability. This attribute provides a one-to-one mapping between an element in the source DTD and an element in the ICADD tagset.

Name: SDAPREF
Content: cdata
Default: Conference group:

How to Use: This is an Accessible Document Design Attribute which, if used, will prepare electronic text for Braille, large print and computer voice capability. This attribute contains generated fixed text strings or counters for prefixed text. It may specify a processing instruction calling for intervention by a Braille specialist.

CONFNAME

Short Description: **Conference name**

How to Use: Specifies the name of a conference.

Example of Usage:

```
<confname>Biomechanics Conference on the Spine
```

Content Type: mixed

Contained in: CONFGRP

Contains: #PCDATA

Attributes:

Name: SDAFORM
Content: cdata
Default: para

How to Use: This is an Accessible Document Design Attribute which, if used, will prepare electronic text for braille, large print and computer voice capability. This attribute provides a one-to-one mapping between an element in the source DTD and an element in the ICADD tagset.

Name: SDAPREF
Content: cdata
Default: Conference name:

How to Use: This is an Accessible Document Design Attribute which, if used, will prepare electronic text for Braille, large print and computer voice capability. This attribute contains generated fixed text strings or counters for prefixed text. It may specify a processing instruction calling for intervention by a Braille specialist.

CONTRACT

Short Description: **Contract number**

How to Use: Specifies the contract or grant number.

Example of Usage:

```
<contract>Grant number 35&ndash;34
```

Content Type: mixed

Contained in: PUBFRONT

Contains: #PCDATA

Attributes:

Name: SDAFORM
Content: cdata
Default: para

How to Use: This is an Accessible Document Design Attribute which, if used, will prepare electronic text for braille, large print and computer voice capability. This attribute provides a one-to-one mapping between an element in the source DTD and an element in the ICADD tagset.

Name: SDAPREF
Content: cdata
Default: Contract or grant number:

How to Use: This is an Accessible Document Design Attribute which, if used, will prepare electronic text for Braille, large print and computer voice capability. This attribute contains generated fixed text strings or counters for prefixed text. It may specify a processing instruction calling for intervention by a Braille specialist.

CORPAUTH

Short Description: **Corporate author**

How to Use: Specifies the oranization responsible for the creation of all or some of the intellectual or artistic content of the work.

Example of Usage:

```
<corpauth><orgname>America Association for the Advancement of Science
<street>1155 Sixteenth Street, N.W.<city>Washington<state>DC<postcode>20036
```

Content Type: element

Contained in: GLOSSARY, INDEX, AFTERWRD, NOTES, VITA, APPENDIX, TSTUB, CELL, NOTE, FOOTNOTE, CITATION, DD, ITEM, BQ, P, SUBSECT6, SUBSECT5, SUBSECT4, SUBSECT3, SUBSECT2, SUBSECT1, SECTION, CHAPTER, PART, AUTHGRP, FOREWORD, INTRO, PREFACE, ACK, DED, ABSTRACT, SUPMATL

Contains: ORGNAME, ORGDIV, STREET, CITY, STATE, COUNTRY, POSTCODE, SAN, EMAIL, POSTBOX, PHONE

Attributes:

Name: ID
Content: id
Default: #IMPLIED

How to Use: Uniquely identifies the corporate author. May be used to cross-reference to within the document.

Name: SDAFORM

Content: cdata
Default: au

How to Use: This is an Accessible Document Design Attribute which, if used, will prepare electronic text for braille, large print and computer voice capability. This attribute provides a one-to-one mapping between an element in the source DTD and an element in the ICADD tagset.

COUNTRY

Short Description: **Country**

How to Use: Specifies the country.

Example of Usage:

```
<country>United States of America
```

Example of Usage:

```
<country cnycode="44">
```

Content Type: mixed

Contained in: LOCATION, ORGADDR, INDADDR, CPYRTNME, CPYRTCLR, REPRINT, SPONSOR, PUBNAME, AVAIL, CORPAUTH, AFF, SCHOOL, AUTHOR

Contains: #PCDATA

Attributes:

Name: CNYCODE
Content: name
Default: #IMPLIED

How to Use: Specifies the ISO 3166 country code.

CPYRT

Short Description: **Copyright**

How to Use: Begins the copyright notice for the document.

Content Type: element

Contained in: PUBFRONT

Contains: DATE, CPYRTNME

Attributes:

Name: SDAFORM
Content: cdata
Default: para

How to Use: This is an Accessible Document Design Attribute which, if used, will prepare electronic text for braille, large print and computer voice capability. This attribute provides a one-to-one mapping between an element in the source DTD and an element in the ICADD tagset.

Name: SDAPREF
Content: cdata
Default: <?SDATRANS>Copyright notice:

How to Use: This is an Accessible Document Design Attribute which, if used, will prepare electronic text for Braille, large print and computer voice capability. This attribute contains generated fixed text strings or counters for prefixed text. It may specify a processing instruction calling for intervention by a Braille specialist.

CPYRTCLR

Short Description: **Copyright clearance center**

How to Use: Specifies the statement of payment of necessary fees to appropriate party which is the copyright clearance center information.

Content Type: element

Contained in: CPYRT

Contains: ORGNAME, ORGDIV, STREET, CITY, STATE, COUNTRY, POSTCODE, SAN, EMAIL, POSTBOX, PHONE

Attributes:

Name: SDAFORM
Content: cdata
Default: para

How to Use: This is an Accessible Document Design Attribute which, if used, will prepare electronic text for braille, large print and computer voice capability. This attribute provides a one-to-one mapping between an element in the source DTD and an element in the ICADD tagset.

Name: SDAPREF
Content: cdata
Default: Copyright clearance center:

How to Use: This is an Accessible Document Design Attribute which, if used, will prepare electronic text for Braille, large print and computer voice capability. This attribute contains generated fixed text strings or counters for prefixed text. It may specify a processing instruction calling for intervention by a Braille specialist.

CPYRTNME

Short Description: **Copyright notice-name**

How to Use: Specifies the name of the copyright holder at the time of publication.

Content Type: element

Contained in: CPYRT

Contains: ORGNAME, SURNAME, FNAME, ORGDIV, DEGREE, ROLE, AFF, STREET, CITY, STATE, COUNTRY, POSTCODE, SAN, EMAIL, POSTBOX, PHONE

DATE

Short Description: **Date**

How to Use: Begins a date. The type of date entered depends on the location in the document. For example, a date entered in the copyright section is a copyright date; a date entered in a citation is the publication date; a date entered in the publication's front matter is the document's publication date.

Content Type: mixed

Contained in: GLOSSARY, INDEX, AFTERWRD, NOTES, VITA, APPENDIX, TSTUB, CELL, NOTE, FOOTNOTE, CITATION, DD, ITEM, BQ, P, SUBSECT6, SUBSECT5, SUBSECT4, SUBSECT3, SUBSECT2, SUBSECT1, SECTION, CHAPTER, PART, CONFGRP, CPYRT, PUBFRONT, FOREWORD, INTRO, PREFACE, ACK, DED, ABSTRACT, SUPMATL, FRONT

Contains: #PCDATA

Attributes:

Name: TYPE
Content: (1 | 2 | 3 | 4 | 5)

Default: #IMPLIED

How to Use: Specifies the format of the date. Suggestions by this ISO standard are that a value of 1 = compliant with ISO 8601:1988; 2 = mm-dd-yy; 3 = mm/dd/yy; 4 = dd-mm-yy; 5 = month day year. If more or other options are necessary, this list may be extended in the DTD or the document type declaration subset.

Name: SDAPREF
Content: cdata
Default: Date:

How to Use: This is an Accessible Document Design Attribute which, if used, will prepare electronic text for Braille, large print and computer voice capability. This attribute contains generated fixed text strings or counters for prefixed text. It may specify a processing instruction calling for intervention by a Braille specialist.

DD

Short Description: **Definition description**

How to Use: Specifies a definition description within a definition list. It is associated with a term.

Content Type: element

Contained in: DEFLIST

Contains: DATE, P, DEFLIST, ORGADDR, INDADDR, ARTWORK, BQ, LIT, BIBLIST, AUTHOR, CORPAUTH, KEYWORD, KEYPHRAS, POEM, NAMELOC, INDXFLAG, TABLE, LIST, FORMULA, DFORMULA

Attributes:

Name: ID
Content: id
Default: #IMPLIED

How to Use: Uniquely identifies the definition description. May be used to cross-reference to within the document.

Name: SDAFORM
Content: cdata
Default: para

How to Use: This is an Accessible Document Design Attribute which, if used, will prepare electronic text for braille, large print and computer voice capability. This attribute provides a one-to-one mapping between an element in the source DTD and an element in the ICADD tagset.

DDHD

Short Description: **Definition description head**

How to Use: Specifies a definition description head within a definition list.

Content Type: mixed

Contained in: DEFLIST

Contains: #PCDATA, FORMULA, DFORMULA, DFORMGRP, Q, PAGES, EMPH, NOTEREF, FNOTEREF, FIGREF, TABLEREF, ARTREF, APPREF, CITEREF, SECREF, FORMREF, GLOSREF

Attributes:

Name: SDAFORM
Content: cdata
Default: lhead

How to Use: This is an Accessible Document Design Attribute which, if used, will prepare electronic text for braille, large print and computer voice capability. This attribute provides a one-

to-one mapping between an element in the source DTD and an element in the ICADD tagset.

DED

Short Description: **Dedication**

How to Use: Begins the dedication within the front matter.

Example of Usage:

```
<ded>To my father
```

Content Type: element

Contained in: FRONT

Contains: TITLE, DATE, P, DEFLIST, ORGADDR, INDADDR, ARTWORK, BQ, LIT, BIBLIST, AUTHOR, CORPAUTH, KEYWORD, KEYPHRAS, POEM, NAMELOC, INDXFLAG, TABLE, LIST, FORMULA, DFORMULA, SECTION

Attributes:

Name: ID
Content: id
Default: #IMPLIED

How to Use: Uniquely identifies the dedication. May be used to cross-reference to within the document.

Name: SDAPREF
Content: cdata
Default: <h1>Dedication</h1>

How to Use: This is an Accessible Document Design Attribute which, if used, will prepare electronic text for Braille, large print and computer voice capability. This attribute contains generated fixed text strings or counters for prefixed text. It may specify a processing instruction calling for intervention by a Braille specialist.

DEFLIST

Short Description: **Definition list**

How to Use: Begins a definition list which consists of terms and definitions. Optional heads may be used.

Example of Usage:

```
<deflist>
<head>Acronym<ddhd>Meaning
<term>ISO<dd><p>International Organization for Standardization
<term>SGML<dd><p>Standard Generalized Markup Language
<term>NISO<dd><p>National Information Standards Organization
</deflist>
```

Content Type: element

Contained in: GLOSSARY, INDEX, AFTERWRD, NOTES, VITA, APPENDIX, TSTUB, CELL, NOTE, FOOTNOTE, DD, ITEM, BQ, P, SUBSECT6, SUBSECT5, SUBSECT4, SUBSECT3, SUBSECT2, SUBSECT1, SECTION, CHAPTER, PART, FOREWORD, INTRO, PREFACE, ACK, DED, ABSTRACT, SUPMATL

Contains: HEAD, DDHD, DD, TERM

Attributes:

Name: ID
Content: id

Default: #IMPLIED

How to Use: Uniquely identifies the definition list. May be used to cross-reference to within the document.

Name: SDAFORM
Content: cdata
Default: list

How to Use: This is an Accessible Document Design Attribute which, if used, will prepare electronic text for braille, large print and computer voice capability. This attribute provides a one-to-one mapping between an element in the source DTD and an element in the ICADD tagset.

Name: SDAPREF
Content: cdata
Default: <?SDATRANS>Definitions

How to Use: This is an Accessible Document Design Attribute which, if used, will prepare electronic text for Braille, large print and computer voice capability. This attribute contains generated fixed text strings or counters for prefixed text. It may specify a processing instruction calling for intervention by a Braille specialist.

DEGREE

Short Description: **Degree granted**

How to Use: Specifies the type of degree granted.

Example of Usage:

```
<degree>Ph.D.
```

Content Type: mixed

Contained in: INDADDR, CPYRTNME, REPRINT, AUTHOR

Contains: #PCDATA

DFORMGRP

Short Description: **Display formula group**

How to Use: Specifies a group of display formulas. By default, the only content recognized are display formulas which do not recognize SGML markup; the user needs to add the appropriate math DTD if applicable to their implementation.

Content Type: element

Contained in: GLOSSARY, INDEX, AFTERWRD, NOTES, VITA, APPENDIX, TSTUB, CELL, TSUBHEAD, NOTE, FOOTNOTE, EMPH, Q, SERTITLE, SUBJECT, OTHINFO, DD, HEAD, DDHD, TERM, ITEM, BQ, P, SUBSECT6, SUBSECT5, SUBSECT4, SUBSECT3, SUBSECT2, SUBSECT1, SECTION, CHAPTER, PART, TITLE, SUBTITLE, FOREWORD, INTRO, PREFACE, ACK, DED, ABSTRACT, SUPMATL

Contains: DFORMULA

Attributes:

Name: ID
Content: id
Default: #IMPLIED

How to Use: Uniquely identifies the display formula group. May be used to cross-reference to within the document.

Name: NUM
Content: cdata
Default: #IMPLIED

How to Use: Specifies the number of the display formula group.

Name: ALIGN
Content: (LEFT | CENTER | RIGHT)
Default: CENTER

How to Use: Specifies the alignment of the display formula group.

Name: SDAPREF
Content: cdata
Default: <?SDATRANS>Display formula group:

How to Use: This is an Accessible Document Design Attribute which, if used, will prepare electronic text for Braille, large print and computer voice capability. This attribute contains generated fixed text strings or counters for prefixed text. It may specify a processing instruction calling for intervention by a Braille specialist.

DFORMULA

Short Description: **Display formula**

How to Use: Specifies a display formula. By default, this content does not recognize SGML markup; the user needs to add the appropriate math DTD if applicable to their implementation.

Content Type: cdata

Contained in: GLOSSARY, INDEX, AFTERWRD, NOTES, VITA, APPENDIX, DFORMGRP, TSTUB, CELL, TSUBHEAD, NOTE, FOOTNOTE, EMPH, Q, SERTITLE, SUBJECT, OTHINFO, DD, HEAD, DDHD, TERM, ITEM, BQ, P, SUBSECT6, SUBSECT5, SUBSECT4, SUBSECT3, SUBSECT2, SUBSECT1, SECTION, CHAPTER, PART, TITLE, SUBTITLE, FOREWORD, INTRO, PREFACE, ACK, DED, ABSTRACT, SUPMATL

Contains:

Attributes:

Name: ID
Content: id
Default: #IMPLIED

How to Use: Uniquely identifies the display formula. May be used to cross-reference to within the document.

Name: NUM
Content: cdata
Default: #IMPLIED

How to Use: Specifies the number of the display formula.

Name: ALIGN
Content: (LEFT | CENTER | RIGHT)
Default: CENTER

How to Use: Specifies the alignment of the display formula.

Name: ALPHABET
Content: (LATIN | GREEK | CYRILLIC | HEBREW | KANJI)
Default: LATIN

How to Use: Specifies the character set or alphabet used for this element. Modify the DTD as necessary to add new alphabets.

Name: SDAPREF
Content: cdata
Default: <?SDATRANS>Display formula:

How to Use: This is an Accessible Document Design Attribute which, if used, will prepare electronic text for Braille, large print and computer voice capability. This attribute contains generated fixed text strings or counters for prefixed text. It may specify a processing instruction calling for intervention by a Braille specialist.

EDITION

Short Description: **Edition statement**

How to Use: Specifies the edition statement for the document.

Example of Usage:

```
<edition>Third Edition
```

Content Type: mixed

Contained in: PUBFRONT

Contains: #PCDATA

Attributes:

Name: SDAFORM
Content: cdata
Default: para

How to Use: This is an Accessible Document Design Attribute which, if used, will prepare electronic text for braille, large print and computer voice capability. This attribute provides a one-to-one mapping between an element in the source DTD and an element in the ICADD tagset.

Name: SDAPREF
Content: cdata
Default: <?SDATRANS>Edition:

How to Use: This is an Accessible Document Design Attribute which, if used, will prepare electronic text for Braille, large print and computer voice capability. This attribute contains generated fixed text strings or counters for prefixed text. It may specify a processing instruction calling for intervention by a Braille specialist.

EMAIL

Short Description: **Electronic mail address**

How to Use: Specifies an electronic mail address.

Example of Usage:

```
<email>john@doe.world.com
```

Content Type: mixed

Contained in: LOCATION, ORGADDR, INDADDR, CPYRTNME, CPYRTCLR, REPRINT, SPONSOR, PUBNAME, AVAIL, CORPAUTH, AFF, SCHOOL, AUTHOR

Contains: #PCDATA

Attributes:

Name: SDAFORM
Content: cdata
Default: para

How to Use: This is an Accessible Document Design Attribute which, if used, will prepare electronic text for braille, large print and computer voice capability. This attribute provides a one-to-one mapping between an element in the source DTD and an element in the ICADD tagset.

Name: SDAPREF
Content: cdata
Default: Electronic address:

How to Use: This is an Accessible Document Design Attribute which, if used, will prepare

electronic text for Braille, large print and computer voice capability. This attribute contains generated fixed text strings or counters for prefixed text. It may specify a processing instruction calling for intervention by a Braille specialist.

EMPH

Short Description: **Emphasized text**

How to Use: Specifies text that is to be emphasized. The type attribute is used to designate the type of emphasis to be used.

Example of Usage:

```
This is <emph type="1">bold</emph> text.
```

Content Type: mixed

Contained in: TSUBHEAD, EMPH, Q, CLINE, POEMLINE, SERTITLE, SUBJECT, OTHINFO, HEAD, DDHD, TERM, P, TITLE, SUBTITLE

Contains: #PCDATA, FORMULA, DFORMULA, DFORMGRP, Q, PAGES, EMPH, NOTEREF, FNOTEREF, FIGREF, TABLEREF, ARTREF, APPREF, CITEREF, SECREF, FORMREF, GLOSREF

Attributes:

Name: TYPE
Content: (1 | 2 | 3 | 4 | 5 | 6)
Default: #IMPLIED

How to Use: Specifies the type of emphasis. The standard suggests the following emphasis types: 1 = bold; 2 = italic; 3 = bold italic; 4 = underline; 5 = non proportional; and 6 = smallcaps. If more emphasis types are needed, the DTD should be modified.

Name: SDARULE
Content: cdata
Default: [emph type=1] b [emph type=2] it [emph type=(3|4|5|6)] other

How to Use: This is an Accessible Document Design Attribute which, if used, will prepare electronic text for braille, large print and computer voice capability. This attribute provides a mechanism to apply more complex mappings based on the ancestry of the current element.

EXTENT

Short Description: **Extent of work (number of pages)**

How to Use: Specifies the extent of the work, specifically the number of pages.

Content Type: mixed

Contained in: PUBFRONT

Contains: #PCDATA

Attributes:

Name: SDAFORM
Content: cdata
Default: para

How to Use: This is an Accessible Document Design Attribute which, if used, will prepare electronic text for braille, large print and computer voice capability. This attribute provides a one-to-one mapping between an element in the source DTD and an element in the ICADD tagset.

Name: SDAPREF
Content: cdata
Default: Number of pages:

How to Use: This is an Accessible Document Design Attribute which, if used, will prepare

electronic text for Braille, large print and computer voice capability. This attribute contains generated fixed text strings or counters for prefixed text. It may specify a processing instruction calling for intervention by a Braille specialist.

FAX

Short Description: **FAX number**

How to Use: Specifies a fax number.

Example of Usage:

```
<fax>(205)555-1212
```

Content Type: mixed

Contained in: LOCATION, ORGADDR, INDADDR, CPYRTNME, CPYRTCLR, REPRINT, SPONSOR, PUBNAME, AVAIL, CORPAUTH, AFF, SCHOOL, AUTHOR

Contains: #PCDATA

Attributes:

Name: SDAFORM
Content: cdata
Default: para

How to Use: This is an Accessible Document Design Attribute which, if used, will prepare electronic text for braille, large print and computer voice capability. This attribute provides a one-to-one mapping between an element in the source DTD and an element in the ICADD tagset.

Name: SDAPREF
Content: cdata
Default: Fax number:

How to Use: This is an Accessible Document Design Attribute which, if used, will prepare electronic text for Braille, large print and computer voice capability. This attribute contains generated fixed text strings or counters for prefixed text. It may specify a processing instruction calling for intervention by a Braille specialist.

FIG

Short Description: **Figure**

How to Use: Specifies a figure within a figure group. The content of a figure is empty by default. The specific illustration is identified by the name attribute.

Example of Usage:

```
<fig id="fig123" sizex="5" sizey="10" unit="pi" name="mountain">
```

Content Type: empty

Contained in: FIGGRP

Contains:

Attributes:

Name: ID
Content: id
Default: #IMPLIED

How to Use: Uniquely identifies the figure. May be used to cross-reference to within the document.

Name: SIZEX
Content: nutoken

Default: #IMPLIED

How to Use: Specifies the width of the figure.

Name: SIZEY
Content: nutoken
Default: #IMPLIED

How to Use: Specifies the height of the figure.

Name: UNIT
Content: cdata
Default: #IMPLIED

How to Use: Specifies the type of sizes, such as points or picas.

Name: NAME
Content: entity
Default: #IMPLIED

How to Use: Specifies the specific figure. The named figure must be declared as an entity declaration in either the DTD or the document type declaration subset.

Name: SCALE
Content: number
Default: 100

How to Use: Identifies the scaling factor of the figure. By default, it is 100%. Typcically, the scaling factor is used against the width and height of the graphic. For example, if the height and width of the figure is specified as 20 x 30 and the scaling factor is 50, then the size of the figure will be 10 x 15.

Name: SDAPREF
Content: cdata
Default: Figure:

How to Use: This is an Accessible Document Design Attribute which, if used, will prepare electronic text for Braille, large print and computer voice capability. This attribute contains generated fixed text strings or counters for prefixed text. It may specify a processing instruction calling for intervention by a Braille specialist.

Name: SDARULE
Content: cdata
Default: title para

How to Use: This is an Accessible Document Design Attribute which, if used, will prepare electronic text for braille, large print and computer voice capability. This attribute provides a mechanism to apply more complex mappings based on the ancestry of the current element.

FIGGRP

Short Description: **Figure group**

How to Use: Begins a grouping of figures. A figure title may be specified before or after the figure(s).

Example of Usage:

```
<figgrp><title>Swiss Alps
<fig id="fig123" sizex="5" sizey="10" unit="pi" name="mountain"></figgrp>
```

Content Type: element

Contained in:

Contains: TITLE, FIG

FIGREF

Short Description: **Reference to a figure**

How to Use: Specifies a reference to a figure. This tag is used with the rid attribute when the figure and references to them will be numbered automatically.

Example of Usage:

```
<figref rid="fig123">
```

Content Type: mixed

Contained in: TSUBHEAD, EMPH, Q, SERTITLE, SUBJECT, OTHINFO, HEAD, DDHD, TERM, P, TITLE, SUBTITLE

Contains: #PCDATA

Attributes:

Name: ID
Content: id
Default: #IMPLIED

How to Use: Uniquely identifies a figure reference. May be used to cross-reference to within the document.

Name: RID
Content: idref
Default: #REQUIRED

How to Use: This attribute is used to reference a figure. The rid attribute references an id attribute on a figure element.

Name: HYTIME
Content: name
Default: CLINK

How to Use: This indicates a contextual link.

Name: HYNAMES
Content: cdata
Default: rid linkends

How to Use: This indicates a contextual link. Unique identifier attributes are on all elements which may be used as the end of an external or internal link.

Name: SDAFORM
Content: cdata
Default: xref #attrib IDREF

How to Use: This is an Accessible Document Design Attribute which, if used, will prepare electronic text for braille, large print and computer voice capability. This attribute provides a one-to-one mapping between an element in the source DTD and an element in the ICADD tagset.

FNAME

Short Description: **First (given) name**

How to Use: Specifies a first (given) name of an individual.

Example of Usage:

```
<fname>John
<fname>John T.
<fname>J.T.
```

Content Type: mixed

Contained in: INDADDR, CPYRTNME, REPRINT, AUTHOR

Contains: #PCDATA

FNOTEREF

Short Description: **Reference to a footnote**

How to Use: Specifies a reference to a footnote. This tag is used with the rid attribute when the footnote and references to them will be numbered automatically.

Example of Usage:

```
Footnotes may be referenced <fnoteref rid="FN1"> using this element.
```

Content Type: mixed

Contained in: TSUBHEAD, EMPH, Q, SERTITLE, SUBJECT, OTHINFO, HEAD, DDHD, TERM, P, TITLE, SUBTITLE

Contains: #PCDATA

Attributes:

Name: ID
Content: id
Default: #IMPLIED

How to Use: Uniquely identifies a footnote reference. May be used to cross-reference to within the document.

Name: RID
Content: idref
Default: #REQUIRED

How to Use: This attribute is used to reference a footnote. The rid attribute references an id attribute on a footnote element.

Name: HYTIME
Content: name
Default: CLINK

How to Use: This indicates a contextual link.

Name: HYNAMES
Content: cdata
Default: rid linkends

How to Use: This indicates a contextual link. Unique identifier attributes are on all elements which may be used as the end of an external or internal link.

Name: SDAFORM
Content: cdata
Default: xref #attrib IDREF

How to Use: This is an Accessible Document Design Attribute which, if used, will prepare electronic text for braille, large print and computer voice capability. This attribute provides a one-to-one mapping between an element in the source DTD and an element in the ICADD tagset.

FOOTNOTE

Short Description: **Footnote**

How to Use: Specifies a footnote at the point of occurrence. A footnote may be a statement of explanatory text or indication of the basis for an assertion or the source of material quoted. A footnote usually appears at the foot of a page of text.

Example of Usage:

```
Many publications have footnotes imbedded in a paragraph, <footnote id="FN1">
<P>Footnotes may be used to further explain a point.</footnote> Footnotes
are frequently collected at the bottom of the page.
```

Content Type: element

Contained in:

Contains: NO, DATE, DEFLIST, ORGADDR, INDADDR, ARTWORK, BQ, LIT, BIBLIST, AUTHOR, CORPAUTH, KEYWORD, KEYPHRAS, POEM, NAMELOC, INDXFLAG, TABLE, LIST, FORMULA, DFORMULA, P

Attributes:

Name: ID
Content: id
Default: #IMPLIED

How to Use: Uniquely identifies the footnote. May be used to cross-reference to within the document.

Name: SDAFORM
Content: cdata
Default: fn

How to Use: This is an Accessible Document Design Attribute which, if used, will prepare electronic text for braille, large print and computer voice capability. This attribute provides a one-to-one mapping between an element in the source DTD and an element in the ICADD tagset.

FOREWORD

Short Description: **Foreword**

How to Use: Begins the foreword of the document. The foreword consists of introductory remarks preceding the text of a book, written by someone other than the author of the work. It is often used interchangeably with Preface.

Content Type: element

Contained in: FRONT

Contains: TITLE, DATE, P, DEFLIST, ORGADDR, INDADDR, ARTWORK, BQ, LIT, BIBLIST, AUTHOR, CORPAUTH, KEYWORD, KEYPHRAS, POEM, NAMELOC, INDXFLAG, TABLE, LIST, FORMULA, DFORMULA, SECTION

Attributes:

Name: ID
Content: id
Default: #IMPLIED

How to Use: Uniquely identifies the foreword. May be used to cross-reference to within the document.

Name: SDAPREF
Content: cdata
Default: <h1>Foreword</h1>

How to Use: This is an Accessible Document Design Attribute which, if used, will prepare electronic text for Braille, large print and computer voice capability. This attribute contains generated fixed text strings or counters for prefixed text. It may specify a processing instruction calling for intervention by a Braille specialist.

FORMREF

Short Description: **Reference to a formula**

How to Use: Specifies a formula reference. This tag is used with the rid attribute when the formula and references to them will be numbered automatically.

Content Type: mixed

Contained in: TSUBHEAD, EMPH, Q, SERTITLE, SUBJECT, OTHINFO, HEAD, DDHD, TERM, P, TITLE, SUBTITLE

Contains: #PCDATA

Attributes:

Name: ID
Content: id
Default: #IMPLIED

How to Use: Uniquely identifies the formula reference. May be used to cross-reference to within the document.

Name: RID
Content: idref
Default: #REQUIRED

How to Use: This attribute is used to reference a formula. The rid attribute references an id attribute on a formula element.

Name: HYTIME
Content: name
Default: CLINK

How to Use: This indicates a contextual link.

Name: HYNAMES
Content: cdata
Default: rid linkends

How to Use: This indicates a contextual link. Unique identifier attributes are on all elements which may be used as the end of an external or internal link.

Name: SDAFORM
Content: cdata
Default: xref #attrib IDREF

How to Use: This is an Accessible Document Design Attribute which, if used, will prepare electronic text for braille, large print and computer voice capability. This attribute provides a one-to-one mapping between an element in the source DTD and an element in the ICADD tagset.

FORMULA

Short Description: **Mathematical formula**

How to Use: Specifies an in-line formula. By default, this content does not recognize SGML markup; the user needs to add the appropriate math DTD if applicable to their implementation.

Content Type: cdata

Contained in: GLOSSARY, INDEX, AFTERWRD, NOTES, VITA, APPENDIX, TSTUB, CELL, TSUBHEAD, NOTE, FOOTNOTE, EMPH, Q, SERTITLE, SUBJECT, OTHINFO, DD, HEAD, DDHD, TERM, ITEM, BQ, P, SUBSECT6, SUBSECT5, SUBSECT4, SUBSECT3, SUBSECT2, SUBSECT1, SECTION, CHAPTER, PART, TITLE, SUBTITLE, FOREWORD, INTRO, PREFACE, ACK, DED, ABSTRACT, SUPMATL

Contains:

Attributes:

Name: ID
Content: id
Default: #IMPLIED

How to Use: Uniquely identifies the formula. May be used to cross-reference to within the document.

Name: ALPHABET
Content: (LATIN | GREEK | CYRILLIC | HEBREW | KANJI)
Default: LATIN

How to Use: Specifies the character set or alphabet used for this element. Modify the DTD as necessary to add new alphabets.

Name: SDAPREF
Content: cdata
Default: <?SDATRANS>Inline formula:

How to Use: This is an Accessible Document Design Attribute which, if used, will prepare electronic text for Braille, large print and computer voice capability. This attribute contains generated fixed text strings or counters for prefixed text. It may specify a processing instruction calling for intervention by a Braille specialist.

FPAGE

Short Description: **First page**

How to Use: Specifies the first page number of the article (in the original paper version). The first page number need not necessarily be a number.

Example of Usage:

```
<fpage>A17</fpage>
```

Content Type: mixed

Contained in: PUBFRONT

Contains: #PCDATA

FRONT

Short Description: **Front matter**

How to Use: Begins the front matter of the document.

Content Type: element

Contained in: BOOK

Contains: TITLEGRP, AUTHGRP, DATE, PUBFRONT, TOC, FOREWORD, INTRO, PREFACE, ACK, DED, ABSTRACT

GLOSREF

Short Description: **Reference to glossary**

How to Use: Specifies a glossary reference. This tag is used with the rid attribute when the glossary and references to them will be numbered automatically.

Content Type: mixed

Contained in: TSUBHEAD, EMPH, Q, SERTITLE, SUBJECT, OTHINFO, HEAD, DDHD, TERM, P, TITLE, SUBTITLE

Contains: #PCDATA

Attributes:

Name: ID
Content: id
Default: #IMPLIED

How to Use: Uniquely identifies the glossary reference. May be used to cross-reference to within the document.

Name: RID
Content: idref
Default: #REQUIRED

How to Use: This attribute is used to reference a glossary. The rid attribute references an id attribute on the glossary element.

Name: HYTIME
Content: name
Default: CLINK

How to Use: This indicates a contextual link.

Name: HYNAMES
Content: cdata
Default: rid linkends

How to Use: This indicates a contextual link. Unique identifier attributes are on all elements which may be used as the end of an external or internal link.

Name: SDAFORM
Content: cdata
Default: xref #attrib IDREF

How to Use: This is an Accessible Document Design Attribute which, if used, will prepare electronic text for braille, large print and computer voice capability. This attribute provides a one-to-one mapping between an element in the source DTD and an element in the ICADD tagset.

GLOSSARY

Short Description: **Glossary**

How to Use: Specifies the glossary section. The glossary may be an alphabetic listing of unusual, obsolete, dialectical, or technical terms, all concerned with a particular subject or area of interest.

Content Type: element

Contained in: BACK

Contains: TITLE, DATE, P, DEFLIST, ORGADDR, INDADDR, ARTWORK, BQ, LIT, BIBLIST, AUTHOR, CORPAUTH, KEYWORD, KEYPHRAS, POEM, NAMELOC, INDXFLAG, TABLE, LIST, FORMULA, DFORMULA, SECTION, INDXNAME, PAGES

Attributes:

Name: ID
Content: id
Default: #IMPLIED

How to Use: Uniquely identifies the glossary. May be used to cross-reference to within the document.

Name: SDAPREF
Content: cdata
Default: <h1>Glossary</h1>

How to Use: This is an Accessible Document Design Attribute which, if used, will prepare electronic text for Braille, large print and computer voice capability. This attribute contains generated fixed text strings or counters for prefixed text. It may specify a processing instruction calling for intervention by a Braille specialist.

HEAD

Short Description: **Heading**

How to Use: Specifies a heading within a list, definition list, bibliographic list, or table body. Within a definition list, it is the header for the term column.

Content Type: mixed

Contained in: TBODY, BIBLIST, DEFLIST, LIST

Contains: #PCDATA, FORMULA, DFORMULA, DFORMGRP, Q, PAGES, EMPH, NOTEREF, FNOTEREF, FIGREF, TABLEREF, ARTREF, APPREF, CITEREF, SECREF, FORMREF, GLOSREF

Attributes:

Name: SDAFORM
Content: cdata
Default: lhead

How to Use: This is an Accessible Document Design Attribute which, if used, will prepare electronic text for braille, large print and computer voice capability. This attribute provides a one-to-one mapping between an element in the source DTD and an element in the ICADD tagset.

HISTORY

Short Description: **History**

How to Use: Specifies a history statement about the article. It may be a line of data specifying the place or date of composition, or both, or creation of the information in the work; such as a dateline in a newspaper article, submission date.

Content Type: element

Contained in: PUBFRONT

Contains: RECEIVED, ACCEPTED, REVISED

INDADDR

Short Description: **Individual's address**

How to Use: Specifies the address of an individual, e.g., the name, degree, role, address, affiliation, etc. This individual may not be an author.

Content Type: element

Contained in: GLOSSARY, INDEX, AFTERWRD, NOTES, VITA, APPENDIX, TSTUB, CELL, NOTE, FOOTNOTE, DD, ITEM, BQ, P, SUBSECT6, SUBSECT5, SUBSECT4, SUBSECT3, SUBSECT2, SUBSECT1, SECTION, CHAPTER, PART, FOREWORD, INTRO, PREFACE, ACK, DED, ABSTRACT, SUPMATL

Contains: SURNAME, FNAME, DEGREE, ROLE, STREET, CITY, STATE, COUNTRY, POSTCODE, SAN, EMAIL, POSTBOX, PHONE, AFF

Attributes:

Name: SDAFORM
Content: cdata
Default: para

How to Use: This is an Accessible Document Design Attribute which, if used, will prepare electronic text for braille, large print and computer voice capability. This attribute provides a one-to-one mapping between an element in the source DTD and an element in the ICADD tagset.

Name: SDAPREF
Content: cdata
Default: Address:

How to Use: This is an Accessible Document Design Attribute which, if used, will prepare electronic text for Braille, large print and computer voice capability. This attribute contains generated fixed text strings or counters for prefixed text. It may specify a processing instruction calling for intervention by a Braille specialist.

INDEX

Short Description: **Index**

How to Use: Specifies an index within a document. An index is a systematic guide to the contents of a file, document, or group of documents, consisting of an ordered arrangement of terms or other symbols representing the contents and references, code numbers, page numbers, etc., for accessing the contents.

Content Type: element

Contained in: BACK

Contains: TITLE, DATE, P, DEFLIST, ORGADDR, INDADDR, ARTWORK, BQ, LIT, BIBLIST, AUTHOR, CORPAUTH, KEYWORD, KEYPHRAS, POEM, NAMELOC, INDXFLAG, TABLE, LIST, FORMULA, DFORMULA, SECTION, INDXNAME, PAGES

Attributes:

Name: ID
Content: id
Default: #IMPLIED

How to Use: Uniquely identifies the index. May be used to cross-reference to within the document.

Name: SDAPREF
Content: cdata
Default: <h1>Index</h1>

How to Use: This is an Accessible Document Design Attribute which, if used, will prepare electronic text for Braille, large print and computer voice capability. This attribute contains generated fixed text strings or counters for prefixed text. It may specify a processing instruction calling for intervention by a Braille specialist.

INDEXREF

Short Description: **Reference to index item**

How to Use: Specifies a reference to an index item. This tag is used with the rid attribute when the index and references to them will be numbered automatically.

Content Type: mixed

Contained in: TSUBHEAD, EMPH, Q, SERTITLE, SUBJECT, OTHINFO, HEAD, DDHD, TERM, P, TITLE, SUBTITLE

Contains: #PCDATA

Attributes:

Name: ID
Content: id
Default: #IMPLIED

How to Use: Uniquely identifies the index reference. May be used to cross-reference to within the document.

Name: RID

Content: idref
Default: #REQUIRED

How to Use: This attribute is used to reference an index item. The rid attribute references an id attribute on the index element.

Name: HYTIME
Content: name
Default: CLINK

How to Use: This indicates a contextual link.

Name: HYNAMES
Content: cdata
Default: rid linkends

How to Use: This indicates a contextual link. Unique identifier attributes are on all elements which may be used as the end of an external or internal link.

Name: SDAFORM
Content: cdata
Default: xref #attrib IDREF

How to Use: This is an Accessible Document Design Attribute which, if used, will prepare electronic text for braille, large print and computer voice capability. This attribute provides a one-to-one mapping between an element in the source DTD and an element in the ICADD tagset.

INDXFLAG

Short Description: **Index flag**

How to Use: Specifies the index entries. The attributes are used to specify the level of the index entry.

Example of Usage:

```
<indxflag ref1="Transportation" ref2="Air" ref3="Passenger" ref4="First Class">
```

Content Type: empty

Contained in: GLOSSARY, INDEX, AFTERWRD, NOTES, VITA, APPENDIX, TSTUB, CELL, NOTE, FOOTNOTE, DD, ITEM, BQ, P, SUBSECT6, SUBSECT5, SUBSECT4, SUBSECT3, SUBSECT2, SUBSECT1, SECTION, CHAPTER, PART, FOREWORD, INTRO, PREFACE, ACK, DED, ABSTRACT, SUPMATL

Contains:

Attributes:

Name: REF1
Content: cdata
Default: #IMPLIED

How to Use: Specifies the first level index entry reference.

Name: REF2
Content: cdata
Default: #IMPLIED

How to Use: Specifies the second level index entry reference.

Name: REF3
Content: cdata
Default: #IMPLIED

How to Use: Specifies the third level index entry reference.

Name: REF4
Content: cdata

Default: #IMPLIED

How to Use: Specifies the fourth level index entry reference.

INDXNAME

Short Description: **Index term by name**

How to Use: Identifies name terms within an Index. This tag may be used within paragraph text to identify name terms when the index is generated automatically.

Content Type: mixed

Contained in: GLOSSARY, INDEX

Contains: #PCDATA

Attributes:

Name: SDAFORM
Content: cdata
Default: term

How to Use: This is an Accessible Document Design Attribute which, if used, will prepare electronic text for braille, large print and computer voice capability. This attribute provides a one-to-one mapping between an element in the source DTD and an element in the ICADD tagset.

INDXSUBJ

Short Description: **Index term by subject**

How to Use: Identifies subject terms within an Index. This tag may be used within paragraph text to identify subject terms when the index is generated automatically.

Content Type: mixed

Contained in: GLOSSARY, INDEX

Contains: #PCDATA

Attributes:

Name: SDAFORM
Content: cdata
Default: term

How to Use: This is an Accessible Document Design Attribute which, if used, will prepare electronic text for braille, large print and computer voice capability. This attribute provides a one-to-one mapping between an element in the source DTD and an element in the ICADD tagset.

INTRO

Short Description: **Introduction**

How to Use: Begins the introduction of the document. The introduction states the subject and discusses the treatment of the subject of the work.

Content Type: element

Contained in: FRONT

Contains: TITLE, DATE, P, DEFLIST, ORGADDR, INDADDR, ARTWORK, BQ, LIT, BIBLIST, AUTHOR, CORPAUTH, KEYWORD, KEYPHRAS, POEM, NAMELOC, INDXFLAG, TABLE, LIST, FORMULA, DFORMULA, SECTION

Attributes:

Name: ID
Content: id

Default: #IMPLIED

How to Use: Uniquely identifies the introduction. May be used to cross-reference to within the document.

Name: SDAPREF
Content: cdata
Default: <h1>Introduction</h1>

How to Use: This is an Accessible Document Design Attribute which, if used, will prepare electronic text for Braille, large print and computer voice capability. This attribute contains generated fixed text strings or counters for prefixed text. It may specify a processing instruction calling for intervention by a Braille specialist.

ISBN

Short Description: **International Standard Book Number**

How to Use: Specifies the International Standard Book Number (ISBN) number. The ISBN is a four part, ten character code that provides title identification of a specific nonserial publication issued by a particular publisher.

Example of Usage:

```
<isbn>0-387-88621-4
```

Content Type: mixed

Contained in: PUBFRONT

Contains: #PCDATA

Attributes:

Name: SDAFORM
Content: cdata
Default: para

How to Use: This is an Accessible Document Design Attribute which, if used, will prepare electronic text for braille, large print and computer voice capability. This attribute provides a one-to-one mapping between an element in the source DTD and an element in the ICADD tagset.

Name: SDAPREF
Content: cdata
Default: ISBN:

How to Use: This is an Accessible Document Design Attribute which, if used, will prepare electronic text for Braille, large print and computer voice capability. This attribute contains generated fixed text strings or counters for prefixed text. It may specify a processing instruction calling for intervention by a Braille specialist.

ISSN

Short Description: **International Standard Serial Number**

How to Use: Specifies the ISSN number. The International Standard Serial Number is an eight character code that provides title identification of serial publications.

Content Type: mixed

Contained in: PUBFRONT

Contains: #PCDATA

Attributes:

Name: SDAFORM
Content: cdata

Default: para

How to Use: This is an Accessible Document Design Attribute which, if used, will prepare electronic text for braille, large print and computer voice capability. This attribute provides a one-to-one mapping between an element in the source DTD and an element in the ICADD tagset.

Name: SDAPREF
Content: cdata
Default: ISSN:

How to Use: This is an Accessible Document Design Attribute which, if used, will prepare electronic text for Braille, large print and computer voice capability. This attribute contains generated fixed text strings or counters for prefixed text. It may specify a processing instruction calling for intervention by a Braille specialist.

ISSUEID

Short Description: **Issue identification**

How to Use: Specifies the issue identification information pertaining to the issue. The information is necessary for basic bibliogrphic identification.

Content Type: element

Contained in: SERPUBFR

Contains: ISSUENO, ISSUEPT, SUPPLID

ISSUENO

Short Description: **Issue number**

How to Use: Specifies the number of the issue.

Content Type: mixed

Contained in: ISSUEID

Contains: #PCDATA

ISSUEPT

Short Description: **Issue part**

How to Use: Specifies the issue part for the identification of the issue.

Content Type: mixed

Contained in: ISSUEID

Contains: #PCDATA

ITEM

Short Description: **Item**

How to Use: Specifies an item within a list. In order to have a subordinate list, an item may contain a list.

Example of Usage:

```
<list type="1"><head>Types of Fruit
<item><p>Apples
<list type="2"><item><p>Red<item><p>Green</list>
<item><p>Oranges
<item><p>Grapes
<list type="2"><item><p>Red<item><p>Green<item><p>Black</list>
</list>
```

Content Type: element

Contained in: LIST

Contains: DATE, P, DEFLIST, ORGADDR, INDADDR, ARTWORK, BQ, LIT, BIBLIST, AUTHOR, CORPAUTH, KEYWORD, KEYPHRAS, POEM, NAMELOC, INDXFLAG, TABLE, LIST, FORMULA, DFORMULA

Attributes:

Name: ID
Content: id
Default: #IMPLIED

How to Use: Uniquely identifies an item in a list. May be used to cross-reference to within the document.

Name: SDAFORM
Content: cdata
Default: litem

How to Use: This is an Accessible Document Design Attribute which, if used, will prepare electronic text for braille, large print and computer voice capability. This attribute provides a one-to-one mapping between an element in the source DTD and an element in the ICADD tagset.

KEYPHRAS

Short Description: **Key phrase**

How to Use: Specifies a key phrase in the document.

Example of Usage:

```
<keyphras>very important</keyphras>
```

Content Type: mixed

Contained in: GLOSSARY, INDEX, AFTERWRD, NOTES, VITA, APPENDIX, TSTUB, CELL, NOTE, FOOTNOTE, DD, ITEM, BQ, P, SUBSECT6, SUBSECT5, SUBSECT4, SUBSECT3, SUBSECT2, SUBSECT1, SECTION, CHAPTER, PART, FOREWORD, INTRO, PREFACE, ACK, DED, ABSTRACT, SUPMATL

Contains: #PCDATA

Attributes:

Name: SDAFORM
Content: cdata
Default: term

How to Use: This is an Accessible Document Design Attribute which, if used, will prepare electronic text for braille, large print and computer voice capability. This attribute provides a one-to-one mapping between an element in the source DTD and an element in the ICADD tagset.

KEYWORD

Short Description: **Key word**

How to Use: Specifies a key word in the document.

Example of Usage:

```
<keyword>SGML
```

Content Type: mixed

Contained in: GLOSSARY, INDEX, AFTERWRD, NOTES, VITA, APPENDIX, TSTUB, CELL, NOTE, FOOTNOTE, DD, ITEM, BQ, P, SUBSECT6, SUBSECT5, SUBSECT4, SUBSECT3, SUBSECT2, SUBSECT1, SECTION, CHAPTER, PART, FOREWORD, INTRO, PREFACE, ACK, DED, ABSTRACT, SUPMATL

Contains: #PCDATA

Attributes:

Name: SDAFORM
Content: cdata
Default: term

How to Use: This is an Accessible Document Design Attribute which, if used, will prepare electronic text for braille, large print and computer voice capability. This attribute provides a one-to-one mapping between an element in the source DTD and an element in the ICADD tagset.

LCCARDNO

Short Description: **Library of Congress card number**

How to Use: Specifies the Library of Congress card number. This provides access to a complete catalog record for the work.

Content Type: mixed

Contained in: PUBFRONT

Contains: #PCDATA

Attributes:

Name: SDAFORM
Content: cdata
Default: para

How to Use: This is an Accessible Document Design Attribute which, if used, will prepare electronic text for braille, large print and computer voice capability. This attribute provides a one-to-one mapping between an element in the source DTD and an element in the ICADD tagset.

Name: SDAPREF
Content: cdata
Default: LC card number:

How to Use: This is an Accessible Document Design Attribute which, if used, will prepare electronic text for Braille, large print and computer voice capability. This attribute contains generated fixed text strings or counters for prefixed text. It may specify a processing instruction calling for intervention by a Braille specialist.

LIST

Short Description: **Any Type of List**

How to Use: Begins a list.

Example of Usage:

```
<list type="1"><head>Types of Cheese
<item>Cheddar
<item>Swiss
<item>Gruyere
</list>
```

Content Type: element

Contained in: GLOSSARY, INDEX, AFTERWRD, NOTES, VITA, APPENDIX, TSTUB, CELL, NOTE, FOOTNOTE, DD, ITEM, BQ, P, SUBSECT6, SUBSECT5, SUBSECT4, SUBSECT3, SUBSECT2, SUBSECT1, SECTION, CHAPTER, PART, FOREWORD, INTRO, PREFACE, ACK, DED, ABSTRACT, SUPMATL

Contains: HEAD, ITEM

Attributes:

Name: ID
Content: id
Default: #IMPLIED

How to Use: Uniquely identifies a list. May be used to cross-reference to within the document.

Name: TYPE
Content: (1 | 2 | 3 | 4 | 5 | 6)
Default: #IMPLIED

How to Use: Specifies the type of list. Suggested list types are the following: 1 specifies an arabic list, 2 is an alphabetic list, 3 is a roman numbered list, 4 is a bulleted list, 5 is an unlabelled list. Note: If more list types are needed, then they should be added to the list of choices in the DTD.

Name: SDAFORM
Content: cdata
Default: list

How to Use: This is an Accessible Document Design Attribute which, if used, will prepare electronic text for braille, large print and computer voice capability. This attribute provides a one-to-one mapping between an element in the source DTD and an element in the ICADD tagset.

Name: SDAPREF
Content: cdata
Default: [list type=1]#set (item,#count(item,1)) [list type=2]#set (item,#count(item,A)) [list type=3]#set (item,#count(item,I)) [list type=4]#set (item,#count(item,*)) [list type=5]#set (item,#count(item,-))

How to Use: This is an Accessible Document Design Attribute which, if used, will prepare electronic text for Braille, large print and computer voice capability. This attribute contains generated fixed text strings or counters for prefixed text. It may specify a processing instruction calling for intervention by a Braille specialist.

LIT

Short Description: **Literal Text**

How to Use: Specifies text in which the spaces and line endings should be preserved as keyed. For example, it might be used to specify computer commands. The end tag should be on the same line as the last line of the element to avoid creation of undesired lines.

Content Type: cdata

Contained in: GLOSSARY, INDEX, AFTERWRD, NOTES, VITA, APPENDIX, TSTUB, CELL, NOTE, FOOTNOTE, DD, ITEM, BQ, P, SUBSECT6, SUBSECT5, SUBSECT4, SUBSECT3, SUBSECT2, SUBSECT1, SECTION, CHAPTER, PART, FOREWORD, INTRO, PREFACE, ACK, DED, ABSTRACT, SUPMATL

Contains:

Attributes:

Name: SDAFORM
Content: cdata
Default: lit

How to Use: This is an Accessible Document Design Attribute which, if used, will prepare

electronic text for braille, large print and computer voice capability. This attribute provides a one-to-one mapping between an element in the source DTD and an element in the ICADD tagset.

LOCATION

Short Description: **Location**

How to Use: Specifies the address information for the conference or for the publisher. The type of content specified is determined by the context the element is used in.

Example of Usage:

```
<confgrp><confname>Literary Conference
<location><city>Chicago<state>Illinois<country>USA
</confgrp>
```

Content Type: element

Contained in: CITATION, CONFGRP, PUBFRONT

Contains: STREET, CITY, STATE, COUNTRY, POSTCODE, SAN, EMAIL, POSTBOX, PHONE

Attributes:

Name: SDAFORM
Content: cdata
Default: para

How to Use: This is an Accessible Document Design Attribute which, if used, will prepare electronic text for braille, large print and computer voice capability. This attribute provides a one-to-one mapping between an element in the source DTD and an element in the ICADD tagset.

Name: SDAPREF
Content: cdata
Default: Location:

How to Use: This is an Accessible Document Design Attribute which, if used, will prepare electronic text for Braille, large print and computer voice capability. This attribute contains generated fixed text strings or counters for prefixed text. It may specify a processing instruction calling for intervention by a Braille specialist.

LPAGE

Short Description: **Last page**

How to Use: Specifies the last page number of the article (in the original paper version). The last page number need not necessarily be a number.

Example of Usage:

```
<lpage>B20</page>
```

Content Type: mixed

Contained in: PUBFRONT

Contains: #PCDATA

MISC

Short Description: **Miscellaneous date**

How to Use: Specifies any date necessary for internal use.

Example of Usage:

```
<misc><p>This article arrived electronically in TeX.</p>
<date>16 November 1993</date></misc>
```

Content Type: element

Contained in: HISTORY

Contains: P, DATE

MSN

Short Description: **Monographic series number**

How to Use: Specifies the monographic series number.

Example of Usage:

```
<msn>EMP #3
```

Content Type: mixed

Contained in: CITATION, TITLEGRP

Contains: #PCDATA

NAMELOC

Short Description: **Named location (of a link)**

How to Use: Assigns a local ID to the named objects in the name list.

Content Type: element

Contained in: GLOSSARY, INDEX, AFTERWRD, NOTES, VITA, APPENDIX, TSTUB, CELL, NOTE, FOOTNOTE, DD, ITEM, BQ, P, SUBSECT6, SUBSECT5, SUBSECT4, SUBSECT3, SUBSECT2, SUBSECT1, SECTION, CHAPTER, PART, FOREWORD, INTRO, PREFACE, ACK, DED, ABSTRACT, SUPMATL

Contains: NMLIST

Attributes:

Name: HYTIME
Content: name
Default: NAMELOC

How to Use: This indicates a contextual link.

Name: ID
Content: id
Default: #REQUIRED

How to Use: Uniquely identifies the name location of a link. May be used to cross-reference to within the document.

Name: ORDERING
Content: (ORDERED | NOORDER)
Default: NOORDER

How to Use: Specifies whether the order of the locations are significant.

Name: SET
Content: (SET | NOTSET)
Default: NOTSET

How to Use: Specifies whether to make a set multiple by ignoring duplicates.

Name: AGGLOC
Content: (AGGLOC | AGGLINK | NAGG)
Default: NAGG

How to Use: Specifies whether there are multiple locations in an aggregate.

Name: SDAPREF
Content: cdata
Default: <?SDATRANS>Nameloc:

How to Use: This is an Accessible Document Design Attribute which, if used, will prepare electronic text for Braille, large print and computer voice capability. This attribute contains generated fixed text strings or counters for prefixed text. It may specify a processing instruction calling for intervention by a Braille specialist.

NMLIST

Short Description: **List of named objects**

How to Use: Specifies the list of local ID or entity names in the name location.

Content Type: mixed

Contained in: NAMELOC

Contains: #PCDATA

Attributes:

Name: HYTIME
Content: name
Default: NMLIST

How to Use: This indicates a contextual link.

Name: NAMETYPE
Content: (ENTITY | ELEMENT)
Default: ENTITY

How to Use: Specifies whether the list is made up of entity names or IDs of elements.

Name: OBNAMES
Content: (OBNAMES | NOBNAMES)
Default: NOBNAMES

How to Use: Specifies whether or not the objects are treated as names.

Name: SDAPREF
Content: cdata
Default: <?SDATRANS>Namelist:

How to Use: This is an Accessible Document Design Attribute which, if used, will prepare electronic text for Braille, large print and computer voice capability. This attribute contains generated fixed text strings or counters for prefixed text. It may specify a processing instruction calling for intervention by a Braille specialist.

NO

Short Description: **Number**

How to Use: Specifies a number. The number is used to specify the number of whatever content it is contained in, e.g., a number within a section is a section number.

Example of Usage:

```
<chapter><no>1
<title>Chapter Title
```

Content Type: mixed

Contained in: APPENDIX, TABLE, NOTE, FOOTNOTE, CITATION, SUBSECT6, SUBSECT5, SUBSECT4, SUBSECT3, SUBSECT2, SUBSECT1, SECTION, CHAPTER, PART, CONFGRP, TITLEGRP

Contains: #PCDATA

NOTE

Short Description: **Note**

How to Use: Specifies a note within text. A note may be a statement explaining the text, providing additional information about the text, or indicating the basis for an assertion, or the source of material quoted (a citation). The placement of a note is totally dependent on the design of the document and the purpose of the note. They may appear at the end of a work as endnotes, at the end of a chapter, at the foot of a page of text as footnotes, or embedded within the text as notes within text.

Example of Usage:

```
<note id="nt2"><p>This article does not endorse any commercial products
mentioned herein.</note>
```

Content Type: element

Contained in:

Contains: NO, DATE, DEFLIST, ORGADDR, INDADDR, ARTWORK, BQ, LIT, BIBLIST, AUTHOR, CORPAUTH, KEYWORD, KEYPHRAS, POEM, NAMELOC, INDXFLAG, TABLE, LIST, FORMULA, DFORMULA, P

Attributes:

Name: ID
Content: id
Default: #IMPLIED

How to Use: Uniquely identifies a note. May be used to cross-reference to within the document.

Name: SDAFORM
Content: cdata
Default: note

How to Use: This is an Accessible Document Design Attribute which, if used, will prepare electronic text for braille, large print and computer voice capability. This attribute provides a one-to-one mapping between an element in the source DTD and an element in the ICADD tagset.

NOTEREF

Short Description: **Reference to a note**

How to Use: Specifies a reference to a note.

Example of Usage:

```
<noteref rid="nt2">
```

Content Type: mixed

Contained in: TSUBHEAD, EMPH, Q, SERTITLE, SUBJECT, OTHINFO, HEAD, DDHD, TERM, P, TITLE, SUBTITLE

Contains: #PCDATA

Attributes:

Name: ID
Content: id
Default: #IMPLIED

How to Use: Uniquely identifies a reference to a note. May be used to cross-reference to within the document.

Name: RID

Content: idref
Default: #REQUIRED

How to Use: This attribute is used to reference a note. The rid attribute references an id attribute on a note element.

Name: HYTIME
Content: name
Default: CLINK

How to Use: This indicates a contextual link.

Name: HYNAMES
Content: cdata
Default: rid linkends

How to Use: This indicates a contextual link. Unique identifier attributes are on all elements which may be used as the end of an external or internal link.

Name: SDAFORM
Content: cdata
Default: xref #attrib IDREF

How to Use: This is an Accessible Document Design Attribute which, if used, will prepare electronic text for braille, large print and computer voice capability. This attribute provides a one-to-one mapping between an element in the source DTD and an element in the ICADD tagset.

NOTES

Short Description: **Notes (Section of a doc.)**

How to Use: Specifies the Notes section within the back matter of a document.

Content Type: element

Contained in: BACK

Contains: TITLE, DATE, P, DEFLIST, ORGADDR, INDADDR, ARTWORK, BQ, LIT, BIBLIST, AUTHOR, CORPAUTH, KEYWORD, KEYPHRAS, POEM, NAMELOC, INDXFLAG, TABLE, LIST, FORMULA, DFORMULA, SECTION

Attributes:

Name: SDAPREF
Content: cdata
Default: <h1>Notes</h1>

How to Use: This is an Accessible Document Design Attribute which, if used, will prepare electronic text for Braille, large print and computer voice capability. This attribute contains generated fixed text strings or counters for prefixed text. It may specify a processing instruction calling for intervention by a Braille specialist.

ORGADDR

Short Description: **Organization address**

How to Use: Groups the address components associated with an organization, or may be used to identify the organizational address when no embedded address components are desired.

Example of Usage:

```
<orgaddr><orgname>Society of Computer Users
<city>New York<state>NY
```

Content Type: element

Contained in: GLOSSARY, INDEX, AFTERWRD, NOTES, VITA, APPENDIX, TSTUB, CELL, NOTE, FOOTNOTE, DD, ITEM, BQ, P, SUBSECT6, SUBSECT5, SUBSECT4, SUBSECT3, SUBSECT2, SUBSECT1, SECTION, CHAPTER, PART, FOREWORD, INTRO, PREFACE, ACK, DED, ABSTRACT, SUPMATL

Contains: ORGNAME, ORGDIV, STREET, CITY, STATE, COUNTRY, POSTCODE, SAN, EMAIL, POSTBOX, PHONE

Attributes:

Name: SDAFORM
Content: cdata
Default: para

How to Use: This is an Accessible Document Design Attribute which, if used, will prepare electronic text for braille, large print and computer voice capability. This attribute provides a one-to-one mapping between an element in the source DTD and an element in the ICADD tagset.

Name: SDAPREF
Content: cdata
Default: Address:

How to Use: This is an Accessible Document Design Attribute which, if used, will prepare electronic text for Braille, large print and computer voice capability. This attribute contains generated fixed text strings or counters for prefixed text. It may specify a processing instruction calling for intervention by a Braille specialist.

ORGDIV

Short Description: **Division within organization**

How to Use: Specifies the division within the organization.

Example of Usage:

```
<orgdiv>Documentation & Training
```

Content Type: mixed

Contained in: ORGADDR, CPYRTNME, CPYRTCLR, REPRINT, SPONSOR, PUBNAME, AVAIL, CORPAUTH, AFF, SCHOOL

Contains: #PCDATA

ORGNAME

Short Description: **Name of organization**

How to Use: Specifies the organization's name.

Example of Usage:

```
<orgname>University of Nebraska
<orgdiv>School of Agriculture
<city>Lincoln<state>NE
```

Content Type: mixed

Contained in: ORGADDR, CPYRTNME, CPYRTCLR, REPRINT, SPONSOR, PUBNAME, AVAIL, CORPAUTH, AFF, SCHOOL

Contains: #PCDATA

OTHINFO

Short Description: **Other bibliographic info**

How to Use: Specifies other miscellaneous information within a citation. This may be used when individual identification of bibliographic reference text elements is unnecessary.

Content Type: mixed

Contained in: CITATION

Contains: #PCDATA, FORMULA, DFORMULA, DFORMGRP, Q, PAGES, EMPH, NOTEREF, FNOTEREF, FIGREF, TABLEREF, ARTREF, APPREF, CITEREF, SECREF, FORMREF, GLOSREF

Attributes:

Name: SDAFORM
Content: cdata
Default: para

How to Use: This is an Accessible Document Design Attribute which, if used, will prepare electronic text for braille, large print and computer voice capability. This attribute provides a one-to-one mapping between an element in the source DTD and an element in the ICADD tagset.

P

Short Description: **Paragraph**

How to Use: Begins a paragraph of text.

Example of Usage:

```
<p>This is the beginning of a paragraph...
```

Content Type: mixed

Contained in: GLOSSARY, INDEX, AFTERWRD, NOTES, VITA, APPENDIX, TSTUB, CELL, NOTE, FOOTNOTE, DD, ITEM, BQ, SUBSECT6, SUBSECT5, SUBSECT4, SUBSECT3, SUBSECT2, SUBSECT1, SECTION, CHAPTER, PART, FOREWORD, INTRO, PREFACE, ACK, DED, ABSTRACT, SUPMATL

Contains: #PCDATA, DATE, DEFLIST, ORGADDR, INDADDR, ARTWORK, BQ, LIT, BIBLIST, AUTHOR, CORPAUTH, KEYWORD, KEYPHRAS, POEM, NAMELOC, INDXFLAG, TABLE, LIST, FORMULA, DFORMULA, DFORMGRP, Q, PAGES, EMPH, NOTEREF, FNOTEREF, FIGREF, TABLEREF, ARTREF, APPREF, CITEREF, SECREF, FORMREF, GLOSREF

Attributes:

Name: ID
Content: id
Default: #IMPLIED

How to Use: Uniquely identifies a paragraph. May be used to cross-reference to within the document.

Name: ALPHABET
Content: (LATIN | GREEK | CYRILLIC | HEBREW | KANJI)
Default: LATIN

How to Use: Specifies the character set or alphabet used for this element. Modify the DTD as necessary to add new alphabets.

Name: SDAFORM
Content: cdata
Default: para

How to Use: This is an Accessible Document Design Attribute which, if used, will prepare electronic text for braille, large print and computer voice capability. This attribute provides a one-

to-one mapping between an element in the source DTD and an element in the ICADD tagset.

PACKAGE

Short Description: **Packaging method**

How to Use: Specifies the term denoting the physical form in which a work is packaged.

Content Type: mixed

Contained in: PUBFRONT

Contains: #PCDATA

Attributes:

Name: SDAFORM
Content: cdata
Default: para

How to Use: This is an Accessible Document Design Attribute which, if used, will prepare electronic text for braille, large print and computer voice capability. This attribute provides a one-to-one mapping between an element in the source DTD and an element in the ICADD tagset.

Name: SDAPREF
Content: cdata
Default: Packaging method:

How to Use: This is an Accessible Document Design Attribute which, if used, will prepare electronic text for Braille, large print and computer voice capability. This attribute contains generated fixed text strings or counters for prefixed text. It may specify a processing instruction calling for intervention by a Braille specialist.

PAGES

Short Description: **Page number(s) of reference**

How to Use: Specifies the page number of the reference, for example, use within a bibliographic reference.

Content Type: mixed

Contained in: GLOSSARY, INDEX, TSUBHEAD, EMPH, Q, SERTITLE, SUBJECT, OTHINFO, CITATION, HEAD, DDHD, TERM, P, TITLE, SUBTITLE

Contains: #PCDATA

Attributes:

Name: SDAFORM
Content: cdata
Default: pp

How to Use: This is an Accessible Document Design Attribute which, if used, will prepare electronic text for braille, large print and computer voice capability. This attribute provides a one-to-one mapping between an element in the source DTD and an element in the ICADD tagset.

PART

Short Description: **Part (Section in a document)**

How to Use: Specifies a part within a document. This is the topmost subordinate unit into which a book may be divided. If the part element is used, chapters would be contained within the parts.

Content Type: element

Contained in: BODY

Contains: NO, DATE, TITLE, P, DEFLIST, ORGADDR, INDADDR, ARTWORK, BQ, LIT, BIBLIST, AUTHOR, CORPAUTH, KEYWORD, KEYPHRAS, POEM, NAMELOC, INDXFLAG, TABLE, LIST, FORMULA, DFORMULA, CHAPTER

Attributes:

Name: SDARULE
Content: cdata
Default: chapter #use SDAPART

How to Use: This is an Accessible Document Design Attribute which, if used, will prepare electronic text for braille, large print and computer voice capability. This attribute provides a mechanism to apply more complex mappings based on the ancestry of the current element.

PHONE

Short Description: **Telephone Number**

How to Use: Specifies a telephone number.

Example of Usage:

```
<phone>1-800-555-1222
```

Content Type: mixed

Contained in: LOCATION, ORGADDR, INDADDR, CPYRTNME, CPYRTCLR, REPRINT, SPONSOR, PUBNAME, AVAIL, CORPAUTH, AFF, SCHOOL, AUTHOR

Contains: #PCDATA

Attributes:

Name: SDAFORM
Content: cdata
Default: para

How to Use: This is an Accessible Document Design Attribute which, if used, will prepare electronic text for braille, large print and computer voice capability. This attribute provides a one-to-one mapping between an element in the source DTD and an element in the ICADD tagset.

Name: SDAPREF
Content: cdata
Default: Phone:

How to Use: This is an Accessible Document Design Attribute which, if used, will prepare electronic text for Braille, large print and computer voice capability. This attribute contains generated fixed text strings or counters for prefixed text. It may specify a processing instruction calling for intervention by a Braille specialist.

POEM

Short Description: **Poem**

How to Use: Specifies lines of poetry within text.

Example of Usage:

```
<poem><poemline>Roses are Red,
<poemline>Violets are Blue,
<poemline>SGML is fun,
<poemline>Let's tag it and run!</poem>
```

Content Type: element

Contained in: GLOSSARY, INDEX, AFTERWRD, NOTES, VITA, APPENDIX, TSTUB, CELL, NOTE, FOOTNOTE, DD, ITEM, BQ, P, SUBSECT6, SUBSECT5, SUBSECT4, SUBSECT3, SUBSECT2, SUBSECT1, SECTION, CHAPTER, PART, FOREWORD, INTRO, PREFACE, ACK, DED, ABSTRACT, SUPMATL

Contains: STANZA, POEMLINE

POEMLINE

Short Description: **Line in a poem**

How to Use: Specifies the lines of text in a poem or stanza. Refer to the POEM element for an example.

Content Type: mixed

Contained in: STANZA, POEM

Contains: #PCDATA, EMPH

POSTBOX

Short Description: **Post office box**

How to Use: Specifies the post office box.

Example of Usage:

```
<postbox>10320
```

Content Type: mixed

Contained in: LOCATION, ORGADDR, INDADDR, CPYRTNME, CPYRTCLR, REPRINT, SPONSOR, PUBNAME, AVAIL, CORPAUTH, AFF, SCHOOL, AUTHOR

Contains: #PCDATA

POSTCODE

Short Description: **Postal code**

How to Use: Specifies the postal code.

Example of Usage:

```
<postcode>12345-0001
<postcode>XN512
```

Content Type: mixed

Contained in: LOCATION, ORGADDR, INDADDR, CPYRTNME, CPYRTCLR, REPRINT, SPONSOR, PUBNAME, AVAIL, CORPAUTH, AFF, SCHOOL, AUTHOR

Contains: #PCDATA

PREFACE

Short Description: **Preface**

How to Use: Begins the preface of the document. The preface consists of a note preceding the text of a book, which states the origin, purpose, and scope of the work(s) contained in the book and sometimes includes acknowledgments of assistance. When written by someone other than the author, it is more properly a Foreword.

Example of Usage:

```
<preface><title>Preface
<p>This book was born out of frustration...
```

Content Type: element

Contained in: FRONT

Contains: TITLE, DATE, P, DEFLIST, ORGADDR, INDADDR, ARTWORK, BQ, LIT, BIBLIST, AUTHOR, CORPAUTH, KEYWORD, KEYPHRAS, POEM, NAMELOC, INDXFLAG, TABLE, LIST, FORMULA, DFORMULA, SECTION

Attributes:

Name: ID
Content: id
Default: #IMPLIED

How to Use: Uniquely identifies a preface. May be used to cross-reference to within the document.

Name: SDAPREF
Content: cdata
Default: <h1>Preface</h1>

How to Use: This is an Accessible Document Design Attribute which, if used, will prepare electronic text for Braille, large print and computer voice capability. This attribute contains generated fixed text strings or counters for prefixed text. It may specify a processing instruction calling for intervention by a Braille specialist.

PRICE

Short Description: **Price**

How to Use: Specifies the price.

Example of Usage:

```
<price>3.95
```

Content Type: mixed

Contained in: PUBFRONT

Contains: #PCDATA

Attributes:

Name: SDAFORM
Content: cdata
Default: para

How to Use: This is an Accessible Document Design Attribute which, if used, will prepare electronic text for braille, large print and computer voice capability. This attribute provides a one-to-one mapping between an element in the source DTD and an element in the ICADD tagset.

Name: SDAPREF
Content: cdata
Default: Price:

How to Use: This is an Accessible Document Design Attribute which, if used, will prepare electronic text for Braille, large print and computer voice capability. This attribute contains generated fixed text strings or counters for prefixed text. It may specify a processing instruction calling for intervention by a Braille specialist.

PUBFRONT

Short Description: **Publisher's front matter**

How to Use: Begins the publisher's front matter. It groups the elements that are inserted by the publisher; e.g., publisher's unique identification number, copyright notice, etc.

Content Type: element

Contained in: FRONT

Contains: DATE, SPONSOR, CONTRACT, REPRINT, CPYRT, PUBNAME, LOCATION, CONFGRP, AVAIL, CODEN, ACQNO, ISBN, LCCARDNO, REPORTID, EDITION, VOLID, CATALOG, ACIDFREE, PRICE, EXTENT, PACKAGE

PUBID

Short Description: **Publisher's unique id number**

How to Use: Specifies the publisher's identification number. This is used to determine whether work being received duplicates data already in the receiving system.

Content Type: mixed

Contained in: PUBFRONT

Contains: #PCDATA

Attributes:

Name: SDAFORM
Content: cdata
Default: para

How to Use: This is an Accessible Document Design Attribute which, if used, will prepare electronic text for braille, large print and computer voice capability. This attribute provides a one-to-one mapping between an element in the source DTD and an element in the ICADD tagset.

Name: SDAPREF
Content: cdata
Default: Publisher's ID number:

How to Use: This is an Accessible Document Design Attribute which, if used, will prepare electronic text for Braille, large print and computer voice capability. This attribute contains generated fixed text strings or counters for prefixed text. It may specify a processing instruction calling for intervention by a Braille specialist.

PUBNAME

Short Description: **Publisher name**

How to Use: Specifies the publisher's name.

Example of Usage:

```
<pubname><orgname>ACME Publishing Company</pubname>
```

Content Type: element

Contained in: PUBFRONT

Contains: ORGNAME, ORGDIV, STREET, CITY, STATE, COUNTRY, POSTCODE, SAN, EMAIL, POSTBOX, PHONE

Attributes:

Name: SDAFORM
Content: cdata
Default: para

How to Use: This is an Accessible Document Design Attribute which, if used, will prepare electronic text for braille, large print and computer voice capability. This attribute provides a one-to-one mapping between an element in the source DTD and an element in the ICADD tagset.

Name: SDAPREF

Content: cdata
Default: Publisher:

How to Use: This is an Accessible Document Design Attribute which, if used, will prepare electronic text for Braille, large print and computer voice capability. This attribute contains generated fixed text strings or counters for prefixed text. It may specify a processing instruction calling for intervention by a Braille specialist.

Q

Short Description: **Quotation, in-line**

How to Use: Specifies an in-line quotation. It is a short quotation that occurs within running text to be enclosed in quotation marks. Quotations may be nested.

Example of Usage:

```
<q>All the world's a stage...</q>
```

Content Type: mixed

Contained in: TSUBHEAD, EMPH, Q, SERTITLE, SUBJECT, OTHINFO, HEAD, DDHD, TERM, P, TITLE, SUBTITLE

Contains: #PCDATA, FORMULA, DFORMULA, DFORMGRP, Q, PAGES, EMPH, NOTEREF, FNOTEREF, FIGREF, TABLEREF, ARTREF, APPREF, CITEREF, SECREF, FORMREF, GLOSREF

Attributes:

Name: ID
Content: id
Default: #IMPLIED

How to Use: Uniquely identifies a quotation. May be used to cross-reference to within the document.

Name: ALPHABET
Content: (LATIN | GREEK | CYRILLIC | HEBREW | KANJI)
Default: LATIN

How to Use: Specifies the character set or alphabet used for this element. Modify the DTD as necessary to add new alphabets.

Name: SDAPREF
Content: cdata
Default: %SDASUFF;

How to Use: This is an Accessible Document Design Attribute which, if used, will prepare electronic text for Braille, large print and computer voice capability. This attribute contains generated fixed text strings or counters for prefixed text. It may specify a processing instruction calling for intervention by a Braille specialist.

RECEIVED

Short Description: **Received date**

How to Use: Specifies the date the article was received by the publisher. This information is part of the article's history statement.

Content Type: element

Contained in: HISTORY

Contains: DATE

REPORTID

Short Description: **Report identifier**

How to Use: Specifies the report identifier. This is the complete, formatted alphanumeric designation most uniquely identifying a report.

Content Type: mixed

Contained in: PUBFRONT

Contains: #PCDATA

Attributes:

Name: SDAFORM
Content: cdata
Default: para

How to Use: This is an Accessible Document Design Attribute which, if used, will prepare electronic text for braille, large print and computer voice capability. This attribute provides a one-to-one mapping between an element in the source DTD and an element in the ICADD tagset.

Name: SDAPREF
Content: cdata
Default: Report identifier:

How to Use: This is an Accessible Document Design Attribute which, if used, will prepare electronic text for Braille, large print and computer voice capability. This attribute contains generated fixed text strings or counters for prefixed text. It may specify a processing instruction calling for intervention by a Braille specialist.

REPRINT

Short Description: **Reprint source**

How to Use: Specifies the source (organization or individual) to request a reprint of the article from.

Example of Usage:

```
<reprint>
<orgname>National Information Standards Organization
```

Content Type: element

Contained in: PUBFRONT

Contains: ORGNAME, SURNAME, FNAME, ORGDIV, DEGREE, ROLE, AFF, STREET, CITY, STATE, COUNTRY, POSTCODE, SAN, EMAIL, POSTBOX, PHONE

Attributes:

Name: SDAFORM
Content: cdata
Default: para

How to Use: This is an Accessible Document Design Attribute which, if used, will prepare electronic text for braille, large print and computer voice capability. This attribute provides a one-to-one mapping between an element in the source DTD and an element in the ICADD tagset.

Name: SDAPREF
Content: cdata
Default: Reprint source:

How to Use: This is an Accessible Document Design Attribute which, if used, will prepare electronic text for Braille, large print and computer voice capability. This attribute contains generated fixed text strings or counters for prefixed text. It may specify a processing instruction calling for intervention by a Braille specialist.

REVISED

Short Description: **Revised date**

How to Use: Specifies the date the article was revised in the history statement.

Content Type: element

Contained in: HISTORY

Contains: DATE

ROLE

Short Description: **Role indicator**

How to Use: Identifies the nature of the person's contribution to the work or a corporation's contribution to the work.

Example of Usage:

```
<role>Series Editor
<role>Sponsor
```

Content Type: mixed

Contained in: INDADDR, CPYRTNME, REPRINT, AUTHOR

Contains: #PCDATA

ROW

Short Description: **Table row**

How to Use: Specifies a row within the body of a table.

Content Type: element

Contained in: TBODY

Contains: TSTUB, CELL

Attributes:

Name: SDAFORM
Content: cdata
Default: row

How to Use: This is an Accessible Document Design Attribute which, if used, will prepare electronic text for braille, large print and computer voice capability. This attribute provides a one-to-one mapping between an element in the source DTD and an element in the ICADD tagset.

SAN

Short Description: **Standard address number**

How to Use: Specifies the standard address number which is a unique identifying number assigned to every address of every group, organization, or individual involved in or serving the book industry.

Content Type: mixed

Contained in: LOCATION, ORGADDR, INDADDR, CPYRTNME, CPYRTCLR, REPRINT, SPONSOR, PUBNAME, AVAIL, CORPAUTH, AFF, SCHOOL, AUTHOR

Contains: #PCDATA

Attributes:

Name: SDAFORM
Content: cdata
Default: para

How to Use: This is an Accessible Document Design Attribute which, if used, will prepare electronic text for braille, large print and computer voice capability. This attribute provides a one-to-one mapping between an element in the source DTD and an element in the ICADD tagset.

Name: SDAPREF
Content: cdata
Default: Standard address number:

How to Use: This is an Accessible Document Design Attribute which, if used, will prepare electronic text for Braille, large print and computer voice capability. This attribute contains generated fixed text strings or counters for prefixed text. It may specify a processing instruction calling for intervention by a Braille specialist.

SCHOOL

Short Description: **Degree granting institution**

How to Use: Specifies the school or university.

Example of Usage:

```
<school><orgname>University of Nebraska
<orgdiv>School of Agriculture
<city>Lincoln <state>NE
```

Content Type: element

Contained in: INDADDR, CPYRTNME, REPRINT, AUTHOR

Contains: ORGNAME, ORGDIV, STREET, CITY, STATE, COUNTRY, POSTCODE, SAN, EMAIL, POSTBOX, PHONE

SECREF

Short Description: **Reference to a section**

How to Use: Specifies a section reference. This tag is used with the attribute when the section and references to them will be numbered automatically. There is no content allowed when the attribute is used.

Example of Usage:

```
<secref rid="s25">
```

Content Type: mixed

Contained in: TSUBHEAD, EMPH, Q, SERTITLE, SUBJECT, OTHINFO, HEAD, DDHD, TERM, P, TITLE, SUBTITLE

Contains: #PCDATA

Attributes:

Name: ID
Content: id
Default: #IMPLIED

How to Use: Uniquely identifies a section reference. May be used to cross-reference to within the document.

Name: RID
Content: idref

Default: #REQUIRED

How to Use: This attribute is used to reference an section. The rid attribute references an id attribute on a section element.

Name: HYTIME
Content: name
Default: CLINK

How to Use: This indicates a contextual link.

Name: HYNAMES
Content: cdata
Default: rid linkends

How to Use: This indicates a contextual link. Unique identifier attributes are on all elements which may be used as the end of an external or internal link.

Name: SDAFORM
Content: cdata
Default: xref #attrib IDREF

How to Use: This is an Accessible Document Design Attribute which, if used, will prepare electronic text for braille, large print and computer voice capability. This attribute provides a one-to-one mapping between an element in the source DTD and an element in the ICADD tagset.

SECTION

Short Description: **Section**

How to Use: Specifies a section within a chapter of a document.

Example of Usage:

```
<section id="s25"><title>Installation
<subsect1 id="ss7"><title>Parts
<p>This is a paragraph describing...
```

Content Type: element

Contained in: GLOSSARY, INDEX, AFTERWRD, NOTES, VITA, APPENDIX, CHAPTER, FOREWORD, INTRO, PREFACE, ACK, DED, ABSTRACT, SUPMATL

Contains: NO, DATE, TITLE, P, DEFLIST, ORGADDR, INDADDR, ARTWORK, BQ, LIT, BIBLIST, AUTHOR, CORPAUTH, KEYWORD, KEYPHRAS, POEM, NAMELOC, INDXFLAG, TABLE, LIST, FORMULA, DFORMULA, SUBSECT1

Attributes:

Name: ID
Content: id
Default: #IMPLIED

How to Use: Uniquely identifies the section. May be used to cross-reference to within the document.

Name: SDABDY
Content: names
Default: TITLE H2

How to Use: This is an Accessible Document Design Attribute which, if used, will prepare electronic text for braille, large print and computer voice capability. This attribute provides a mapping depending on the use of the element in context.

Name: SDAPART
Content: names
Default: TITLE H3

How to Use: This is an Accessible Document Design Attribute which, if used, will prepare

electronic text for braille, large print and computer voice capability. This attribute provides a mapping depending on the use of the element in context.

SERBACK

Short Description: **Serial back matter**

How to Use: Specifies the beginning of the back matter of a serial.

Content Type: element

Contained in: SERIAL

Contains: ACK, VITA, GLOSSARY

SERBODY

Short Description: **Serial body matter**

How to Use: Specifies the beginning of the body matter of a serial. The serial body consists of serial parts or sections.

Content Type: element

Contained in: SERIAL

Contains: SERPART, SERSEC

SERFRONT

Short Description: **Serial front matter**

How to Use: Specifies the beginning of the front matter of a serial. The serial front consists of a title, a subtitle, an alternate title, serial publisher's front matter and a table of contents.

Content Type: element

Contained in: SERIAL

Contains: TITLE, STITLE, ALTTITLE, SERPUBFR, TOC

SERIAL

Short Description: **Serial document type**

How to Use: Specifies the beginning of a serial document. It contains articles.

Inclusion Elements: ASEQNTL, ADVERT, FIGGRP, FOOTNOTE, NOTE

Content Type: element

Contained in:

Contains: SERFRONT, SERBODY, SERBACK

Attributes:

Name: ID
Content: id
Default: #IMPLIED

How to Use: Uniquely identifies the serial publication. May be used to cross-reference to within the document.

Name: SDAFORM
Content: cdata
Default: serial

How to Use: This is an Accessible Document Design Attribute which, if used, will prepare electronic text for braille, large print and computer voice capability. This attribute provides a one-

to-one mapping between an element in the source DTD and an element in the ICADD tagset.

SERPART

Short Description: **Part in a serial**

How to Use: Specifies the beginning of a part within a serial. The serial body consists of serial parts or serial sections. A serial part element might be used for specifying a Department or Special Features part of a publication.

Content Type: element

Contained in: SERBODY

Contains: TITLE, ARTICLE, DATE, KEYWORD, KEYPHRAS, P, DEFLIST, ORGADDR, INDADDR, ARTWORK, BQ, LIT, BIBLIST, AUTHOR, CORPAUTH, POEM, NAMELOC, INDXFLAG, TABLE, LIST, FORMULA, DFORMULA, DFORMGRP

SERPUBFR

Short Description: **Publisher's front matter in a serial**

How to Use: Specifies the front matter for the information inserted by the publisher in a serial.

Content Type: element

Contained in: SERFRONT

Contains: DATE, REPRINT, CPYRT, PUBNAME, LOCATION, CONFGRP, AVAIL, CODEN, ACQNO, ACIDFREE, PRICE, EXTENT, ISSUEID, LCCARDNO, REPORTID, EDITION, VOLID, CATALOG, PACKAGE

SERSEC

Short Description: **Section in a serial**

How to Use: Specifies a serial section within a serial part or a serial body.

Content Type: element

Contained in: SERPART, SERBODY

Contains: TITLE, ARTICLE, DATE, KEYWORD, KEYPHRAS, P, DEFLIST, ORGADDR, INDADDR, ARTWORK, BQ, LIT, BIBLIST, AUTHOR, CORPAUTH, POEM, NAMELOC, INDXFLAG, TABLE, LIST, FORMULA, DFORMULA

SERTITLE

Short Description: **Title, (monographic) series**

How to Use: Specifies the title of a serial.

Content Type: mixed

Contained in: CITATION, TITLEGRP

Contains: #PCDATA, FORMULA, DFORMULA, DFORMGRP, Q, PAGES, EMPH, NOTEREF, FNOTEREF, FIGREF, TABLEREF, ARTREF, APPREF, CITEREF, SECREF, FORMREF, GLOSREF

Attributes:

Name: SDAFORM
Content: cdata
Default: ti

How to Use: This is an Accessible Document Design Attribute which, if used, will prepare electronic text for braille, large print and computer voice capability. This attribute provides a one-to-one mapping between an element in the source DTD and an element in the ICADD tagset.

SPONSOR

Short Description: **Conference sponsor**

How to Use: Specifies the contract or grant sponsor for the conference or document.

Example of Usage:

```
<sponsor>University of Colorado
```

Content Type: element

Contained in: CONFGRP, PUBFRONT

Contains: ORGNAME, ORGDIV, STREET, CITY, STATE, COUNTRY, POSTCODE, SAN, EMAIL, POSTBOX, PHONE

Attributes:

Name: SDAFORM
Content: cdata
Default: para

How to Use: This is an Accessible Document Design Attribute which, if used, will prepare electronic text for braille, large print and computer voice capability. This attribute provides a one-to-one mapping between an element in the source DTD and an element in the ICADD tagset.

Name: SDAPREF
Content: cdata
Default: (Contract or grant) sponsor:

How to Use: This is an Accessible Document Design Attribute which, if used, will prepare electronic text for Braille, large print and computer voice capability. This attribute contains generated fixed text strings or counters for prefixed text. It may specify a processing instruction calling for intervention by a Braille specialist.

STANZA

Short Description: **Stanza in a Poem**

How to Use: Specifies a stanza in a poem.

Content Type: element

Contained in: POEM

Contains: POEMLINE

STATE

Short Description: **State**

How to Use: Specifies the state.

Example of Usage:

```
<state>Maryland
<state>MD
```

Content Type: mixed

Contained in: LOCATION, ORGADDR, INDADDR, CPYRTNME, CPYRTCLR, REPRINT, SPONSOR, PUBNAME, AVAIL, CORPAUTH, AFF, SCHOOL, AUTHOR

Contains: #PCDATA

STITLE

Short Description: **Serial Subtitle**

How to Use: Begins a subtitle in the serial front matter.

Content Type: mixed

Contained in: SERFRONT

Contains: #PCDATA, FORMULA, DFORMULA, DFORMGRP, Q, PAGES, EMPH, NOTEREF, FNOTEREF, FIGREF, TABLEREF, ARTREF, APPREF, CITEREF, SECREF

Attributes:

Name: ALPHABET
Content: (LATIN | GREEK | CYRILLIC | HEBREW | KANJI)
Default: LATIN

How to Use: Specifies the character set or alphabet used for this element. Modify the DTD as necessary to add new alphabets.

Name: SDAFORM
Content: cdata
Default: ti

How to Use: This is an Accessible Document Design Attribute which, if used, will prepare electronic text for braille, large print and computer voice capability. This attribute provides a one-to-one mapping between an element in the source DTD and an element in the ICADD tagset.

STREET

Short Description: **Street**

How to Use: Specifies the street address.

Example of Usage:

```
<street>1600 Research Boulevard
```

Content Type: mixed

Contained in: LOCATION, ORGADDR, INDADDR, CPYRTNME, CPYRTCLR, REPRINT, SPONSOR, PUBNAME, AVAIL, CORPAUTH, AFF, SCHOOL, AUTHOR

Contains: #PCDATA

SUBJECT

Short Description: **Subject**

How to Use: Specifies the subject within a citation.

Content Type: mixed

Contained in: CITATION

Contains: #PCDATA, FORMULA, DFORMULA, DFORMGRP, Q, PAGES, EMPH, NOTEREF, FNOTEREF, FIGREF, TABLEREF, ARTREF, APPREF, CITEREF, SECREF, FORMREF, GLOSREF

Attributes:

Name: SDAFORM
Content: cdata
Default: it

How to Use: This is an Accessible Document Design Attribute which, if used, will prepare electronic text for braille, large print and computer voice capability. This attribute provides a one-to-one mapping between an element in the source DTD and an element in the ICADD tagset.

SUBSECT1

Short Description: **Subsection level 1**

How to Use: Specifies a first level subsection. It is subordinate to a Section.

Content Type: element

Contained in: SECTION

Contains: NO, DATE, TITLE, P, DEFLIST, ORGADDR, INDADDR, ARTWORK, BQ, LIT, BIBLIST, AUTHOR, CORPAUTH, KEYWORD, KEYPHRAS, POEM, NAMELOC, INDXFLAG, TABLE, LIST, FORMULA, DFORMULA, SUBSECT2

Attributes:

Name: ID
Content: id
Default: #IMPLIED

How to Use: Uniquely identifies the subsection. May be used to cross-reference to within the document.

Name: SDABDY
Content: names
Default: TITLE H3

How to Use: This is an Accessible Document Design Attribute which, if used, will prepare electronic text for braille, large print and computer voice capability. This attribute provides a mapping depending on the use of the element in context.

Name: SDAPART
Content: names
Default: TITLE H4

How to Use: This is an Accessible Document Design Attribute which, if used, will prepare electronic text for braille, large print and computer voice capability. This attribute provides a mapping depending on the use of the element in context.

SUBSECT2

Short Description: **Subsection level 2**

How to Use: Specifies a second level subsection. It is subordinate to a first level subsection.

Content Type: element

Contained in: SUBSECT1

Contains: NO, DATE, TITLE, P, DEFLIST, ORGADDR, INDADDR, ARTWORK, BQ, LIT, BIBLIST, AUTHOR, CORPAUTH, KEYWORD, KEYPHRAS, POEM, NAMELOC, INDXFLAG, TABLE, LIST, FORMULA, DFORMULA, SUBSECT3

Attributes:

Name: ID
Content: id
Default: #IMPLIED

How to Use: Uniquely identifies the subsection. May be used to cross-reference to within the document.

Name: SDABDY
Content: names
Default: TITLE H4

How to Use: This is an Accessible Document Design Attribute which, if used, will prepare electronic text for braille, large print and computer voice capability. This attribute provides a mapping depending on the use of the element in context.

Name: SDAPART
Content: names
Default: TITLE H5

How to Use: This is an Accessible Document Design Attribute which, if used, will prepare electronic text for braille, large print and computer voice capability. This attribute provides a mapping depending on the use of the element in context.

SUBSECT3

Short Description: **Subsection level 3**

How to Use: Specifies a third level subsection. It is subordinate to a second level subsection.

Content Type: element

Contained in: SUBSECT2

Contains: NO, DATE, TITLE, P, DEFLIST, ORGADDR, INDADDR, ARTWORK, BQ, LIT, BIBLIST, AUTHOR, CORPAUTH, KEYWORD, KEYPHRAS, POEM, NAMELOC, INDXFLAG, TABLE, LIST, FORMULA, DFORMULA, SUBSECT4

Attributes:

Name: ID
Content: id
Default: #IMPLIED

How to Use: Uniquely identifies the subsection. May be used to cross-reference to within the document.

Name: SDABDY
Content: names
Default: TITLE H5

How to Use: This is an Accessible Document Design Attribute which, if used, will prepare electronic text for braille, large print and computer voice capability. This attribute provides a mapping depending on the use of the element in context.

Name: SDAPART
Content: names
Default: TITLE H6

How to Use: This is an Accessible Document Design Attribute which, if used, will prepare electronic text for braille, large print and computer voice capability. This attribute provides a mapping depending on the use of the element in context.

SUBSECT4

Short Description: **Subsection level 4**

How to Use: Specifies a fourth level subsection. It is subordinate to a third level subsection.

Content Type: element

Contained in: SUBSECT3

Contains: NO, DATE, TITLE, P, DEFLIST, ORGADDR, INDADDR, ARTWORK, BQ, LIT, BIBLIST, AUTHOR, CORPAUTH, KEYWORD, KEYPHRAS, POEM, NAMELOC, INDXFLAG, TABLE, LIST, FORMULA, DFORMULA, SUBSECT5

Attributes:

Name: ID
Content: id
Default: #IMPLIED

How to Use: Uniquely identifies the subsection. May be used to cross-reference to within the document.

Name: SDABDY
Content: names
Default: TITLE H6

How to Use: This is an Accessible Document Design Attribute which, if used, will prepare electronic text for braille, large print and computer voice capability. This attribute provides a mapping depending on the use of the element in context.

Name: SDAPART
Content: names
Default: TITLE B

How to Use: This is an Accessible Document Design Attribute which, if used, will prepare electronic text for braille, large print and computer voice capability. This attribute provides a mapping depending on the use of the element in context.

SUBSECT5

Short Description: **Subsection level 5**

How to Use: Specifies a fifth level subsection. It is subordinate to a fourth level subsection.

Content Type: element

Contained in: SUBSECT4

Contains: NO, DATE, TITLE, P, DEFLIST, ORGADDR, INDADDR, ARTWORK, BQ, LIT, BIBLIST, AUTHOR, CORPAUTH, KEYWORD, KEYPHRAS, POEM, NAMELOC, INDXFLAG, TABLE, LIST, FORMULA, DFORMULA, SUBSECT6

Attributes:

Name: ID
Content: id
Default: #IMPLIED

How to Use: Uniquely identifies the subsection. May be used to cross-reference to within the document.

Name: SDABDY
Content: names
Default: TITLE B

How to Use: This is an Accessible Document Design Attribute which, if used, will prepare electronic text for braille, large print and computer voice capability. This attribute provides a mapping depending on the use of the element in context.

Name: SDAPART
Content: names
Default: TITLE B

How to Use: This is an Accessible Document Design Attribute which, if used, will prepare electronic text for braille, large print and computer voice capability. This attribute provides a mapping depending on the use of the element in context.

SUBSECT6

Short Description: **Subsection level 6**

How to Use: Specifies a sixth level subsection. It is subordinate to a fifth level subsection.

Content Type: element

Contained in: SUBSECT5

Contains: NO, DATE, TITLE, P, DEFLIST, ORGADDR, INDADDR, ARTWORK, BQ, LIT, BIBLIST, AUTHOR, CORPAUTH, KEYWORD, KEYPHRAS, POEM, NAMELOC, INDXFLAG, TABLE, LIST, FORMULA, DFORMULA

Attributes:

Name: ID
Content: id
Default: #IMPLIED

How to Use: Uniquely identifies the subsection. May be used to cross-reference to within the document.

Name: SDABDY
Content: names
Default: TITLE B

How to Use: This is an Accessible Document Design Attribute which, if used, will prepare electronic text for braille, large print and computer voice capability. This attribute provides a mapping depending on the use of the element in context.

Name: SDAPART
Content: names
Default: TITLE B

How to Use: This is an Accessible Document Design Attribute which, if used, will prepare electronic text for braille, large print and computer voice capability. This attribute provides a mapping depending on the use of the element in context.

SUBTITLE

Short Description: **Subtitle**

How to Use: Specifies a subtitle.

Content Type: mixed

Contained in: TITLEGRP

Contains: #PCDATA, FORMULA, DFORMULA, DFORMGRP, Q, PAGES, EMPH, NOTEREF, FNOTEREF, FIGREF, TABLEREF, ARTREF, APPREF, CITEREF, SECREF, FORMREF, GLOSREF

Attributes:

Name: SDAFORM
Content: cdata
Default: h1

How to Use: This is an Accessible Document Design Attribute which, if used, will prepare electronic text for braille, large print and computer voice capability. This attribute provides a one-to-one mapping between an element in the source DTD and an element in the ICADD tagset.

SUPMATL

Short Description: **Available supporting material**

How to Use: Identifies any available supplemental data, such as an original manuscript.

Content Type: element

Contained in: FRONT

Contains: TITLE, DATE, P, DEFLIST, ORGADDR, INDADDR, ARTWORK, BQ, LIT, BIBLIST, AUTHOR, CORPAUTH, KEYWORD, KEYPHRAS, POEM, NAMELOC, INDXFLAG, TABLE, LIST, FORMULA, DFORMULA, SECTION

Attributes:

Name: SDAFORM
Content: cdata
Default: para

How to Use: This is an Accessible Document Design Attribute which, if used, will prepare electronic text for braille, large print and computer voice capability. This attribute provides a one-to-one mapping between an element in the source DTD and an element in the ICADD tagset.

Name: SDAPREF
Content: cdata
Default: Supporting material:

How to Use: This is an Accessible Document Design Attribute which, if used, will prepare electronic text for Braille, large print and computer voice capability. This attribute contains generated fixed text strings or counters for prefixed text. It may specify a processing instruction calling for intervention by a Braille specialist.

SUPPLID

Short Description: **Supplement to issue ID**

How to Use: Specifies the supplemental information to the issue identification.

Content Type: mixed

Contained in: ISSUEID

Contains: #PCDATA

SURNAME

Short Description: **Surname**

How to Use: Specifies the surname (last name) of an individual.

Example of Usage:

```
<author><fname>Carl Gustav <surname>Jung
```

Content Type: mixed

Contained in: INDADDR, CPYRTNME, REPRINT, AUTHOR

Contains: #PCDATA

TABLE

Short Description: **Table**

How to Use: Specifies the beginning of a table.

Content Type: element

Contained in: GLOSSARY, INDEX, AFTERWRD, NOTES, VITA, APPENDIX, TSTUB, CELL, NOTE, FOOTNOTE, DD, ITEM, BQ, P, SUBSECT6, SUBSECT5, SUBSECT4, SUBSECT3, SUBSECT2, SUBSECT1, SECTION, CHAPTER, PART, FOREWORD, INTRO, PREFACE, ACK, DED, ABSTRACT, SUPMATL

Contains: NO, TBODY, TITLE

Attributes:

Name: ID
Content: id
Default: #IMPLIED

How to Use: Uniquely identifies the table. May be used to cross-reference to within the document.

Name: SDAFORM
Content: cdata
Default: table

How to Use: This is an Accessible Document Design Attribute which, if used, will prepare electronic text for braille, large print and computer voice capability. This attribute provides a one-to-one mapping between an element in the source DTD and an element in the ICADD tagset.

Name: SDARULE
Content: cdata
Default: title h3 head hdcell

How to Use: This is an Accessible Document Design Attribute which, if used, will prepare electronic text for braille, large print and computer voice capability. This attribute provides a mechanism to apply more complex mappings based on the ancestry of the current element.

Name: SDAPREF
Content: cdata
Default: <?SDATRANS>

How to Use: This is an Accessible Document Design Attribute which, if used, will prepare electronic text for Braille, large print and computer voice capability. This attribute contains generated fixed text strings or counters for prefixed text. It may specify a processing instruction calling for intervention by a Braille specialist.

TABLEREF

Short Description: **Reference to a table**

How to Use: Specifies a table reference. This tag is used with the rid attribute when the table and references to them will be numbered automatically.

Content Type: mixed

Contained in: TSUBHEAD, EMPH, Q, SERTITLE, SUBJECT, OTHINFO, HEAD, DDHD, TERM, P, TITLE, SUBTITLE

Contains: #PCDATA

Attributes:

Name: ID
Content: id
Default: #IMPLIED

How to Use: Uniquely identifies a table reference. May be used to cross-reference to within the document.

Name: RID
Content: idref
Default: #REQUIRED

How to Use: This attribute is used to reference a table. The rid attribute references an id attribute on a table element.

Name: HYTIME
Content: name
Default: CLINK

How to Use: This indicates a contextual link.

Name: HYNAMES
Content: cdata
Default: rid linkends

How to Use: This indicates a contextual link. Unique identifier attributes are on all elements which may be used as the end of an external or internal link.

Name: SDAFORM
Content: cdata
Default: xref #attrib IDREF

How to Use: This is an Accessible Document Design Attribute which, if used, will prepare electronic text for braille, large print and computer voice capability. This attribute provides a one-to-one mapping between an element in the source DTD and an element in the ICADD tagset.

TBODY

Short Description: **Table body**

How to Use: Specifies the beginning of the body of a table.

Content Type: element

Contained in: TABLE

Contains: HEAD, TSUBHEAD, ROW

Attributes:

Name: SDAFORM
Content: cdata
Default: tbody

How to Use: This is an Accessible Document Design Attribute which, if used, will prepare electronic text for braille, large print and computer voice capability. This attribute provides a one-to-one mapping between an element in the source DTD and an element in the ICADD tagset.

TERM

Short Description: **Defined Term**

How to Use: Specifies a term within a definition list. A definition description defines the term.

Content Type: mixed

Contained in: DEFLIST

Contains: #PCDATA, FORMULA, DFORMULA, DFORMGRP, Q, PAGES, EMPH, NOTEREF, FNOTEREF, FIGREF, TABLEREF, ARTREF, APPREF, CITEREF, SECREF, FORMREF, GLOSREF

Attributes:

Name: ID
Content: id
Default: #IMPLIED

How to Use: Uniquely identifies a term within a definition list. May be used to cross-reference to within the document.

Name: SDAFORM
Content: cdata
Default: term

How to Use: This is an Accessible Document Design Attribute which, if used, will prepare electronic text for braille, large print and computer voice capability. This attribute provides a one-to-one mapping between an element in the source DTD and an element in the ICADD tagset.

TITLE

Short Description: **Title**

How to Use: Begins a title. The type of title depends on the location of the tag in the data stream, e.g. a tag following the section tag is a section title.

Content Type: mixed

Contained in: GLOSSARY, INDEX, AFTERWRD, NOTES, VITA, APPENDIX, TABLE, FIGGRP, CITATION, SUBSECT6, SUBSECT5, SUBSECT4, SUBSECT3, SUBSECT2, SUBSECT1, SECTION, CHAPTER, PART, TITLEGRP, FOREWORD, INTRO, PREFACE, ACK, DED, ABSTRACT, SUPMATL

Contains: #PCDATA, FORMULA, DFORMULA, DFORMGRP, Q, PAGES, EMPH, NOTEREF, FNOTEREF, FIGREF, TABLEREF, ARTREF, APPREF, CITEREF, SECREF, FORMREF, GLOSREF

Attributes:

Name: ALPHABET
Content: (LATIN | GREEK | CYRILLIC | HEBREW | KANJI)
Default: LATIN

How to Use: Specifies the character set or alphabet used for this element. Modify the DTD as necessary to add new alphabets.

Name: PURPOSE
Content: (NORMAL | RUN)
Default: NORMAL

How to Use: Specifies whether this is a normal or running title.

Name: SDAFORM
Content: cdata
Default: ti

How to Use: This is an Accessible Document Design Attribute which, if used, will prepare electronic text for braille, large print and computer voice capability. This attribute provides a one-to-one mapping between an element in the source DTD and an element in the ICADD tagset.

TITLEGRP

Short Description: **Title group**

How to Use: Begins a group of titles for the document.

Content Type: element

Contained in: FRONT

Contains: MSN, SUBTITLE, SERTITLE, NO, TITLE

TOC

Short Description: **Table of contents**

How to Use: Specifies the occurrence or location of the table of contents for the document. The content is empty which assumes it is automatically generated. Note: If the table of contents is not generated automatically, then the appropriate elements need to be added to the DTD.

Content Type: empty

Contained in: FRONT

Contains:

Attributes:

Name: SDAFORM
Content: cdata
Default: list

How to Use: This is an Accessible Document Design Attribute which, if used, will prepare electronic text for braille, large print and computer voice capability. This attribute provides a one-to-one mapping between an element in the source DTD and an element in the ICADD tagset.

Name: SDAPREF
Content: cdata

Default: <?SDATRANS>Contents

How to Use: This is an Accessible Document Design Attribute which, if used, will prepare electronic text for Braille, large print and computer voice capability. This attribute contains generated fixed text strings or counters for prefixed text. It may specify a processing instruction calling for intervention by a Braille specialist.

TSTUB

Short Description: **Table stub**

How to Use: Specifies a table stub within the row. The table stub is the cell in the first column of the row.

Content Type: element

Contained in: ROW

Contains: DATE, P, DEFLIST, ORGADDR, INDADDR, ARTWORK, BQ, LIT, BIBLIST, AUTHOR, CORPAUTH, KEYWORD, KEYPHRAS, POEM, NAMELOC, INDXFLAG, TABLE, LIST, FORMULA, DFORMULA

Attributes:

Name: SDAFORM
Content: cdata
Default: stubcell

How to Use: This is an Accessible Document Design Attribute which, if used, will prepare electronic text for braille, large print and computer voice capability. This attribute provides a one-to-one mapping between an element in the source DTD and an element in the ICADD tagset.

TSUBHEAD

Short Description: **Table column subordinate head**

How to Use: Specifies the subheading for the body of a table.

Content Type: mixed

Contained in: TBODY

Contains: #PCDATA, FORMULA, DFORMULA, DFORMGRP, Q, PAGES, EMPH, NOTEREF, FNOTEREF, FIGREF, TABLEREF, ARTREF, APPREF, CITEREF, SECREF, FORMREF, GLOSREF

Attributes:

Name: SDAFORM
Content: cdata
Default: hdcell

How to Use: This is an Accessible Document Design Attribute which, if used, will prepare electronic text for braille, large print and computer voice capability. This attribute provides a one-to-one mapping between an element in the source DTD and an element in the ICADD tagset.

VITA

Short Description: **Curriculum vita**

How to Use: Specifies the curriculum vita within the back matter of the document.

Content Type: element

Contained in: BACK

Contains: TITLE, DATE, P, DEFLIST, ORGADDR, INDADDR, ARTWORK, BQ, LIT, BIBLIST, AUTHOR, CORPAUTH, KEYWORD, KEYPHRAS, POEM, NAMELOC, INDXFLAG, TABLE, LIST, FORMULA, DFORMULA, SECTION

VOLID

Short Description: **Volume identifier**

How to Use: Specifies the volume identifier.

Content Type: mixed

Contained in: PUBFRONT

Contains: #PCDATA

Attributes:

Name: SDAFORM
Content: cdata
Default: para

How to Use: This is an Accessible Document Design Attribute which, if used, will prepare electronic text for braille, large print and computer voice capability. This attribute provides a one-to-one mapping between an element in the source DTD and an element in the ICADD tagset.

Name: SDAPREF
Content: cdata
Default: Volume identifier:

How to Use: This is an Accessible Document Design Attribute which, if used, will prepare electronic text for Braille, large print and computer voice capability. This attribute contains generated fixed text strings or counters for prefixed text. It may specify a processing instruction calling for intervention by a Braille specialist.

Annex C
(informative)

Examples

C.1 Example of a marked up Book

The following is an extract from a book marked up in accordance with this International Standard. Used with permission. Copyright by Aspen Publishers Inc.

```
<!DOCTYPE BOOK SYSTEM "iso12083-book.dtd"
[
<!ENTITY copy CDATA "copyright symbol">
<!ENTITY deg CDATA "degree symbol">
<!ENTITY e CDATA ". . .">
<!ENTITY minus CDATA "minus sign">
<!ENTITY ndash CDATA "ndash sign">
]>

<BOOK>
<FRONT><TITLEGRP>
<TITLE>Organizational Burnout in Health Care Facilities</TITLE>
<SUBTITLE>Strategies for Prevention and Change
</SUBTITLE>
</TITLEGRP>
<AUTHGRP><AUTHOR><FNAME>Earl A.</FNAME>
<SURNAME>Simendinger</SURNAME>
<DEGREE>Ph.D.</DEGREE>
<ROLE>President and Chief Executive Officer</ROLE>
<AFF><ORGNAME>St. Luke's Hospital</ORGNAME>
<CITY>San Francisco</CITY>
<STATE>California</STATE>
</AFF></AUTHOR>
<AUTHOR><FNAME>Terence F.</FNAME>
<SURNAME>Moore</SURNAME>
<ROLE>President</ROLE>
<AFF><ORGNAME>Mid-Michigan Health Care Systems, Inc.</ORGNAME>
<CITY>Midland</CITY>
<STATE>Michigan</STATE></AFF>
</AUTHOR>
</AUTHGRP>
<DED>
<TITLE>To our parents</TITLE>
<P>Albert A. Moore and Marilla H. Moore and Earl A. Simendinger, M.D., and Leah M.
Simendinger</P></DED>
<FOREWORD><TITLE>Foreword</TITLE>
<P>This book is not a prescription for professional success in the competitive
```

```
health care industry. It is, rather, a series of observations and studies of
various aspects of organizational dynamics that must be recognized by health care
managers, particularly those in senior positions.</P>

<P>Chapter 9 focuses on the strategic planning process and its importance to
organizational viability. A planning process that integrates the major groups
within a hospital (board, administration, and medical staff) is absolutely
essential if the human and material resources available to the institution are
to be used in the most effective way possible. What is often perceived as a lack
of leadership in a hospital is actually a lack of comprehensive planning.</P>
</FOREWORD>
<PREFACE><TITLE>Preface</TITLE>

<P>Several years ago a friend of ours, Lee Zadra, asked us to document the
reasons why some hospitals lose <Emph type="2">altitude</Emph>, and what can be done to
rejuvenate them. Specifically, he asked, <Q>Why do organizations burn out?</Q>
We are concerned about our industry and our colleagues and hope that greater
attention will be focused on the process of organizational burnout in health care
literature, in seminars, and in professional meetings. This is a start.</P>

<AUTHOR><FNAME>Earl A.</FNAME>
<SURNAME>Simendinger</SURNAME>
<DEGREE>Ph.D.</DEGREE></AUTHOR>
<AUTHOR><FNAME>Terence F.</FNAME>
<SURNAME>Moore </SURNAME></AUTHOR>
</PREFACE>
<ACK>
<TITLE>Acknowledgments</TITLE>
<P>We wish to extend our deep appreciation to David Zuza, Director of Corporate
Planning for Mid-Michigan Health Care Systems, who contributed Chapter Nine;
&e; us in initiating and completing this project.</P>
</ACK>
<TOC>
</FRONT>
<BODY>
<CHAPTER><NO>1</NO>
<TITLE>Introduction to Organizational Burnout</TITLE>

<P>Organizational burnout is not simply the result of personal burnout. Although
the subject of personal burnout has received considerable attention in the past
ten or fifteen years, &e; when its total output is less than the sum of the
inputs. Burnout can occur when (1) an organization's leaders burn out, (2) its
nonsupervisory employees burn out, or (3) neither the leaders nor the employees
burn out, but there is a systems or <emph type="2">circuit</emph> failure--usually related to
ineffective communications or the lack of clearly defined organizational goals
accepted by the employees. &e;</P>

<SECTION><TITLE>Characteristics of Burned Out Organizations</TITLE>

<P>Certain characteristics are common to almost all hospitals that have
significant gaps between their performance and their potential.</P>

<SUBSECT1><TITLE>Bickering</TITLE>

<P>Of all the characteristics of organizational burnout manifested in hospitals,
```

```
&e;</P>

<P>Bickering is open and frequent. A great deal of time is wasted &e; and burn
up an inordinate amount of time and energy.</P>
</SUBSECT1>
<SUBSECT1><TITLE>Sense of Resignation</TITLE>

<P>The burned out organization appears to be resigned &e; but whose legs will
not buckle under his opponent's punch.</P>

<P>A sense of resignation &e; the chief executive officer of a 350-bed hospital
before he would be placed on a consulting status went into a two-year <emph type="2">glide
pattern</emph>. &e; administration is scrambling to catch up.</P>

<P>Another administrator who was in his early sixties &e; to retirement age
without working.</P></SUBSECT1></SECTION>

<SECTION><TITLE>Organizational Failure vs. Organizational Success</TITLE>

<P>As mentioned earlier, organizational burnout is not the same as total failure
of the hospital. The actual <emph type="2">death</emph> of a hospital is relatively rare, but
has been well analyzed by Connely, Pointer, and Ruschlin.<FNOTEREF rid="fn1">1</FNOTEREF> &e; most
of
which pertain to some aspect of utilization:
<LIST TYPE="4">
<ITEM><P>number of admissions</P></ITEM>
<ITEM><P>average daily census</P></ITEM>
<ITEM><P>percent occupancy</P></ITEM>
<ITEM><P>total expense</P></ITEM>
<ITEM><P>payroll expense</P></ITEM>
<ITEM><P>admissions per bed</P></ITEM>
</LIST>
</P>
<P>The mean bed capacity for the care of adults in the twenty-three failed
hospitals that were studied was 33 beds, &e; the smaller hospitals. As Connely
and his associates said,
<BQ>
<P>The conclusions of the study, while admittedly tentative and requiring
much additional investigation, suggest that hospital control and size are
associated with failure; that hospital utilization (as measured by admissions,
average daily census and percent occupancy) is highly associated with failure;
and that percent occupancy and total expense jointly may
<emph type="2">explain</emph> a considerable portion of the dependent variable.<FNOTEREF
rid="fn2">2</FNOTEREF></P>
</BQ>These findings are compelling reasons &e; or <emph type="2">sell out</emph> to even larger
systems.</P>
</SECTION>
<SECTION><TITLE>Notes</TITLE>
<FOOTNOTE id="fn1">
<NO>1</NO>
<P><BIBLIST><CITATION id="cite1"><TITLE>Health Service Research</TITLE>
<AUTHOR><FNAME>Lloyd</FNAME>
<SURNAME>Connely</SURNAME></AUTHOR>
<AUTHOR><FNAME>Dennis</FNAME>
<SURNAME>Pointer</SURNAME></AUTHOR>
<AUTHOR><FNAME>Hirsh</FNAME>
```

```
<SURNAME>Ruschlin</SURNAME></AUTHOR>
<SERTITLE>Viability and Hospital
Failure: Methodology Considerations and Empirical Evidence</SERTITLE>
<OTHINFO>13 (Spring 1978): 27&ndash;36</OTHINFO></CITATION></BIBLIST></P></FOOTNOTE>
<FOOTNOTE id="fn2">
<NO>2</NO>
<P><BIBLIST><CITATION id="cite2"><TITLE>Ibid 34.</TITLE></CITATION></BIBLIST></P>
</FOOTNOTE>
</SECTION>
</CHAPTER>
<CHAPTER><NO>2</NO>
<TITLE>The Process of Organizational Burnout: An Interpretive Model</TITLE>

<P>There is some correlation between executive burnout and different forms of
organizational burnout. &e; the organization influences the behavior of
executives, which causes their burnout.</P>

<P>From a broad conceptual viewpoint, an organization &e; the foundation of
this new interpretive entropic theory.</P>

<SECTION><TITLE>The Theory of Entropy</TITLE>

<P>To explain why organizations may burn out and eventually die, it is essential
first to understand a concept adapted from a classic systems
theory-entropy.<FNOTEREF rid="fn1">1</FNOTEREF> A completely closed system, &e; it is essentially
a perpetual motion machine.</P>

<P>The wristwatch becomes an open system when it depends on a depleting power
source, e.g., a battery. &e; This dependency on external resources makes the
watch an open system.</P>

<P>This loss-of-energy process is entropy. &e; An organization generally
requires more negentropy than entropy because it is impossible to predict
when, where, or how entropic forces may arise in the organization's day-to-day
operations.</P>

<P>The entropic process is even present in open systems. &e; for a given
period of time produces one of three results:
<DEFLIST>
<TERM>E&deg;</TERM>
<DD><P>representing the degree of entropy in an organization, results in a
negative number.</P></DD>
<TERM>SS</TERM>
<DD><P>representing a state of maintenance in which input equals output,
is zero.</P></DD>
<TERM>N&deg;</TERM>
<DD><P>representing the degree to which the organization is experiencing
negentropy, is a positive number.</P></DD></DEFLIST></P>

<P>This theory can also be described as a water container with two openings
(Figure 2-1). &e; if the waterline is rising, the organization is experiencing
negentropy.</P>
</SECTION>
<SECTION><TITLE>The Burnout Process</TITLE>

<P>This theory incorporates a five-phase sequential model to explain how and
```

```
why organizations, particularly hospitals, burn out: (1) initiation, (2)
infection, (3) impairment, (4) identification/ disregard, and (5)
ignition/interment.</P>

<SUBSECT1><TITLE>Initiation</TITLE>

<P>An internal or external occurrence &e; was catastrophic for the hospital.</P>

<P>There are several sensing activities &e; Activities that may help
administrators recognize incipient problems include:
<LIST TYPE="4">
<ITEM><P>assessment of the immediate environment. Important information &e;
</P></ITEM>
<ITEM><P>evaluation of routine comparative data. Analysis data
&e;</P></ITEM>
<ITEM><P>examination of non-health agency data. Other agencies. &e;</P></ITEM></LIST>
</P>
<P>A hospital administrator &e; as it became available on the commercial
market.</P>
</SUBSECT1>
<SUBSECT1><TITLE>Ignition/Interment</TITLE>

<P>In the final phase of the burnout process, &e;</P>

<SUBSECT2><TITLE>Curative Process</TITLE>

<P>An organization can use many approaches &e; must be evaluated before a plan
or approach is chosen:
<LIST TYPE="4">
<ITEM><P>assessment of the damage</P></ITEM>
<ITEM><P>length of time that the organization has to recover</P></ITEM>
<ITEM><P>quality of staff </P></ITEM>
<ITEM><P>cost of the recovery process</P></ITEM>
<ITEM><P>extent of competition</P></ITEM></LIST>
</P>
<P>These factors, among others, are important in the recovery decision-making
process and to the ultimate approach selected.
&e; warning alarms that have been shown to work well, however, if properly
placed.</P>

<SUBSECT3><TITLE>Double Loop Learning</TITLE>

<P>A simple and effective process, double loop learning can be helpful &e; and
procedures should be questioned.<FNOTEREF rid="fn1">5</FNOTEREF> Once such activities &e; or even
for need.</P>

<P>The double loop learning concept &e; and updated or revised, if necessary.
</P>
</SUBSECT3>
<SUBSECT3><TITLE>System Verification</TITLE>

<P>Systems can be periodically double-checked by means of &e; in particular the
hospital's position control system, can be double-checked.</P>
</SUBSECT3>
<SUBSECT3><TITLE>Understaffing</TITLE>
```

```
<P>For various economic and cosmetic reasons management may allow &e; are early
warning signs of entropy may be overlooked.</P>

<subsect4>
<TITLE>Notes</TITLE>
<FOOTNOTE>
<NO>1</NO>
<P><BIBLIST><CITATION id="cite4"><TITLE>Entropy, a New World View</TITLE>
<AUTHOR><FNAME>Jeremy</FNAME>
<SURNAME>Rifkin</SURNAME></AUTHOR>
<OTHINFO>(New York: Bantam
Books, 1981), pp.6&ndash;10</OTHINFO></CITATION></BIBLIST></P></FOOTNOTE>
<FOOTNOTE id="fn5">
<NO>5</NO>
<P><BIBLIST><CITATION id="cite5"><TITLE>American Psychologist</TITLE>
<AUTHOR><FNAME>Chris</FNAME>
<SURNAME>Argyris</SURNAME></AUTHOR>
<SERTITLE>Theories of Action That Inhibit Individual Leading</SERTITLE>
<OTHINFO>(September 1976): 638</OTHINFO></CITATION></BIBLIST></P></FOOTNOTE>
</subsect4></SUBSECT3></SUBSECT2></SUBSECT1></SECTION>

</CHAPTER>
<CHAPTER><NO>4</NO>
<TITLE>Implications of Personal Burnout </TITLE>

<P>Burned out personnel, collectively, can burn out their organization.
Certainly, burned out personnel at any level in an organization have a negative
effect on the organization's total performance. Therefore, it is important to
understand what constitutes personal burnout and how it influences individual
and organizational performance.</P>

<SECTION><TITLE>Causes of Personal Burnout</TITLE>

<P>Personal burnout is so closely associated with stress that the two terms are
often used synonymously. There are psychosocial causes of stress, bioecological
causes of stress, and personality causes of stress.</P>

<P>Psychosocial causes of stress include divorce, business readjustment, and
retirement. Bioecological causes of stress include nutritional habits, noise
pollution, and biological rhythms, which
<BQ>
<P>
can be viewed as natural fluctuations in body processes which promote survival
by automatically dictating that periods of high energy be interspersed by
periods of restorative rest. Generally speaking, biological rhythms are fixed
by generations of genetic programming, but they have a built-in flexibility to
allow maximum adaptations, thus increasing survival. As the seasons change, so
does the amount of heat and light imposed on the body, so metabolic and
hormonal adaptation is required. The biological rhythm that controls these
processes has the ability to change-probably using the changing light as a
trigger, although the exact mechanism is not known for certain.
<FNOTEREF rid="fn1">1</FNOTEREF></P></BQ></P>
</SECTION>
<SECTION><TITLE>Are You Burned Out?</TITLE>
```

```
<P>The following quiz is an exercise to determine your personal stage of
burnout:</P>

<P>Look back over the past six months. Have you been noticing changes in
yourself or in the world around you? Think of the office &e; the family &e; social
situations. Allow about 30 seconds for each answer. Then assign it a number from
1 (for no or little change) to 5 (for a great deal of change) to designate the
degree of change you perceive.</P>
<LIST TYPE="4">
<ITEM><P>Do you tire more easily? Feel fatigued rather than energetic?
</P></ITEM>
<ITEM><P>Are people annoying you by telling you, "You don't look so good lately?"
</P></ITEM>
<ITEM><P>Are you working harder and harder and accomplishing less and less?
</P></ITEM>
<ITEM><P>Do you have very little to say to people?
</P></ITEM>
</LIST>

<P>Very roughly. now, place yourself on the Burn-Out Scale. Keep in mind that
this is merely an approximation of where you are, useful as a guide on your way
to a more satisfying life. Don't let a high total alarm you, but pay attention
to it. Burn-out is reversible, no matter how far along it is. The higher number
signifies that the sooner you start being kinder to yourself, the better.
<LIT>
The Burn-Out Scale:

          0-25     You're doing fine.
         26-35     There are things you should be watching.
         36-50     You're a candidate.
         51-65     You are burning out.
         Over 65   You're in a dangerous place, threatening to your physical
                   and mental well-being.</LIT><FNOTEREF rid="fnn">*</FNOTEREF></P>
<FOOTNOTE id="fnn">
<NO>*</NO>
<P><emph type="2">Source:</emph><BIBLIST>
<CITATION id="cite6">
<TITLE>Burn-out: The High Cost of Achievement</TITLE>
<AUTHOR><FNAME>Herbert J.</FNAME>
<SURNAME>Freudenberger</SURNAME>
<DEGREE>Ph.D.</DEGREE></AUTHOR>
<AUTHOR><FNAME>with Geraldine</FNAME>
<SURNAME>Richelson</SURNAME></AUTHOR>
<SERTITLE>Questionnaire and Burn-Out Scale</SERTITLE>
<OTHINFO>Copyright &copy;: 1980 by Herbert J. Freudenberger, Ph.D., and Geraldine
Richelson. Reprinted by permission of Doubleday & Company, Inc.</OTHINFO>
</CITATION></BIBLIST></P></FOOTNOTE>
</SECTION>
<SECTION><TITLE>Coping with Stress</TITLE>

<P>Often described as a silent but pervasive hazard, stress is usually
considered a major contributing factor, if not the primary cause, of numerous
ailments. &e; As one colleague recently commented to a physician who was
complaining about being on call, "What is it like not to be on call for anyone
at anytime for anything?" Stress is not always negative. &e; In other words, an
```

```
individual's attitude can have a positive or negative effect on his or her
reaction to stress.</P>

<P>Howard and several colleagues determined the effectiveness of various
techniques in coping with stress.<FNOTEREF rid="fn1">17</FNOTEREF> They found that the six best
techniques for coping with job stress were as follows:
<LIST TYPE="4">
<ITEM><P>Build resistance by regular sleep, exercise, and good health habits.
</P></ITEM>
<ITEM><P>Compartmentalize work and nonwork life.
</P></ITEM>
<ITEM><P>Work hard on the job, but when at home, learn to blank out job problems.
</P></ITEM>
<ITEM><P>Engage in physical exercise.
</P></ITEM>
<ITEM><P>Talk through problems on the job with peers; have <emph type="2">bitching</emph>
sessions.
</P></ITEM>
<ITEM><P>Withdraw physically from the situation for a while; take a break.
</P></ITEM>
</LIST>

Managers must realize that they cannot do everything that needs to be done,
no matter how well they are organized. Accepting this, executives should focus
on those areas where they can contribute the most.
</P>

<SUBSECT1><TITLE>The Role of the Manager in Preventing Stress</TITLE>

<P>It is not enough for administrators to take care of their own physical and
psychological well-being. They must also ensure that their subordinate managers
are not placed in unduly stressful situations because of their managerial
responsibilities.</P>

<P>It is difficult to say whether hospital administrators are under more
stress than other executives are, but many administrators show signs of aging
faster than their counterparts do. &e; This definition emphasizes the
importance of fitness and good health for the executive.</P>
</SUBSECT1>
<SUBSECT1><TITLE>Ability to Handle Stress and Success</TITLE>

<P>There has been considerable conjecture about why executives in general and
health care executives in particular are successful.<FNOTEREF rid="fn18">18</FNOTEREF> Most
authorities attribute success to specific traits, such as integrity,
intelligence, or communication skills. Argyris, however, indicated that at
least seven characteristics described as <emph type="2">qualities of success</emph> can
be regarded as techniques that top executives use to offset job strain. All
seven were described by Uris:<FNOTEREF rid="fn19">19</FNOTEREF>
<DEFLIST>
<TERM>Frustration tolerance.</TERM>
<DD><P>"All that work and nothing to show for it," is a statement that often
precedes executive rage and frustration. &e;</P></DD>
<TERM>Encouraging participation.</TERM>
<DD><P>The effective executive shucks off pressure by encouraging his
subordinates to share in the control and development of the department. &e;
```

```
</P></DD>
<TERM>Realistic goal setting.</TERM>
<DD><P>It's human nature to try for perfection, particularly when the concept
of efficiency is accepted as a standard. &e;Level of aspiration, in other words, was in line with
capabilities and the realities of the situation.
<FNOTEREF rid="fn">*</FNOTEREF></P></DD>
</DEFLIST>
</P>
<FOOTNOTE id="fn">
<NO>*</NO>
<P>Reprinted with permission from
<BIBLIST>
<CITATION id="cite10">
<TITLE>The Effective Executive</TITLE>
<OTHINFO>pp. 270&ndash;275, by Owen Uris. Copyright
&copy; 1958, McGraw-Hill Book Company.</OTHINFO></CITATION></BIBLIST></P></FOOTNOTE>
</SUBSECT1></SECTION>
<SECTION><TITLE>Top Management Turnover in Hospitals</TITLE>

<P>When a baseball team loses game after game, the coach and perhaps some
players are replaced-seldom does the franchise go out of existence. When the
board of directors perceives an inordinate gap between performance and the
potential for an organization, the chief executive officer and other
administrators often become casualties.</P>

<P>A survey conducted by Witt Associates, a well-known consulting firm,
revealed that, nationally, 17 percent of all hospital administrator turnover
was caused by involuntary termination (Figure 4-1).<FNOTEREF rid="fn20">20</FNOTEREF> &e;The
higher
turnover rate in investor-owned hospitals can, in part, be
attributed to their smaller size and the fact that upwardly mobile hospital
administrators are more likely to move on to larger hospitals.</P>
<figgrp><FIG ID="fg4-1">
</figgrp>
<P>The president of the Massachusetts Hospital Association, David Kinzer,
began analyzing executive turnover in hospitals when he realized that, over
seven years, only 41 percent of the hospitals in Massachusetts had the same
chief executive officer.<FNOTEREF rid="fn21">21</FNOTEREF> Kinzer probed further with his
colleagues
in other hospital associations and found that <emph type="2">survival rates</emph> were even
lower in other states (Table 4-2).</P>

<TABLE><NO>4-2</NO>
<TITLE>Chief Executive Officer Job Changes: 1973&ndash;1980</TITLE>
<TBODY>
<HEAD></HEAD>
<HEAD>Total No. of Hospitals 1980</HEAD>
<HEAD>Net Gain/Loss of Hospitals Since 1973</HEAD>
<HEAD>Total No. of CEO Job Changes 1973&ndash;80</HEAD>
<HEAD>No. of CEOs Still on Job</HEAD>
<HEAD>Survival Rate of CEOs</HEAD>
<ROW>
<TSTUB><P>Texas</P></TSTUB>
<CELL><P>495</P></CELL>
<CELL><P>+20</P></CELL>
<CELL><P>-</P></CELL>
```

```
<CELL><P>108</P></CELL>
<CELL><P>22%</P></CELL></ROW>
<ROW>
<TSTUB><P>Maryland</P></TSTUB>
<CELL><P>49</P></CELL>
<CELL><P>+5</P></CELL>
<CELL><P>42</P></CELL>
<CELL><P>14</P></CELL>
<CELL><P>24%</P></CELL></ROW>
<ROW>
<TSTUB><P>New York</P></TSTUB>
<CELL><P>252</P></CELL>
<CELL><P>&minus;34</P></CELL>
<CELL><P>171</P></CELL>
<CELL><P>81</P></CELL>
<CELL><P>32%</P></CELL></ROW>
<ROW>
<TSTUB><P>Indiana</P></TSTUB>
<CELL><P>115</P></CELL>
<CELL><P>0</P></CELL>
<CELL><P>117</P></CELL>
<CELL><P>29</P></CELL>
<CELL><P>36.5%</P></CELL></ROW>
<ROW>
<TSTUB><P>Missouri</P></TSTUB>
<CELL><P>159</P></CELL>
<CELL><P>&minus;2</P></CELL>
<CELL><P>138</P></CELL>
<CELL><P>58</P></CELL>
<CELL><P>37%</P></CELL></ROW>
<ROW>
<TSTUB><P>California</P></TSTUB>
<CELL><P>511</P></CELL>
<CELL><P>+20</P></CELL>
<CELL><P>-</P></CELL>
<CELL><P>190</P></CELL>
<CELL><P>37%</P></CELL></ROW>
<ROW>
<TSTUB><P>Ohio</P></TSTUB>
<CELL><P>197</P></CELL>
<CELL><P>0</P></CELL>
<CELL><P>123</P></CELL>
<CELL><P>74</P></CELL>
<CELL><P>37.5%</P></CELL></ROW>
<ROW>
<TSTUB><P>Tennessee</P></TSTUB>
<CELL><P>165</P></CELL>
<CELL><P>+5</P></CELL>
<CELL><P>130</P></CELL>
<CELL><P>64</P></CELL>
<CELL><P>39%</P></CELL></ROW>
<ROW>
<TSTUB><P>Michigan</P></TSTUB>
<CELL><P>204</P></CELL>
<CELL><P>&minus;25</P></CELL>
```

```
<CELL><P>176</P></CELL>
<CELL><P>82</P></CELL>
<CELL><P>40%</P></CELL></ROW>
<ROW>
<TSTUB><P>Pennsylvania</P></TSTUB>
<CELL><P>314</P></CELL>
<CELL><P>&minus;2</P></CELL>
<CELL><P>167</P></CELL>
<CELL><P>76</P></CELL>
<CELL><P>40%</P></CELL></ROW>
<ROW>
<TSTUB><P>Massachusetts</P></TSTUB>
<CELL><P>120</P></CELL>
<CELL><P>&minus;18</P></CELL>
<CELL><P>84</P></CELL>
<CELL><P>49</P></CELL>
<CELL><P>41%</P></CELL></ROW>
</TBODY>
</TABLE>
<P>The next logical step for Kinzer was to examine the causes for the
turnover in chief executive officers. &e; Kinzer stated that even those figures
are misleading. Many so-called <emph type='2'>retirements</emph> are actually departures in
which administrators just packed their bags and fled, vowing publicly that
they will never again have anything to do with hospitals.</P>

<P>Most likely, all these terminations are not the direct result of some
well-defined cause relating to executive failure or increased organizational
burnout; regardless, they remind one of the jingle about the good driver who
died:
<LIT>
    He was right,
    Dead right,
    As he sped along.
    But he is just
    as dead as if he had been wrong.</LIT></P>
</SECTION>
<SECTION><TITLE>Conclusion</TITLE>

<P>Personal burnout that affects organizations adversely may occur when
employees are allowed to remain in a position of authority long after they
have reached their prime (common when the owner is the chief executive
officer) or when individuals throughout the organization suffer physical and
mental burnout. &e; Doing so reduces the potential for organizational
burnout.</P>

</SECTION>
<SECTION><TITLE>Notes</TITLE>
<FOOTNOTE id='fnn1'>
<NO>1</NO>
<P><BIBLIST><CITATION id='cite22'>
<TITLE>Controlling Stress and Tension</TITLE>
<AUTHOR><FNAME>Daniel</FNAME>
<SURNAME>Girdano</SURNAME></AUTHOR>
<AUTHOR><FNAME>George</FNAME>
<SURNAME>Everly</SURNAME></AUTHOR>
```

```
<OTHINFO>(Englewood Cliffs, NJ: Prentice-Hall, 1979),
86.</OTHINFO></CITATION></BIBLIST></P></FOOTNOTE>
<FOOTNOTE id="fn17">
<NO>17</NO>
<P>
<BIBLIST>
<CITATION id="cite23">
<TITLE>paper presented at the Second International Symposium on the Management of
Stress, Toronto, Canada, November, 1980</TITLE>
<AUTHOR><FNAME>John H.</FNAME>
<SURNAME>Howard</SURNAME></AUTHOR>
</CITATION></BIBLIST></P></FOOTNOTE>
<FOOTNOTE id="fn18">
<NO>18</NO>
<P>See, for example,
<BIBLIST>
<CITATION id="cite24">
<TITLE>Hospital and Health Services Administration</TITLE>
<AUTHOR><FNAME>Terence F.</FNAME>
<SURNAME>Moore</SURNAME></AUTHOR>
<AUTHOR><FNAME>Walter</FNAME>
<SURNAME>Wentz </SURNAME></AUTHOR>
<SERTITLE>Administrative Success: Key Ingredients</SERTITLE>
<OTHINFO>Special II, (1981):85&ndash;93.</OTHINFO></CITATION></BIBLIST></P></FOOTNOTE>

<FOOTNOTE id="fn19">
<NO>19</NO>
<P><BIBLIST><CITATION id="cite25"><TITLE>The Effective Executive</TITLE>
<AUTHOR><FNAME>Owen</FNAME>
<SURNAME>Uris</SURNAME></AUTHOR>
<OTHINFO>(New York: McGraw-Hill, 1958),
270&ndash;275.</OTHINFO></CITATION></BIBLIST></P></FOOTNOTE>
<FOOTNOTE id="fn20">
<NO>20</NO>
<P><BIBLIST><CITATION id="cite26"><TITLE>Modern Healthcare</TITLE>
<AUTHOR><FNAME>John</FNAME>
<SURNAME>Witt</SURNAME></AUTHOR>
<SERTITLE>17% of CEO's Fired Revealing Pressure of the Job </SERTITLE>
<OTHINFO>12 (August 1982): 103&ndash;106.</OTHINFO></CITATION></BIBLIST></P></FOOTNOTE>
<FOOTNOTE id="fn21">
<NO>21</NO>
<P><BIBLIST><CITATION id="cite27"><TITLE>Hospital and Health Services Administration</TITLE>
<AUTHOR><FNAME>David</FNAME>
<SURNAME>Kinzer</SURNAME></AUTHOR>
<SERTITLE>Turnover of Hospital Chief Executive Officers: A Hospital
Association Perspective</SERTITLE>
<OTHINFO>(May-June 1982):60&ndash;64.</OTHINFO></CITATION></BIBLIST></P></FOOTNOTE>
</SECTION></CHAPTER></BODY>
<BACK>
<AFTERWRD>
<TITLE>Epilogue</TITLE>

<P>The conceptual framework on which we base our theories and comments is
supported by data that we have gathered through many years as hospital
administrators and a thorough literature review. &e; Detailed studies of hospitals
that have deteriorated organizationally might be useful, for example, if properly
```

```
researched and described.</P>

<P>One of our country's greatest assets is its health care system, which is
unparalleled by that of any other country in the world. &e; Many hospitals and
hospital administrators have difficulties not because they cannot solve their
problems, but because they cannot see their problems.</P>
</AFTERWRD>
<INDEX>
<TITLE>Index</TITLE>
<LIST TYPE="1">
<ITEM><P>Ability to handle stress</P></ITEM>
<ITEM><P>Abuse of power </P></ITEM>
<ITEM><P>Accent on quality </P></ITEM>
<ITEM><P>Analysis
<LIST TYPE="2">
<ITEM><P><emph type="2">See also</emph> Assessment; Evaluation; Review</P></ITEM>
<ITEM><P>project</P></ITEM>
<ITEM><P>SWOT</P></ITEM>

</LIST></P></ITEM>
<ITEM><P>Zalenick, Abraham</P>
</ITEM></LIST></INDEX>
</BACK></BOOK>
```

C.2 Example of a marked up Article

The following is an extract from the article "Combustion of Refuse-Derived Fuels in a Specifically Developed High-Intensity Thermal Device" as printed in Resources and Conservation. Used with permission. Copyright 11(1985) by Elsevier Science Publishers B.V., Amsterdam.

```
<!DOCTYPE ARTICLE SYSTEM "iso12083-article.dtd"
[
<!ENTITY deg CDATA "degree" -- degree symbol -- >
<!ENTITY e CDATA ". . ." -- ellipsis -- >
]>

<ARTICLE>
<FRONT><TITLEGRP><TITLE>Combustion of Refuse-Derived Fuels in a Specifically Developed High-
intensity Thermal Device </TITLE></TITLEGRP>
<AUTHGRP>
<AUTHOR><FNAME>S.
</FNAME>
<SURNAME>Arosio
</SURNAME></AUTHOR>
<AUTHOR><FNAME>A.</FNAME>
<SURNAME>Crescenti
</SURNAME></AUTHOR>
<AUTHOR><FNAME>G.</FNAME>
<SURNAME>Sotgia
</SURNAME></author>
<AFF><ORGNAME>Politecnio di Milano</ORGNAME>
<ORGDIV>Dipartmento di Energetica
```

```
</ORGDIV>
<POSTCODE>20133</POSTCODE>
<CITY>Milano</CITY>
<COUNTRY>Italy</COUNTRY></AFF>
</AUTHGRP>

<ABSTRACT><TITLE>Abstract</TITLE>
<P>The aim of this research was to investigate the possibility of using
unconventional fuels, such as refuse-derived fuel (RDF) or industry by-
products, in small to medium combustion units. &e; The RDF used was of two
types: one from a plant in Rome and the other from an experimental plant in
Milan.</P>
<P>The combustion device was designed for high thermal load, high temperature
and special gas flow patterns &e; Operation was at temperatures from 1000&deg;
to 1200&deg; C at residence times of 1.2 to 1.5 s.</P></ABSTRACT></FRONT>

<BODY>
<CHAPTER><TITLE>Introduction</TITLE>
<P>The early results of this project have been reported
<CITEREF rid='cite1'>[1-4]</CITEREF>. &e;
The temperature inside the combustion chamber reached only 800&deg; C.</P>
<P>Two different types of RDF, both fluff, were used. &e; There was a trend of
falling efficiency at higher ratios of RDF.</P>

<SECTION>
<TITLE>Objectives</TITLE>
<P>The objectives of the later, work reported, here included experimentation
with a new specially designed high-intensity <emph type='1'>adiabatic</emph> combustion
chamber installed immediately before the boiler. &e;</P>
<P>The <emph type='1'>adiabatic</emph> combustor &e; which theoretically permits
100% RDF to be used, once steady-state conditions are reached
<CITEREF rid='cite8'>[8]</CITEREF>. &e; </P></SECTION>

<SECTION>
<TITLE>Test Conditions</TITLE>
<P>The main test conditions of the boiler were:
<LIST>
<ITEM><P>maximum total power input: 250 kw (0.90 GJ/h);</P> </ITEM>
<ITEM><P>maximum RDF power input: 60%; </P></ITEM>
<ITEM><P>minimum RDF power input: 22%; </P></ITEM>
<ITEM><P>combustion chamber temperature: 1000-1200&deg; C.</P></ITEM>
</LIST></P>
<P>All tests were performed at Bacharach index values lower than two
&e; due to
the thermal losses was evaluated. </P></SECTION>

<SECTION>
<TITLE>Experimental Results</TITLE>
<P>In order to evaluate the pollutant generation in both cases tests were
carried out in two different conditions: with a plant at (1) steady temperature
(1000&deg; C) and at (2) rising temperature. Efficiencies were calculated only
at steady temperatures. </P>

<SUBSECT1>
<TITLE>Results at steady temperature</TITLE>
```

```
<SUBSECT2>
<TITLE>Boiler efficiencies</TITLE>
<P>Boiler efficiencies were considered &e; leaving the total power input to vary
according to the RDF consumption.</P>
<P>Figures 5 and 6 show the efficiencies at 6 and 9 kg/h oil flow rates. &e; and
35% and 55% respectively in the second case.</P></SUBSECT2>

<SUBSECT2>
<TITLE>Pollutants formation</TITLE>
<P>Tables 3 and 4 give the values &e; the value of the pH of the condensate.</P>
</SUBSECT2></SUBSECT1>

<SUBSECT1>
<TITLE>Results at rising temperatures</TITLE>

<SUBSECT2>
<TITLE>Pollutants formation</TITLE>
<P>A trend of pollutant formation as a function of combustor temperature is
shown in Fig. 8. &e; resulting from the increased volumetric flow rates.</P>
</SUBSECT2></SUBSECT1></SECTION>

<SECTION>
<TITLE>Conclusions</TITLE>
<P>The results obtained in the special combustor, &e; and calorific
values. &e;</P>
<P>It was possible to get higher RDF ratios of power to mass input using the
combustor upstream of the boiler instead of using the boiler alone. The highest
RDF ratio used in this series was 100% of the total power input.</P>

<BIBLIST>
<HEAD>References</HEAD>
<CITATION id="cite1">
<NO>1</NO>
<TITLE>Recupero di massa e di energia dai rifiuti: gli orientamenti
internazionali emergenti, la misura e la prevenzione del loro impatto
ambientale.</TITLE>
<AUTHOR>
<FNAME>L.</FNAME>
<SURNAME>Cassitto</SURNAME>
</AUTHOR>

<SUBJECT>Congress: SEP Pollution 1980</SUBJECT>
<LOCATION><CITY>Padua</CITY></LOCATION>
<DATE>April 21-24,1980</DATE></CITATION>

<CITATION id="cite8">
<NO>10</NO>
<TITLE>Chemical Process Principles, Parts I and II</TITLE>
<AUTHOR>
<FNAME>O.A.</FNAME>
<SURNAME>Hougen</SURNAME></AUTHOR>
<AUTHOR><FNAME>K.M.</FNAME>
<SURNAME>Watson</SURNAME></AUTHOR>
<AUTHOR><FNAME>R.A.</FNAME>
```

```
<SURNAME>Ragak</SURNAME></AUTHOR>
<DATE>1959</DATE>
<CORPAUTH><ORGNAME>J. Wiley & Sons Inc.</ORGNAME>
<CITY>New York</CITY></CORPAUTH>
</CITATION></BIBLIST></SECTION></CHAPTER></BODY></ARTICLE>
```

Annex D

(informative)

Designation of Maintenance Agency

Questions concerning the implementation of this standard should be sent to the ANSI/NISO/ISO 12083 Maintenance Agency:

Electronic Publishing Special Interest Group (EPSIG)
Graphic Communications Association
100 Daingerfield Road
Alexandria, VA 22314 USA

Telephone: 703-519-8185
Fax: 703-548-2867
Email: epsig@aol.com

NISO Standard Evaluation Form

Standards are intended to be useful. However, information on where, when, and how standards are used, and with what results, is difficult to obtain. The purpose of this form is to provide users of this document with a convenient way to communicate about that use to those responsible for the NISO Standard. Your feedback can have an important effect, not only on future versions of this NISO Standard, but on the way other NISO Standards are created. If you have used (or are planning to use) this NISO Standard in any way, please complete this form and return it at your earliest convenience. Thank you for helping us to improve the NISO Standards you use.

1. **How did you learn about this NISO Standard?** (Details are appreciated.)

 ____ Written citation/reference. Source: ____________________

 ____ Promotional literature. Type: ____________________

 ____ Referral from a colleague. Industry: ____________________

 ____ Other, please specify: ____________________

2. **Are you using/planning to use this NISO Standard in any way, and to what extent?**

 ____ Full use (unmodified) ____ Modified use

 ____ Partial use (unmodified) ____ No use

3. **In what kind of environment(s) will this NISO Standard be used?**

 ____ Governmental ____ Nonprofit (academic/educational)

 ____ Personal ____ Nonprofit (other), please specify:

 ____ For profit ____________________

4. **During what year will this NISO Standard first be used?** ____________________

5. **How would you rate this NISO Standard in terms of:**

	Poor	Fair	Good	Very Good	Excellent	No Opinion
Readability	1	2	3	4	5	6
Presentation	1	2	3	4	5	6
Application	1	2	3	4	5	6

6. **How could this NISO Standard be improved in terms of its presentation, readability, application, etc.?**

 ____

 ____

 ____

7. **Would you be interested in working on revisions to this NISO Standard or on other NISO Standards in the same area?** ____ Yes ____ No

8. **This form was completed by:**

 Name and title ____________________

 Organization ____________________

 Address ____________________

 City/State/Zip ____________________

 Telephone ____________________

Please return this form to: **National Information Standards Organization**
4733 Bethesda Avenue, Suite 300
Bethesda, MD 20814
Fax: (301) 654-1721